The Great War and
the Search for a Modern Order,
A History of the American People and
Their Institutions, 1917–1933

The Great War
and the Search
for a Modern Order,
A History of
the American People
and Their Institutions,
1917–1933

ELLIS W. HAWLEY

University of Iowa

Under the General Editorship
of Vincent P. Carosso

St. Martin's Press
New York

Preface

America at the beginning of 1917 was a nation mobilizing for war. It was also a nation potentially capable of developing the world's first mass-consumption economy. And institutionally and ideologically, it was a nation facing one of the central problems of industrial societies with liberal-democratic commitments. For a quarter of a century it had been shifting power to a new set of organizational and technical elites, thus undermining traditional forces of discipline and social integration. But it had yet to develop new institutions capable of assuring that the new sources of authority would be used to further the ends of liberal democracy and national progress. For these institutions the quest was continuing, though punctuated by dire warnings about the evils of statist intervention, bureaucratic centralism, and market subversion.

My purpose in the following pages is to reexamine America's historical development during the years from 1917 to 1933, focusing in particular on wartime mobilization and action, the rise and collapse of the world's first mass-consumption economy, and the continued search for a modern managerial order geared to the realization of liberal ideals. This search, to be sure, moved away from the paths projected by the New Nationalists and New Freedomites of the prewar period. But from the wartime experience came an enhanced vision of enlightened private orders enlisted in the national service and working

v

with public agencies to advance the common good, and the economic expansion of the postwar period seemed to support this vision. It was not until the subsequent economic contraction had unmasked the weaknesses in New Era ideology and practice that the search moved onto other paths. Even then it could not ignore the legacy left by New Era organizers and policy makers. Much of what followed would consist of increased support for those still seeking to realize the New Era vision, and much that did break from this pattern would be limited and shaped by the organizational framework erected between 1917 and 1933.

This is not to say that I propose to ignore the reaction, alienation, and moral blight commonly emphasized in histories of the 1920s. Behind the popular mythology that surrounds these are substantial realities, which I hope to convey. But the focus in what follows is not on Bohemians, Babbitts, and bootleggers. Nor is it on alienated cultural critics, incipient New Dealers, or intolerant nativists and fundamentalists. It centers instead on the development of managerial institutions and values, drawing particularly from the work of historians who have come to regard that development as constituting the core of modern American history. Underlying such treatment is the view that the 1920s are best understood not as the Indian summer of an outmoded order or even as the seedtime of the reforms of the New Deal but rather as the premature spring of the kind of modern capitalism that would take shape in the America of the 1940s and 1950s. The importance of the 1920s, I have come to believe, lies in the ideological and institutional foundations then laid for post–1940 developments, and in this sense they may well constitute the more innovative and significant of the two interwar decades.

The underlying ideas and judgments expressed in this book have taken shape through a dozen years of study, research, and teaching. In ways too numerous to detail, I am indebted to students, colleagues, and archivists, in the latter category especially to those who have made available the rich resources on this period housed at the Herbert Hoover Presidential Library. In addition, I am indebted to a number of path-breaking scholars who have helped me to see the period in new ways and from new perspectives. In particular, I have been influenced by the work of Robert H. Wiebe, Samuel P. Hays, Louis Galambos, Alfred D. Chandler, William Appleman Williams, Joan Hoff Wilson,

Robert F. Himmelberg, Barry D. Karl, Robert H. Zieger, Robert D. Cuff, Carl P. Parrini, Edwin T. Layton, Grant McConnell, Philippe Schmitter, and Charles S. Maier. I have also learned much from other scholars, among them Michael J. Hogan, Melvyn P. Leffler, Bruce A. Lohoff, David Burner, Craig Lloyd, Burton Kaufman, Robert H. Van Meter, Martin L. Fausold, Murray Rothbard, Gerald D. Nash, Peri Arnold, and Haggai Hurvitz. And finally, I want to express my gratitude to Vincent P. Carosso for his encouragement, support, and editorship, to Bertrand Lummus for his patience with my failures to meet deadlines, and to my wife, Sofia, for her tolerance and good temper while the book was being written.

Ellis W. Hawley
Iowa City, Iowa
December 22, 1978

Contents

Editor's Introduction

In less than a generation, the twentieth century will belong entirely to the past. Many of the great personalities and events of the first half of the century already seem remote. To Americans born after World War II and to many others as well, Theodore Roosevelt is little more than a name and a picture in a history book, a bespectacled president with a mustache and a broad and toothy grin. Few people living today remember the young, dynamic Roosevelt—the popular hero of San Juan Hill, the first president to visit a foreign country (Panama) during his term of office and to ride in an automobile. And, indeed, the America of TR's day has all but disappeared.

Since 1901, when Roosevelt assumed the presidency, urbanization and industrialization have wrought profound changes in the United States. At the turn of the century the population was 76 million. Fewer than 40 percent lived in urban areas of 2,500 or more; and although American cities were growing rapidly, only six had a population of a half-million or more, and only three had reached or surpassed a million. In 1900, for the first time, the number of industrial wage earners exceeded the number of farmers and farm laborers, and the value of manufactured goods produced by the nation's workers was more than twice the $4.7 billion attributed to agriculture. The loosely organized, largely agricultural country of less than a half-century earlier was on the way to becoming a tightly integrated, highly industrialized, urban nation. But the road would be far from smooth or straight, and American society would experience unalterable changes over the next eight decades.

By 1970 the nation's population had grown to 205 million, and nearly 74 percent of the people had come to live in cities and their ever-expanding suburbs. Urbanization had changed the face of America, creating vast new metropolitan areas that linked city upon city into huge megalopolises, or "urban conglomerates." Similarly, the continued growth of big business transformed the economic landscape. The United States Steel Corporation, founded in 1901, was the country's first billion-dollar firm; by 1970 over a hundred such corporate leviathans existed. Only a few businesses in 1900 commanded a national market; in the 1970s large corporate enterprises dominated nearly every sector of the nation's economy, and many of these giants exercised increasing might abroad. Industrialism also helped alter the nation's international status. In 1900 the United States, despite its recently acquired overseas possessions, was still a new power of limited influence outside the Western Hemisphere. Following World War II it became one of the two superpowers.

But power, like industrial leadership—the twin developments hailed by many at the turn of the century as signaling the beginning of a new era in the nation—made other observers uneasy. The steady growth of large businesses, the rapidly expanding cities, and increased involvement in international affairs would inevitably create vast changes in American life. Turn-of-the-century commentators and politicians focused on many of the central issues that have faced the American people ever since: how to adapt institutions and policies to the needs of an industrial society; how to protect the environment while promoting material progress; how to provide an equitable and humane judicial system; how to deal with racial and ethnic diversity; how to preserve the nation's security in an increasingly turbulent world and contribute, at the same time, to international peace and stability. The four volumes in this series present America's attempts to respond to such challenges.

Professor Hawley's work, the second volume in the series, examines the sixteen years from 1917 to 1933, a time when the American people participated in a world war, helped establish a new international order, and sought to reorganize their domestic affairs to meet the challenges and opportunities of a modern, technologically advanced, industrial and capitalist society dedicated to the liberal-democratic principles enunciated by its eighteenth-century founders. The story of these years—mobilization at home, victory on the battlefields of northern France, failure to secure an enduring structure for maintaining peace, political and economic disorder abroad, and the emergence and collapse at home of what Professor Hawley calls "the world's first mass-consumption economy"—is treated fully, with keen insights, and in novel ways.

Unlike traditional syntheses of these years, which view the era as either the eclipse of progressivism or the "seedbed" of the New Deal, Professor Hawley's account seeks to explain and evaluate this important period on its own terms, appraising carefully its strengths and weaknesses. The central, unifying force of these years is neither political reaction nor business conservatism, the twin themes around which so much of the era's history is written, but rather, as Professor Hawley suggests, the development, legitimization, and use of new managerial and bureaucratic institutions, led by organizational and technical experts, dedicated to solving the nation's peacetime problems and advancing the common good. The organizational framework established during these years owed much to wartime experience, when "enlightened partnerships" of public and private policy makers worked together to mobilize the country for war. Adapting wartime organizational and administrative structures and practices to peacetime problems proved difficult. The deep depression that followed the stock market debacle of October 1929 seriously undermined the New Era system; but, as Professor Hawley shows, the quest for a "new liberalism" to be realized through corporative institutions not only persisted but helped shape much of the country's subsequent institutional development.

Based upon the most recent scholarship, particularly the works of the new organizational or managerial school of historians, this volume brings together new information and insights on the major issues facing the American people from World War I to the beginning of the New Deal: social modernization, cultural fragmentation, Wilsonian and Republican internationalism. Professor Hawley's survey of these years also adds considerably to our knowledge of Herbert Hoover's central role in shaping national policy, first as Secretary of Commerce, then as President. Not the least of its merits is the volume's perceptive analysis of the era's alternative and competing social perceptions and prescriptions—left, center, right. Here, then, is a clear, concise, balanced, and interestingly written analysis of a significant and controversial period in the nation's history, a time of high jinks and serious search for a better life for more people. Professor Hawley brings new understanding to the entire era.

Vincent P. Carosso

The Great War and
the Search for a Modern Order,
A History of the American People and
Their Institutions, 1917–1933

CHAPTER 1

The Heritage of a Progressive Era

At 8:35 P.M. on April 2, 1917, President Woodrow Wilson ascended the Speaker's platform to address a joint session of the American Congress. When the unprecedented applause had subsided, he began reading from a manuscript held firmly in both hands, peeling off each page as he finished and pausing occasionally for new rounds of cheering. First came an indictment of German actions, of the new policy under which "vessels of every kind" were to be "sent to the bottom without warning and without thought of help or mercy for those on board." This, he declared, was a "war against all nations" and a "challenge to all mankind." Next came a linking of these wrongs to a larger and irrepressible conflict between autocracy and democracy, an argument that neutrality was no longer possible in a world where the peace and freedom of everyone were threatened by irresponsible autocrats. And finally came a call to action. It was necessary not only to right wrongs but to "make the world safe for democracy," and America, as a great democratic nation, must necessarily fight for the principles that gave her birth and happiness. "God helping her," she could "do no other."

In Congress a few members still argued for peace, notably Representatives Jeanette Rankin and Claude Kitchin and Senator Robert M. La Follette. But four days later, at 1:18 P.M. on April 6, the President signed a war resolution that had passed the Senate by a vote

1

of 82 to 6 and the House of Representatives by 373 to 50. Some thirty-two months after the onset of the Great War in Europe, a conflict that Wilson himself had labeled "the most terrible and disastrous of all wars," the United States had become a full-fledged belligerent. And looking back from later vantage points, a good many historians and participants would come to feel that the war period constituted a great watershed in the history of the American nation and the civilization of which it was a part. For some it was the dividing line between an era of reform and one of reaction, for others the threshold of a new urban and managerial order, and for still others the end of a promising epoch of human progress. For the particularly nostalgic, the quarter-century before the war would become the "happiest period in ten centuries of Western civilization," the quarter-century that followed an era in which the forces of progress were nearly submerged by irrational destruction and socioeconomic malignancies.

Nor is it easy to quarrel with such perceptions. In many ways the world of 1919 was a different world from that of 1914, and clearly the America of Warren Harding and Calvin Coolidge was not the America that had elected Theodore Roosevelt and Woodrow Wilson. Yet if the nation was entering upon a new stage of its history, it was also bringing with it a heritage that would continue to shape and limit the unfolding of that history. The major concerns of the prewar years had revolved around the challenges posed by industrialization, urbanization, and immigration. It was the search for new institutions to cope with these challenges that had produced much of what was called "progressive reform." And while the paths along which this search moved were altered by the war experience, the quest itself persisted and continued to shape both the institutions and the political behavior of the 1920s. Nor did the other developments of the postwar years constitute anything approaching complete breaks with the past. In the light of recent research, it is now clear that such phenomena as the technological and moral revolutions, the advent of a mass consumption economy, and the revolts staged by urban minorities and cultural rebels all had their roots in the prewar era.

A history of post-1917 America, then, must begin with an examination of the era that preceded it and the heritage that this era transmitted to its successor. In particular, it is necessary to look at the economic transformation that had taken place by 1917, at the institutional and ideological responses to this change, and at the social and cultural tensions seeking resolution. And beyond this, it is necessary to look at the rise of America to world power and at the process through which the quest for a new order at home became tied up with the quest for a new and more progressive international order.

THE ECONOMIC HERITAGE

By 1917, of course, the American nation had already passed through a remarkable period of economic change, an era that had witnessed the rapid transformation of a land of farmers, villages, and small enterprisers into one of factory production, burgeoning cities, and new and powerful masters of industry and finance. In 1870 some 72 percent of America's 40,000,000 people had lived on the land or in rural villages, some 53 percent of her work force had consisted either of farmers or farm laborers, and only her railroad companies had approached the status of big business. By 1917 the rural population had grown, but that of the nation as a whole had expanded much more rapidly. Swelled both by natural increases and by a massive influx of immigrants, it had reached a total of 103,000,000, approximately half of whom were now living in urban places. And of the work force in 1917, a force that had come to consist increasingly of employees rather than the self-employed, only 27 percent remained engaged in agricultural pursuits. On the eve of their participation in the Great War that had begun in 1914, Americans had become a predominantly industrial and urban people, and with the acquisition of new tools and new forms of economic organization their output and productivity had undergone a remarkable growth. The national product in 1917 was nearly eight times as large as it had been in 1870, and output per person was nearly three times as large.

Contrary to some expectations, moreover, this growth had continued even after the frontier was closed and the railroads were built. In the two decades prior to the war, America had taken the lead in developing new industries committed to the mass production and consumption of consumer durables and middle-class services. These had become the "new frontier," and while a part of their growth could be attributed to the size of the American market and the American middle class, some of it was undoubtedly due to the activities and policies of key industrialists. In the American context they had been able to escape the restraining hand of business restrictionists and exploit the potential for new growth.

One side of their activities was the installation of revolutionary production techniques. By 1910 improvements in machine tools and new techniques of "scientific management," developed and popularized by such management engineers as Frederick W. Taylor, had laid the groundwork for striking advances in productivity. And beginning in 1913, something approaching a new system of production had taken shape at the Ford Motor Company. Concentrating on a standardized product, the company had installed a technique of continuous assembly, one that involved continuously moving conveyors, minute specialization of labor, and rigorous coordination. In Henry Ford's own words, it focused upon a manufacturing project "the principles of power, accuracy, economy, system, continuity and speed," and one result was a Model T that eventually sold for less than one third of its previous price.

The other side of the new economy was the introduction of mass marketing techniques. If the new growth was to continue, consumers must be willing and able to buy large quantities of goods once regarded as luxuries, and to achieve this result a variety of strategies was already being deployed. One strategy was to cut distribution costs, primarily through economies of scale, high-volume operations, and the elimination of middlemen. A second was mass advertising designed to create new wants and overcome ingrained spending habits. A third was new forms of consumer credit that allowed would-be purchasers to buy items that could not be bought out of current income. And finally there was the disposition of a new set of managers to raise the wage level and hence the purchasing power of worker-consumers. Again Henry Ford was a pioneer. In a much-heralded move in 1914, he had raised the pay of his workers to a minimum daily rate of $5 while reducing their work day from nine to eight hours.

Rise of the middle class

Also growing by 1917 was another sector of the economy that would become increasingly prominent in the postwar years, a sector devoted to the provision of mass services and mass cultural and recreational activities. Taking shape between the older high and folk cultures was a new mass or middle culture, and catering to its wants and needs was an expanding array of both private and public organizations. Already, for example, motion pictures was emerging as a huge industry based on entertainment. Already professional sports, with baseball leading the way, were becoming large business enterprises. And already in the process of rapid expansion were such fields as health care, secondary and higher education, a press tailored to mass tastes, and the service trades catering to tourists and travelers.

Growth, then, was still under way. Americans in 1917 had inherited an economy that was entering upon a new stage of expansion, becoming more productive, and in spite of its limitations providing an increasingly rich material life for a majority of people. Yet the two decades prior to the war had been anything but decades of satisfaction with economic performance. Growth had also involved a shattering of older social relationships and the emergence of new problems of squalor and misery, corruption and exploitation, monopolistic combinations and destructive economic warfare. These aspects of the process had generated waves of protest and discontent, and from the 1890s on, as dissatisfaction was crystallized first by an economic crisis and then by a wave of muckraking, there had been a running attack on those who regarded such developments as the inevitable costs of progress.

In essence, the attack had challenged the notion that resources and product shares were being efficiently and equitably allocated through an autonomous and apolitical market system. Some men, it was believed, had acquired substantial power over the process, power that was being used in antisocial and unproductive ways. And the result had been both efforts at market restoration and efforts to find and install a better substitute for market allocation. The years from 1890 to 1917 had brought not only a new antitrust bureaucracy charged with maintaining competitive relationships but also an array of regulatory commissions and public enterprises; and perhaps of greater importance for the war and postwar years, those prewar decades had witnessed the emergence of private organizational elites and claims that they could serve as the builders of a new and better social order. What some historians have called the "organizational revolution" was well under way by 1917, a "revolution" that was shifting power and status from old-style entrepreneurs and community leaders to the leaders of financial institutions, corporate bureaucracies, and functional or occupational organizations. And to understand post–1917 developments, it is necessary to understand the major features of this organizational heritage.

THE ORGANIZATIONAL HERITAGE

In the business sphere, in particular, the search for greater order and stability had brought forth three new elites, each aspiring to the role once filled by master entrepreneurs and leaders of local communities. For many businessmen the great enemies had become "social chaos," "destructive competition," and "defective coordination." It was these social disorders that were threatening both liberty and progress, and in different ways the developments that brought forth master financiers, systematic managers, and associational bureaucracies were all responses to these perceptions of social need and group interest.

In the background of the first development lay the wreckage engendered by the panic of 1893 and the concurrent rise of powerful investment banks, especially such organizations as the House of Morgan and Kuhn, Loeb and Company. Understandable desires to mitigate "destructive competition" developed simultaneously with institutions capable of controlling a large share of the savings stream; and the result, as these institutions were used to mobilize the capital needed for mergers and reorganization, was a consolidation movement going far beyond that of the 1880s. Out of it had come a regrouping of the railroads, a set of super-corporations dominating their respective industries, and a system of interlocking investments and directorates that allowed financial leaders to exert considerable control over managerial decisions. Agitation against this "money power," moreover, had not brought its dissolution. On the contrary, the new financial elite had won substantial acceptance as part of a new and more socially conscious national leadership. During the panic of 1907 it had been called upon to check economic demoralization. Subsequently it had become a partner of the State Department in efforts to stabilize troublesome areas abroad, and under the new Federal Reserve Act of 1913 it was to work with public representatives in exercising expert and apolitical controls over the money supply and credit availability.

Meanwhile, a second and at times competing elite was also emerging, primarily in the large corporate organizations with their expanding array of technical specialists coordinated and directed by professional administrators. Here a new "managerial elite" was taking shape, with credentials not of mere wealth but of training and organizational expertise. And addressing both the desire for continued economic development and the concern with its social impact, the leaders of the new elite were offering themselves as the instruments through which an orderly and healthy growth could be organized and directed. Given positions of greater influence, it was argued, they could transform an exploitive and wasteful system into one characterized by humane and uplifting efficiency, and in the decade preceding 1917 there was a growing disposition to lodge power in their hands.

The third development in the business sphere, also a major feature of the two decades preceding the war, was an immense growth of business associations. Businessmen organized partly for defensive reasons, especially for protection against labor unionizers, political reformers, and rival business organizations. But at the same time they also organized to achieve greater mastery over their environment and enhance their power to predict, plan, and control economic behavior. By 1917 these impulses toward organized cooperation had produced hundreds of industrial and trade associations, many with continuing programs and professional staffs. Here was another expanding private bureaucracy, concerned with negotiating jurisdictional boundaries between its units and establishing machinery that could coordinate their activities. And emerging from these concerns was a further array of cooperative business councils and national coordinators. Of particular importance was the formation in 1912 of the United States Chamber of Commerce, designed as an association of associations and offering itself as a tool through which organized business could serve the cause of national progress.

In the meantime, as businessmen organized, other groups also tried to develop similar structures. In agriculture the collapse of populism had been followed by a wave of association building, organizing the more business-like farmers into commodity associations and farm bureaus. In the labor field an elite of skilled workers had turned to "business unionism," developing in spite of employer resistance a network of business-oriented craft unions joined together in the American Federation of Labor. Among the new managers and technicians a variety of professional and technical societies took shape, and in the field of social work a new array of professionally directed charity and uplift organizations were replacing or absorbing the older philanthropic and charitable agencies. The watchwords of the progressive era were "organization" and "professionalism," and for many Americans the "organizers" and "professionalizers" had become the new agents of social progress.

As this social reorganization took place, it helped to stimulate a reorganization and transformation of political institutions. Moving beyond demands for honest and economical government, the new organizational elites had sought managerial aids and allies in the public sector, thus helping to bring into being a variety of technical, fact-finding, and promotional agencies. And seeking a government more responsive to their interests and needs, they had supported reforms designed to break up the older partisan organizations and city machines, shift policy making to administrators and technical experts, and provide themselves with regularized access to the arenas of decision making. American government at the end of the progressive era had not yet been completely "rescued" from the practitioners of mass and party politics; nor had it escaped the tendency for expanding governmental bureaucracies to develop their own drives for power and growth. But to a large extent its meaningful political units had become those generated by the "organizational revolution" rather than those described in the civics books.

Institutionally, then, the America of the prewar period was a society reorganizing around functional identities, shifting power to new orga-

New Freedom = legislation
New Nationalism = National Regulatory Agencies

nizational elites, and forging rationalizations to justify these changes. For better or worse, the land that had idealized yeomen farmers and rugged individualists was becoming a land of corporate organization, bureaucratic systematizers, and associational activities. And while some believed that the new forms of association must necessarily lead either to a new tyranny or to a socialist commonwealth, the more general assumption was that they could be contained within the framework of a liberal democracy. The benefits of the "organizational revolution," so progressive theorists were insisting, could be obtained without sacrificing the essentials of America's liberal heritage. There could be a viable "middle way" between the prescriptions of classical liberalism and those of its socialist critics, and by 1917 several forms of this "new liberalism" had taken shape and were being offered as the road to progress along which Americans should seek to move.

VISIONS OF A NEW LIBERALISM

In one such prescription a market place that was now succumbing to restrictive organization was to be revitalized through governmental action. The "nightwatchman state" of classical liberalism would give way to active and continuous governmental intervention, primarily to keep the market place expanding, deprive would-be monopolists of their anticompetitive weapons, and break up conspiracies for restraint of trade. In this way, it was argued, the discipline and safeguards of an "unseen hand" could be reestablished and sustained. There could be, in the words of Woodrow Wilson, a "new freedom" under which society would again reward "brains and efficiency" rather than "water-logged giants." And after Wilson articulated this view in the presidential campaign of 1912, he had sought to provide the needed governmental tools. Such was the aim of the Clayton and the Federal Trade Commission acts in 1914 and of other legislation that dealt with trade barriers and unfair competitive advantage.

For some progressives, however, such a prescription was more suited to the nineteenth than the twentieth century. It amounted, according to Theodore Roosevelt, to "a kind of rural toryism," incapable of realizing the uplifting and liberating abundance made possible by modern technology. And from 1905 on, as the workings of the antitrust laws became a major political issue, a second and competing prescription also took shape. Designated as a "new nationalism," it called for the creation of a national regulatory and welfare apparatus that might achieve the liberal ends no longer attainable through nineteenth-century institutions. Underlying it was the assumption that a new kind of governmental bureaucracy, staffed with professional experts and responsive to a properly enlightened people, could become the instrument not only of greater efficiency and productivity but also of better social adaptation to economic change. This had been the approach advocated by the Progressive party in 1912; and while it had initially lost out to the "new freedom," its advocates were heartened by Wilson's subsequent support of special farm aids, protective labor laws, an expert tariff commission, and the legalization of export combines.

Also discussed during this period was a third prescription, one that looked upon statism as a "drug" that could destroy social creativity and adaptability yet agreed that the attainment of liberal ends now required a regulatory and welfare apparatus. The answer, according to this third theory, lay in cooperative institutions that would allow each functional bloc in society to see its proper role and work with other blocs to realize a new abundance and an ordered freedom. It lay neither in antitrust action nor governmental direction but rather in a "new individualism" developed and disciplined in private associations and guided through scientific inquiries and coordinating councils. Such was the road to progress advocated by the National Civic Federation and other promoters of "social cooperation," and by 1916 it was a prescription particularly congenial to the new technical professions, efficiency movements, and association builders.

In the immediate prewar period, moreover, economic difficulties combined with concerns about radicalism, statism, and European developments to propel this form of a "new liberalism" to the fore. Convinced that social action was needed yet fearful of where governmental intervention could lead, a variety of organizational leaders had begun articulating a nonstatist and nonradical alternative to classical liberalism. The period had brought forth "solutions" of this sort for the problems of unemployment, industrial waste, and "destructive competition," for the problems posed by labor-capital conflict and industrial violence, and for the problems stemming from new developments abroad. The answer to all of these, it was being argued, was not in strong government but rather in the consignment of social duties to properly enlightened private orders, in the creation of machinery through which these orders could act together for the common good, and in the generation of knowledge upon which enlightened decision makers could draw. The role of the truly progressive state was to serve as the agent or "midwife" for bringing such arrangements into being, and public policy did seem to be moving in this direction. Through such bodies as the Commission on Industrial Relations, the National Foreign Trade Council, and the Council of National Defense the state was being linked to the new organizational blocs in society and used to legitimize a quasi-public role for private "partners" and "copartnerships."

Ideologically, then, the heritage of the progressive era consisted of continuing commitments to a liberal order coupled with growing doubts that it could be realized through the classical prescriptions and with competing efforts to design mechanisms of greater effectiveness. Although America was not without its radicals and reactionaries, the great majority continued to look upon private property and opportunity for advancement as essential to social progress. And while the "old liberalism" continued to have its adherents, it was clearly in decline. The central debate had become that between advocates of a "new freedom," a "new nationalism," and a "new individualism"; and it remained to be seen which of these or what combination of them could reconcile the new economy and the organizational revolution with the nation's liberal heritage.

THE HERITAGE OF ETHNOCULTURAL TENSIONS

Also inherited from the progressive era was a set of ethnocultural tensions that would become central features of the postwar period. In the years from 1886 to 1916 nearly nineteen million immigrants had entered the United States, mostly from eastern and southern Europe and mostly with religions, cultural traditions, and ways of life that diverged markedly from those of northern Europe and Anglo-America. Overwhelmingly they were Roman Catholic or Jewish, and hence suspect in a society that had developed an informal Protestant establishment. Overwhelmingly too they were "uprooted" peasants or agricultural laborers who had brought with them heritages that hampered their functioning in urban settings. And most had located in such settings. Such opportunities as they could find had been not in rural or frontier areas but in the great industrial metropolises of the Northeast. There much of the new industrial working class had come to consist of these "new immigrants," and this transformation had not only heightened class and ethnocultural divisions within the cities. It had also strengthened the antiurban attitudes of the hinterland.

 Added to the disintegrating effects of rapid industrialization and urbanization, then, were the tensions and anxieties generated by a largely immigrant labor force whose traditions, values, and ideals clashed with those of the host society. To those with roots in an older America, order seemed to be dissolving into chaos. Collapsing, so it seemed, were not only the traditional structures for ordering economic and social life but also the religious and cultural traditions upon which national well-being allegedly rested. And alarmed by what they felt to be the corrupting and disorganizing effects of the cultures that were being imported with their new industrial labor, many Americans were inclined to listen to those who were preaching bigotry, intolerance, and discrimination. In the name of progress, patriotism, or a pseudo-scientific racism, they lent their support to measures that would either "Americanize" the new ethnic minorities or bar them from positions of influence and from competition with "real Americans."

In its harsher forms this anti-immigrant or nativist sentiment found expression in such organizations as the American Protective Association. But it also had a softer side, seeking through education and reform to rescue worthy immigrants from their benighted conditions. And it was this softer side that permeated much of prewar progressivism. It helped to spark the attacks on urban political machines, big city vices, and working class saloons. It fostered new kinds of vocational education, social work, and citizenship training;

and rejecting the notion that all should be welcome in the "land of new opportunity," its adherents lent their support to measures that would not only reduce the number of incoming immigrants but also select those most amenable to "Americanization." Only a few progressives placed much value on the cultures that were being imported, and still fewer came to regard cultural pluralism rather than assimilation into the dominant culture as the democratic and liberal solution.

At best, however, such actions had produced a tenuous and uneasy compromise between majority demands and minority aspirations. They had not brought the kind of "melting" that dissolved ethnic loyalties and cleavages or the kind required to make nativists feel secure and unthreatened. In the political arena the continued tensions were reflected in bitter contests over such issues as prohibition, immigration restriction, and parochial schools. And by 1917 all indications were that the tensions were mounting rather than receding. Although the war and postwar experiences would add to them, one could already discern a loss of support for the softer solutions, increased resistance and activism by urban ethnic groups, and the beginnings of the nativist crusade that would become so prominent in the political and social life of the 1920s.

Also mounting at the time were the tensions inherent in a system that professed liberal democracy yet still denied it to most of the ten million Americans who had black skins. Along this fault line, efforts to achieve social peace had been built around the Tuskegeeism of Booker T. Washington, a formula that relegated blacks to the status of an "emerging race" and stressed advancement through vocational training rather than through political action or demands for social equality. Yet in practice the formula had brought neither peace nor much improvement in black living standards. In the South political disfranchisement and formalized segregation were accompanied by a growing use of lynching and violence as methods of race control. And among blacks, the decade preceding the war witnessed both a growing criticism of Tuskegeeism and an increasing migration from the rural South to the urban North. In these developments lay the bases for new forms of black protest and activism. But at the same time they would also spark new efforts to keep blacks "in their place," new defenses of discrimination and white supremacy, and a general spread of racial violence to the North.

At issue as well in 1917 were the arrangements governing the status of women and their role in a properly ordered society. From 1912 on, a wide variety of women's groups had coalesced behind the movement for equal suffrage; and while some saw this primarily as an aid to attaining political and moral reforms, others viewed it as one step toward ending all forms of sexual discrimination and discrediting the social myths that narrowly circumscribed feminine opportunities and behavior. Accompanying political militance were movements to reform women's dress, family relationships, and the double standard for sexual and social behavior. During and after the war, these movements and the reaction against them would continue to form another major source of cultural conflict.

Freedom for women was in fact only part of a larger protest against Victorian ideals and the cultural establishment that had helped to sustain them. By 1917 the city had become not only the home of discordant ethnic minorities and feminine liberationists but also the spawning ground of a new cultural "modernism" that attacked the very notion that art should promote established moral principles. In Greenwich Village the vanguard of the cultural rebellion had proclaimed a "New Renaissance," one that would allegedly free creative individuals from restrictive traditions and usher in a "new freedom," a "new literature," a "new art," a "new morality." Indeed almost anything "new" was to be celebrated and praised, especially if it embodied the virtues of spontaneity, intuition, and sensuality; and artistic endeavor now was to be either its own reason for being or an instrument for changing national sensibilities. Much that would flourish in the 1920s had its roots in this prewar assault on "genteel" traditions and standards, and much of the cultural fragmentation that would characterize modern America was already becoming discernible. As "modernists" and "traditionalists" fought over the custody of high culture, both were losing contact with the emerging popular culture to which large numbers of middle-class Americans were turning.

Culturally, then, the heritage of the progressive era consisted of mounting tensions between the established order of the Victorian age and the challenges posed by the new immigration, the new activism of submerged minorities and social subordinates, and the new attitudes emanating from cultural "modernists" and promoters of a pleasure ethic. These were tensions that many Americans still hoped to resolve. But for the most part, the prewar formulas for doing this had brought only uneasy and tenuous compromises. The America that entered the Great War was a potential candidate for bitter and divisive ethnocultural conflict, and the developments that followed would result in much of this potential being realized.

THE HERITAGE OF PROGRESSIVE DIPLOMACY

As America entered the war, it was also a country that had gone through what one historian has called its "first great revolution in foreign policy." In the 1890s a policy of continental isolationism had given way to a new imperialism; and while the impulse toward acquiring and managing colonies had quickly faded, the progressive presidents had continued to be active interventionists in the international arena. Under Theodore Roosevelt the Caribbean had been turned into an "American lake," the navy had continued to grow, and the United States had become an active participant in big power politics. Under William Howard Taft the diplomatic establishment had been used to push American capital into new areas, ostensibly for purposes of uplifting and stabilizing them. And under Woodrow Wilson a renunciation of this "dollar diplomacy" had been accompanied by new forms of trade promotion, a policy of withholding recognition from morally reprehensible regimes, and military interventions in Santo Domingo, Haiti, and Mexico. For much of America the isolationist creed retained great appeal. But gradually the nation had also acquired a set of policy makers who were no longer inclined to uplift by example or merely to react to developments abroad. America's power, they insisted, must be used to shape its international environment and promote international progress, and with the support of a variety of interested groups they were attempting to translate these ideas into practice.

Running through much of this new outlook was a vision of America taking its place among the great powers and joining with them to bring civilization and progress to the backward areas of the world. America, in essence, was to become part of the competitive process through which the world's rulers and "policemen" were selected, demonstrating its fitness for the role and taking up the duties and responsibilities that went with it. Yet it was also assumed that this competitive process would not lead to a major world conflagration, that it could be contained and ordered within a framework of rational negotiations, international rules, and peace-keeping mechanisms. Those who emerged from the process and took up their international duties would be equipped to build these barriers against irrational and destructive behavior. And America, it was thought, could bring a special competence to the task. Its previous isolation from Europe, its achievements in domestic governance, and its freedom from the irrational hatreds and "entangling alliances" of the European past had all made it a nation to which the European powers might look for moral leadership and disinterested guidance. Such were the arguments often made by the American peace movements, and one side of progressive diplomacy had concentrated on the production of arbitration agreements, cooling-off treaties, and other peace-keeping mechanisms.

Despite such claims, however, the United States had not remained entirely aloof from the alliance systems that had divided Europe into two armed camps. Between 1900 and 1913 American relations with Britain had steadily improved, while those with Germany had rapidly deteriorated. America's interests, so its diplomats had come to believe, were generally compatible with a British-dominated Atlantic and with British trade and balance-of-power politics; they were not compatible with the German bid for imperial glory. And while most Americans did not believe that the Anglo-German rivalry would end in a resort to arms, it was already clear that if such a war did come, the United States was likely to be tied to the British system rather than to its German rival. It could, of course, attempt to serve as mediator or as the builder of a new system. But success in such endeavors would require either the transformation of Germany or drastic changes in the way that Americans perceived their own interests and those of the Western world.

In 1914, then, as an obscure assassination in the Balkans activated Europe's competing alliances and brought the unexpected war, the sympathies of most Americans and especially of those in charge of foreign policy were with Britain and France. And in the months that followed, as British propaganda played upon American emotions and British sea power insured that American merchants could trade only with one side, these sympathies became stronger and more intense. Growing numbers of Americans came to see the Central Powers—Germany, Austria-Hungary, Turkey, and Bulgaria—as aggressor nations seeking to conquer and enslave democratic peoples; and while the other major Allies—Russia, Italy, and Japan—were difficult to perceive as champions of democracy, their imperialistic ambitions aroused far less concern. Although British violations of neutral rights brought protests from the United States, the notes were usually couched in friendly language without threats of reprisal. They had no major effects on British policy or on American provisioning of the Allies, and such friction as they did engender failed to curb a growing conviction that America could not permit a German victory. Such administration leaders as Robert Lansing, Walter Hines Page, and Edward House became early advocates of intervention on the British side; and while Wilson vacillated between commitments to the Allied cause and the idea of a "peace without victory," he was clearly opposed to actions that might contribute to the defeat of Britain and France. The chief spokesman for noninvolvement was Secretary of State William Jennings Bryan. It was Bryan who led the criticism of America's biased neutrality; and when he was replaced by Lansing in 1915—his resignation coming as a protest against Wilson's position on maritime rights—the nation moved closer to intervention.

By 1916 American nonbelligerence had come to hinge on Germany's willingness to withhold its submarines from effective use and allow the United States to function as an Allied arsenal and granary. From early 1915 on the United States had insisted that naval warfare be conducted in accordance with rules of visit and search that submarines could not meet; and in the face of American protests, the Germans had given the *Arabic* and *Sussex* pledges (the former in September 1915 and the latter in May of the following year) committing themselves not to sink unresisting passenger or merchant vessels without warning and rescue operations. This arrangement, however, was not destined to endure. It rested on the German hope that a favorable peace might be negotiated, perhaps in a conference called by President Wilson. When this hope faded, German policy makers decided upon an effort to starve the British into submission even if this meant full-scale American belligerence. On January 31, 1917, the German government informed the United States of its intention to resume unrestricted submarine warfare, and from this decision war quickly followed. On February 3 Wilson announced the severance of diplomatic relations; on March 1 the State Department released proof of German intrigues for an alliance with Mexico; on March 18 German submarines sank three American merchant vessels with heavy loss of life; and on March 20 the President's Cabinet was unanimous in urging a declaration of war. On March 21 the President issued a call for a special session of Congress, and on April 2, the day the session convened, he delivered his war message.

Viewed from almost any angle, the movement into war represented a failure of progressive diplomacy. The events of 1914 had given the lie to assumptions about great power behavior, and those of early 1917 had demonstrated America's inability either to correct the unexpected misbehavior or to escape its consequences. Yet the custodians of the new diplomacy now proposed to turn one of history's darkest hours into a new beginning. As early as September of 1914 Walter Hines Page had come to look upon the war as a blessing, as an opportunity, in other words, to strangle "the Hohenzollern idea" and destroy the German militarism that had become the chief obstacle in the path of human progress. And it was this view of the matter that Wilson now used to sanctify and ennoble the resort to arms. In essence, the war that progressive diplomacy had failed to prevent was now perceived as a "progressive war," a struggle through which the forces of light and progress would destroy the great obstacle in their path, redeem past errors and failures, and build institutions capable of realizing the progressive dream. In Wilson's most famous words, it would not only make the world "safe for democracy" but also "end all wars" and bring "peace and safety to all nations."

In other areas, too, the effort to turn seeming regression into a new beginning quickly became evident. While some Americans deplored and resisted the militarization of American society, others viewed it not only as a requirement for survival but as a stepping stone to the social order that a progressive era had envisioned but failed to achieve. A system of war management, they came to believe, could be adapted to the peacetime management of social progress, and the story of this attempted adaptation would form one of the central themes of the postwar era.

CHAPTER 2

The War to End Wars, 1917–1918

If the progressive era laid the basis for modern America, the war experience of 1917 and 1918 catalyzed the process of organizational change and set the pattern for future economic and social management. It brought, above all, a new reliance upon the private organizational elites that had emerged in the prewar years. For as old institutions failed the test of military exigency, it was these elites who built a system capable of breaking the deadlock in Europe and forcing Germany to sue for peace. They emerged in command of the administrative network that the war helped to develop. And while efforts to adapt this network to the solution of peacetime problems would encounter numerous difficulties and setbacks, such efforts would remain at the core of future American development. The story of America at war was a story of courage and misery in the trenches of northern France, of heightened xenophobia and intolerance at home, and of a diplomacy that aroused expectations it could not fulfill. But above all, it was the story of a people organizing themselves in ways that would shape their future destiny.

EARLY DECISIONS

In large measure the wartime pressure for organizational change stemmed from two decisions about the type of war that the nation would attempt to fight. In the first place, it was decided, the stream of war matériel moving across the Atlantic must be substantially expanded. America must seek, in particular, to meet the urgent requests of the Allies for new credits, more ships, and a larger flow of foodstuffs. And second, it was decided shortly thereafter, the United States must raise a large expeditionary force and deploy it in France. Without such actions, so the reasoning ran, the war could not be brought to a successful conclusion; nor could America expect to play a major role in shaping the peace. The consequences, however, were to subject the economy to massive demands for a new type of consumption, and from the outset it was widely conceded that trying to meet these through existing economic and political institutions was likely to bring economic chaos and social breakdown. Temporarily at least, America would have to construct its own version of the war collectivism to which Europeans had turned.

For the raising of military manpower, this meant conscription; and despite protests about "Prussianization," Congress proceeded to follow the President's recommendations, defeating efforts to force reliance upon volunteer units and enacting a selective service law. This, so it was said, constituted "modern democracy" in action. It was a system at once efficient, equitable, and functionally reliable. And partly because the prewar movement for compulsory military training had paved the way, implementation of the law proved easier than expected. When June 5 was proclaimed Registration Day, Senator James Reed of Missouri predicted that the nation's cities would be "running red with blood." But nothing of the sort happened. On the appointed day, some 9,660,000 American males between the ages of twenty-one and thirty-one went to their polling places. There they were "exhorted by their mayors, prayed for by their clergymen, and wept over by sundry females," after which they filled out the proper forms and awaited the decisions of local draft boards. Eventually the draft boards would register over 24,000,000 men between the ages of eighteen and forty-five, and of these about 2,800,000 would be inducted. Approximately 2,000,000 more volunteered, thus bringing the total who saw service to about 4,800,000.

The government also moved quickly to establish special agencies of information management and thought control. On April 13 the veteran journalist George Creel took charge of a Committee on Public Information, whose primary tasks were to manage war information, mobilize public opinion behind war measures, and "sell the war" to those not yet convinced of its justice and necessity. In operation it quickly organized a system of "self-censorship" for the newspapers and began turning out a steady stream of releases, posters, films, speeches, pamphlets, and other materials. As Creel saw it, he was running " the world's greatest adventure in advertising." But for those who refused to buy the product or tried to offer competing images, there was little toleration. With official encouragement a number of "loyalty" organizations sprang up to catch domestic traitors, expose "slackers" and "shirkers," and force would-be dissenters into line. And with presidential support Congress moved promptly to make legal sanctions available. In June of 1917 it passed the Espionage Act, providing heavy penalties for "false statements with intent to interfere with the operation or success of the military or naval forces" and empowering the Postmaster General to withhold mail privileges from any materials "advocating or urging treason, insurrection, or forcible resistance to any law of the United States."

To the conscription of money there was more resistance. But after heated debates over how the burden should be distributed, Congress produced a War Revenue Act that raised both income and excise taxes and allowed approximately 31 percent of the war's cost to be met from current revenue. The remainder, a sum that would eventually total about $23,000,000,000, was borrowed, partly through the sale of war bonds to the public and partly through the exchange of such bonds for newly created bank credit. To curb private demands for capital, the Federal Reserve Board also created a special Capital Issues Committee with subcommittees in each Federal Reserve district. At first its machinery operated on a voluntary basis, but later it received legal authority to block the employment of capital in nonessential enterprises.

Meanwhile, the country was also groping its way toward new mechanisms that could reduce the competition for scarce materials and bring production into line with the new demands. The mere placing of orders through competitive bidding, so most leaders had concluded, could not bring this about, at least not without excessive costs and ruinous delays. Yet it would also be difficult and dangerous, if not impossible, to build a state bureaucracy equal to the task. The

"American way," so Wilson was being told, was through voluntary cooperation between public agencies and enlightened private organizations. It was an approach that could reduce the wastes and disorder of laissez-faire without incurring the costs and dangers of state control. And the way to proceed, the President was further advised, was to build on the prewar Council of National Defense and its ties to the leadership of functional blocs and private institutions.

By early fall administrative and legislative action had brought several of these exercises in public-private cooperation into being. In May the President had entrusted the organization of a food program to Herbert Hoover, recently director of the Commission for Relief in Belgium. In July the Council of National Defense created a new War Industries Board responsible for the functioning of key raw material and manufacturing industries. In August the Lever Act not only gave a statutory basis and new powers to the Food Administration but authorized the creation of a separate program for fuels. And in early October the President established a War Trade Board to control exports and imports and wage economic warfare against the enemy. In addition, a reorganized Shipping Board was entrusted to Edward Hurley, one of the prewar period's most articulate spokesmen for business-government cooperation; and a Railroads' War Board had assumed the task of reordering rail traffic. Although production bottlenecks and bureaucratic disorders were still much in evidence, the nation was being organized along lines that would eventually be hailed as eminently workable. And while much was made of the expanding public sector, the heart of the new order was a network of cooperating industrial committees that linked the war agencies to private organizations and drew upon both public and private power to enforce agreements reached by consultation and bargaining. It was through mechanisms of this sort that the nation was attempting to adjust production, distribution, and consumption to war needs.

Adopting such an approach also meant official encouragement and support for the association building that antitrusters had previously looked upon as unhealthy. Under pressure from the war administrators, the Department of Justice granted antitrust immunity to combinations certified to be in the public interest, and in areas previously unorganized, public officials often took the lead in promoting private

partners to whom administrative duties could be delegated. The result
was both the formation of new industrial associations and the consolidation of existing ones, the goal being a private body that could be
recognized as the "government" for its particular economic sector.
And although Congress attempted to legislate against the quasi-official
status of such bodies, the resulting strictures did little more than force
a reorganization of the committee system that linked them to the war
agencies. In the fall of 1917 the initial array of cooperative committees
gave way to a new and allegedly less corruptible system of war service
committees acting under the supervision of the United States Chamber
of Commerce.

Where labor associations fitted into this picture was more controversial. But by late 1917 a series of decisions had directed government policy toward working with and through "enlightened" unions
rather than trying to suppress unionization or to extend military
conscription to the industrial sphere. The goal, so it was early
declared, was to achieve full utilization of manpower without depriv-
ing workers of rights and living standards already won. And to achieve
this goal the war agencies proceeded to recognize the leaders and
unions of the American Federation of Labor as legitimate partners
worthy of joining with business and public representatives to implement war programs and determine suitable wages and working conditions. Radical and obstructionist unions, on the other hand, were to
have their organizations destroyed. In September 1917, after a series
of bitter conflicts in the copper industry, federal authorities conducted
a mass raid on the offices of the Industrial Workers of the World,
arrested the union's leaders, and used the wartime statutes to convict
and imprison some ninety-five of them. Subsequently, mob attacks on
what remained of the IWW and like-minded groups became common.

THE WAR ECONOMY IN ACTION

When Congress reconvened in early December, it could take note of
several layers of organizational growth. Yet performance was clearly
below expectations, and during the ensuing winter, as one crisis

followed another, the organizational machinery came under severe criticism from the public and from congressional investigators. On December 26 a monstrous transportation snarl brought federal seizure and operation of the railroads. Two days later the worst blizzard in forty-one years aggravated both the transportation and fuel crises. In mid-January the Fuel Administration was forced to close eastern business plants for a five-day period and for nine subsequent Mondays. And through it all, bitter quarrels developed on the labor front and over the issues of priorities, pricing, and purchasing. It seemed "such a hopeless tangle," wrote Bernard Baruch, then a Wall Street broker who was in charge of developing raw materials controls, that men who were offered war positions refused to take them and those in charge of the war agencies were eager to leave.

Gradually, however, federal orders did untangle the transportation difficulties, and between February and July of 1918 a series of actions brought greater effectiveness while retaining much of the reliance on private organizational resources. On March 4 Baruch became head of a strengthened and more effective War Industries Board. Shortly thereafter the heads of the principal war agencies began meeting with the President as a War Cabinet, thus providing a higher degree of coordination and integration. In addition, Congress established a War Finance Corporation to mobilize and allocate needed capital; the Shipping Board's controls and programs began operating more smoothly; the Postmaster General was put in charge of the telegraph and telephone industries; and to handle the problems that had developed in the labor field, the President established two new bodies that were to become models for future federal action. One was a National War Labor Board, made up of labor, management, and public representatives and charged with fostering collective bargaining and resolving labor disputes. The other was a War Labor Policies Board, established to serve as a coordinator and harmonizer for the labor and welfare programs that had been undertaken in particular industrial sectors. During the winter crisis there had been much support for taking the direction of the war effort out of the President's hands and lodging it in an independent body. But by April such proposals were fading, and in May the administration succeeded in getting through the Overman Act, a measure giving the President almost unlimited power to organize the nation's resources.

While these actions were being taken, the Food Administration was also engaged in dramatic operations that were making Herbert Hoover the best known of the nation's war managers. Operating under the Lever Act, it had organized the food industries for collective action, forcing dissenters into line through its licensing powers and using governmental marketing agencies to hold prices at specified levels and enforce industrial agreements. But of greater concern to the general populace, it was also attempting to organize farmers for greater productivity, consumers for greater conservation, and communities for action against profiteers. Working with the Department of Agriculture, it had drawn farm groups into the machinery through which incentive prices and production goals were set and had subjected them to infinite variations on the theme of "Food Will Win the War." It had conducted massive pledge campaigns, enlisting the support of individual households for Wheatless Mondays, Meatless Tuesdays, and Porkless Thursdays and Saturdays. And it had urged and helped communites to form "price interpretation boards" that compiled and published lists of those engaged in unfair pricing.

The system that had emerged by the summer of 1918 was far from being completely satisfactory. Shippers were still dissatisfied with the Railroad Administration. Consumers complained about profiteering and the rising cost of living. Antitrusters worried about a government-fostered system of "trusts." Northern and western interests disliked Wilson's concessions to powerful southern congressmen and their regional constituencies. And disgruntled business, labor, and farm groups saw themselves as being unfairly rewarded. Yet production and delivery graphs were moving upward now, lending credibility to the claim that America was meeting war needs through a system that still left much decision making in private hands. The food program, after all, was able to triple the export of foodstuffs. The coal shortage did yield to the price pegging and other ministrations of the Fuel Administration. And while the projected flow of new ships and aircraft was just getting under way as the war ended in November 1918, the overall output of war goods, measured in constant 1914 dollars, rose from $4,100,000,000 in 1917 to $9,700,000,000 in 1918.

As finally organized, the war machinery did bring greater harmony to industrial relations—partly, to be sure, through suppression and draft threats, but also through better working conditions, collective bargaining agreements, and wage and profit policies that shifted much of the war's burden to those living on savings or relatively fixed incomes. Government support for a basic eight-hour day with time and a half for overtime made this the established practice in most industries. Similar support for reducing worker discontent brought improved factory conditions, expanded programs of employee welfare, and new systems of personnel management. And out of the wage-setting apparatus came increases that allowed the average industrial worker's income to rise a bit more rapidly than the 40-percent jump in the cost of living. Very little of this, however, came at the expense of business profits. Although income, inheritance, and excess profits taxes were substantially increased, the most important "tax" was that from inflation. And from this profits were protected through cost-plus contracts and similar guarantees. Civilian sacrifice was made mostly by fixed-income groups paying higher prices, an arrangement that foreshadowed future formulas for maintaining industrial peace.

In addition, organizational leaders and labor supporters found much to admire in the new arrangements. Unions, so it seemed, had won considerable acceptance, reflected not only in the quasi-governmental positions held by union officials but in an AFL membership that had grown from 2,073,000 in 1916 to 2,726,000 by the end of the war. Trade and industrial associations had blossomed as new joint coordinators of productive effort, indicating a new spirit of cooperation that could yield great social benefits. Engineers, economists, and scientific managers had assumed roles that institutionalized their expertise for society's benefit. And at the center of the system stood a service-minded managerial elite working to integrate the products of the organizational revolution into a harmonious and productive whole. In these respects the system appeared to be a realization of prewar prescriptions for progress rather than a repudiation of them.

THE WAR AND ETHNOCULTURAL CONFLICT

While seeking to integrate organizational blocs, the war managers also urged harmony and cooperation among ethnic and racial groups. Pageants and parades featured "nationalities sections" symbolizing the unity desired, and official propaganda stressed how America had emerged from the amalgamation of many nationalities. In three ways, however, the war had the effect of enhancing ethnocultural conflict rather than reducing it. In the first place, it fostered both ideals and population movements that weakened and produced new battles against the arrangements for keeping subordinate groups in their place. Second, it aroused suspicion and distrust of those ethnic groups that could be identified with foreign enemies or who were in conflict with foreign friends. And third, it spawned a repressive loyalty apparatus that tended to fall into the hands of nativist groups or social traditionalists and be used in their actions against what they regarded as "un-American elements."

As the war proceeded the arrangements governing relations between whites and blacks came under particular stress. On one side, the need for black manpower, the intensified migration of blacks to northern cities, and the official espousal of democratic ideals provided new weapons to support new demands for racial justice. On the other, the defenders of existing arrangements took alarm and reacted with new outpourings of racial abuse and new efforts at race control. Although blacks were drafted and black officers were trained, the armed forces remained segregated institutions in which black units served chiefly as labor battalions. And while blacks benefited from war employment, their arrival in northern cities frequently aroused hostilities that exploded into rioting and violence. At East St. Louis in 1917, nine whites and over forty blacks lost their lives in a riot over employment in a defense plant. By the end of the war there was increased militance on each side, which set the stage for the eruption of the racial violence that would sweep across the country in 1919.

Arrangements defining the status of women and upholding established moral and cultural standards were also under increased stress. As women took up war work and organized themselves for war purposes, they became more insistent upon acquiring political and social rights. And despite last-ditch resistance from southern conservatives and antifeminists, the support for woman suffrage became strong enough to insure congressional passage in 1919. In addition, the war experience made life vastly more difficult for the defenders of Victorian morality and ideals. Although they could seek to shield training camps from prostitution and other vices, they found it increasingly difficult to hold the line against urban sophistication, the new morality, and cultural deviance. To these the war and the breakdown of parochialism that accompanied it gave an added impetus, and among defenders of an older America there was mounting alarm.

Meanwhile, the outpouring of anti-German propaganda was having pronounced effects on Americans who derived from German ancestry or took pride in German culture. In the eyes of Theodore Roosevelt, men who tried to be "both German and American" were "not Americans at all, but traitors to America and tools and servants of Germany against America." Superpatriots attacked German families and organizations. Many states prohibited church services in German and the teaching of German in the public schools. For the duration sauerkraut became "liberty cabbage"; German measles became "liberty measles"; and hundreds of individuals and business firms hastily anglicized their German-sounding names. As one historian has noted, the majority of Americans seemed to lose "not only their tolerance but their sense of humor as well."

Along with the propaganda, moreover, the government continued to develop an elaborate loyalty apparatus directed not only against suspected German-Americans but also against antiwar radicals, dissident Irish-Americans, conscientious objectors, and others charged with obstructing the war effort. In the spring of 1918 Congress passed both a Sabotage and a Sedition act, the former aimed at the remnants of the IWW and the latter forbidding any disloyal or abusive remarks about the United States and its system of government. Under such statutes the Justice and Post Office departments carried on extensive security operations, eventually prosecuting over 2,000 persons. And linked to these operations was an extensive network of state loyalty agencies, local defense councils or committees of public safety, and such cooperating private orders as the National Security League, the American Defense Society, and the American Protective League. As in other areas of war administration, the machinery that evolved tended to collapse distinctions between the public and private sectors, which meant in practice that "disloyalty" was defined and punished not only by legally constituted bodies but by what amounted to vigilante groups. Supplementing the prosecutions were organized lynchings,

Education + schooling during the war era

floggings, tarrings, and other extralegal acts of vengeance, all part of a behavior pattern that would reappear in the postwar Ku Klux Klan.

It was perhaps inevitable, too, that such actions against disloyalty should become confused and intermixed with nativist efforts to restore and maintain "national purity." In any event, nativist leaders frequently appeared as leaders of the loyalty organizations, and in the name of patriotism the country adopted a number of the measures long urged by nativist groups and others concerned with the corrupting effects of the new immigration. In early 1917 a measure establishing literacy requirements for incoming immigrants was passed over the President's veto. In mobilizing the schools for war purposes much emphasis was put upon Americanization programs. And advanced now as an anti-German and efficiency measure as well as a social purifier, prohibition finally became a part of national law. In the summer of 1917 the prohibitionists successfully amended the Lever bill to forbid the use of foodstuffs in the manufacture of distilled liquors; and in December of that year Congress adopted and submitted to the states a constitutional amendment prohibiting the manufacture, sale, or transportation of all alcoholic beverages. The loyalty apparatus was already becoming part of a new nativist, anti-immigrant, and antiurban crusade, one that would purportedly make America safe for "one hundred percent Americans." And the result would be heightened ethnocultural divisions and conflicts in the decade to come.

WAR AIMS AND COALITION DIPLOMACY

While they attempted to enforce domestic harmony, America's wartime leaders were also much concerned with inter-Allied harmony and, beyond that, the international harmony that could bring lasting peace. One goal of wartime diplomacy was a coordinated and effective military effort. The other was the translation of military success into a progressive and stable world order, which meant, above all, finding ways to protect liberal and peace-loving peoples from the twin scourges of German-style imperialism and antiliberal radicalism. On these ends most agreed. But about the means for attaining them, and especially over what would effectively end the German menace to world progress, there was much less consensus.

At the core of Woodrow Wilson's solution was the vision of a democratized enemy, freed of its militaristic and authoritarian proclivities and brought into a new concert of democratic power capable of providing collective security and administering peaceful progress. This was the vision implicit in Wilson's prewar pronouncements on international organization and "peace without victory," and it continued to inform his thought concerning the kind of peace that the United States should seek and help to enforce. It was a vision, however, that clashed with Allied plans for territorial and economic gains and for crushing and limiting German power rather than democratizing it. It also clashed with the propaganda image of a brutal and depraved enemy utterly incapable of participating in democratic processes. And partly because of fears that it would reduce military effectiveness, Wilson was loath during the war to point up these incongruities or insist upon resolving them.

Such fears, however, did not reduce the President to silence, especially in the face of the moral and emotional crisis engendered by the Allied military reverses of late 1917, the revolution of the Bolsheviks in Russia that November, and the subsequent publication of secret Allied treaties by the new Russian rulers. The Allies, so these revealed, had agreed among themselves to partition Turkey, divide up Germany's colonies, and pay for Italian, Japanese, and Rumanian belligerence with territories taken from the Central Powers. They seemed to be only another set of greedy imperialists. And having failed to persuade the Interallied Conference in Paris to formulate a reply, Wilson decided to do so independently. On January 8, 1918, he went before a joint session of Congress to enumerate and explain his famous Fourteen Points.

In this document Wilson specified not only the general principles of a liberal world order but also the changes necessary to free subject peoples from foreign domination. In Points 1 through 5 he called respectively for open diplomacy, freedom of the seas, equality of economic opportunity, reduction of armaments, and the impartial adjustment of colonial claims. Point 6 demanded German evacuation of

Russia and self-determination for the Russian people. Under Points 7 and 8 the Germans were to evacuate Belgium and France and restore Alsace-Lorraine to France. And Points 9 through 13 called for adjusting Italy's boundaries, granting autonomy to the subject nationalities of Austria-Hungary, restoring the Balkan nations that had fought on the Allied side, liberating the subject peoples of the Turkish Empire, and creating a free and independent Poland. Finally, as a capstone to the edifice, Wilson added and stressed a Fourteenth Point. It called for a general association of nations that would afford "mutual guarantees of political independence and territorial integrity to great and small states alike."

In the months that followed, the Fourteen Points became the great manifesto of the war, extensively used as a weapon of propaganda. Yet the European Allies gave no indication that they were willing to use them as a basis for peace. And American behavior, especially the mistrust that American authorities had of interallied bodies and their continued insistence upon remaining an "associate" rather than an "ally," raised strong doubts about the readiness of the United States to participate in a collective security system. Nor was harmony easily achieved on other matters. American insistence upon fielding an independent army in France caused much friction with the British and French. Interallied coordinating bodies were slow to be established and were frequently torn by bitter dissension over shipping and supplies. And there were mutual suspicions that much of the idealistic rhetoric, whether American or European, amounted to a smokescreen for imperial and commercial ambitions.

In addition, differences developed over appropriate responses to Russia's withdrawal from the war and to the internal struggles there. American military leaders strongly opposed any diversion of Allied troops to Russia. But under pressure from the British and French, Wilson finally agreed to limited operations designed to keep supplies out of German hands, assist friendly forces, and rescue a Czech Legion seeking to extricate itself from Russia via the Trans-Siberian Railroad. By September of 1918, American contingents had joined Allied expeditionary forces both in the Russian north, at Murmansk and Archangel, and in Siberia. In the latter expedition Japanese forces were prominent, and the American decision to participate was in part motivated by a desire to curb Japanese ambitions. Although Japan and the United States were now associates in the war against Germany, American diplomacy continued to oppose Japanese expansion in the Far East and was soon having second thoughts about an agreement of November 1917 (the Lansing-Ishii Agreement) under which Japan was recognized to have "special interests" in China.

On September 27, 1918, in conjunction with the launching of a new bond drive, Wilson forcefully reaffirmed the principles that he had enunciated in the Fourteen Points. By this time, however, the tide of battle had turned decisively in favor of the Allies, and Austria-Hungary was already suing for peace. Under the circumstances, the other Allied leaders were less inclined than ever to accept such war aims as their own. And while Wilson seemed to think that their financial dependence on the United States would "force" them to do so, he would soon learn differently.

THE FIGHTING FRONTS

Meanwhile, despite continuing problems on the diplomatic and home fronts, American troops were being transported to France and brought into military action. In May of 1917 General John J. Pershing had been chosen to head the American Expeditionary Force, and in June he arrived in France with some 15,000 American troops. By October the number had grown to 87,000. But action was still confined to defense of a quiet sector of the front east of Verdun. There Pershing had established an American command, and throughout 1917 he successfully resisted efforts to have American soldiers fed into the other Allied armies in small groups.

During the first months after the United States entered the war, the major contribution of Americans to actual fighting was on the seas. There the German submarine campaign had initially seemed to be paying off. By mid-April of 1917 it was sinking ships at a rate of nearly 900,000 tons a month, a rate that could mean the destruction of the British merchant marine, and hence of British fighting power, within six months. Under the circumstances antisubmarine warfare received top priority, both in the deployment of existing forces and in the naval expansion program. And gradually, through a combination of patrolling, convoying, and minelaying, shipping losses were reduced to tolerable levels. They were down to 400,000 tons in December 1917 and less than 200,000 tons by April 1918. The flow of foodstuffs and materials was sustained, and eventually about 2,000,000 American troops crossed the Atlantic and were deployed in France.

By the spring of 1918, however, the American forces numbered only about 300,000, and at this stage it seemed that the Germans might still win the war. The withdrawal of Russia allowed the transfer of large German armies to the Western Front. And beginning on March 21, 1918, the Germans used them to launch a series of major offensives designed to break through the Allied trench systems and end the long defensive stalemate. In the face of these German drives, the Allies established a unified command with General Ferdinand Foch as supreme commander; and with some reluctance, Pershing now agreed to the detachment and use of American units wherever they were most urgently needed. Beginning on May 31, the American Second Division and several marine units helped the French turn back the Germans at Château-Thierry and Belleau Wood, and between July 15 and August 6 some eight American divisions participated in battles that contained the last of the German offensives and forced a German retreat from the Marne River to the Vesle. By early August the German offensive power had been broken, and with American reinforcements now arriving in large numbers, the Allies were rapidly achieving the superiority necessary to take the initiative.

The result was a series of Allied offensives, forcing German retreats along the Somme River, from the area between the Oise and the Aisne, and from western Belgium. Reinforced by new American divisions, the British and French were now sweeping forward; and farther east the newly constituted American First Army was at last involved in operations of its own. In mid-September it attacked and wiped out the German salient at St. Mihiel. Later in the month it undertook the massive Meuse-Argonne offensive, driving north along the Meuse River and through the Argonne forest toward Sedan. And by early November it had destroyed a major portion of the German defense system and contributed substantially to the German decisions that led to the Armistice.

In its military operations the United States suffered far fewer casualties than the other major belligerents. Only 112,432 Americans died while in service; and of these nearly a third died in training camps, many as a consequence of the influenza epidemic that began in September 1918. Clearly the other belligerents bore the major losses associated with the war's trench-line slaughterhouses and the breaking of German military might. Yet the American contribution can be seen as providing the margin of Allied victory. It was a major factor in foiling the German gamble on submarine warfare; it provided the reinforcements needed to contain the last German offensives; and it provided the margin of military superiority that finally broke the stalemate on the Western Front.

PEACE AND BEYOND

Even before the October reversals, the German military command had concluded that only an armistice could keep the Allied armies out of Germany itself. This had been demanded by General Erich Ludendorff as early as September 29; and five days later, following the formation of a new government under Prince Max of Baden, the Germans indicated their willingness to restore peace on the basis of President Wilson's Fourteen Points. An exchange of notes followed, with Wilson insisting on German evacuation of occupied territory, an immediate end to submarine attacks, and proof that the government requesting terms really represented the German people rather than their "military masters and monarchical autocrats." To these conditions a reorganized German government agreed, and on October 23 Wilson turned to the task of obtaining their acceptance by the other belligerents.

This proved difficult. In the American camp General Pershing was now calling for unconditional surrender, and during deliberations in Paris the British, French, and Italians all voiced strong objections to

Wilson's peace proposals. Finally, however, threats that the United States would make a separate peace, coupled perhaps with fears of where the incipient revolution in Germany could lead, produced a conditional acceptance. On November 4 the Allies agreed to a peace based on the Fourteen Points with two reservations, the first being an exclusion of Point 2, in regard to freedom of the seas, and the second stipulating that Germany must pay for all civilian damages caused by its aggression. In addition, it was agreed, the armistice terms must be such as to prevent the Germans from resuming hostilities. As finally worked out, they called for evacuation of all German-occupied territory, renunciation of the German peace treaties with Russia and Rumania, Allied occupation of the German Rhineland, and the surrender of specified quantities of ships, submarines, and war matériel.

Such terms were not what the Germans had hoped for. But by the time they were offered the German condition had become desperate and German leaders saw little alternative to accepting them. By November 7 the other Central Powers had already surrendered, mutiny was sweeping the German navy, and revolution had broken out in Munich. On November 8 a German armistice commission was received by Marshal Foch in his railway coach in the Compiègne Forest, and the following day, while the commission considered Allied terms, Germany became a republic. Under pressure the Kaiser abdicated and subsequently fled to Holland. At 5:15 A.M. on November 11 the German delegates signed the armistice offered them, and less then six hours later, at 11:00 A.M. on November 11, 1918, the Great War came to an end.

As the guns fell silent, jubilant throngs celebrated the coming of peace. Liberal democracy, so it was stated and restated, had triumphed over the forces bent on its destruction. And among those who had helped to organize and administer the instruments of victory, there were many who believed that their handiwork could be adapted to the problems of postwar reconstruction and used to organize and administer peaceful progress. In the government-encouraged labor unions and welfare organizations, in the new network of association and corporate bureaucracies, and in the professional societies of engineers, economists, publicists, and efficiency experts, there were visions of a "new liberalism" in which their particular orders would play key roles. In the foreign trade field, where the Webb-Pomerene Act of April 1918 had already authorized permanent antitrust exemptions for export associations, there were hopes now of adapting much of the War Trade Board machinery to peacetime needs. In the war production agencies, discussions of reconstruction were producing designs for a continuing social cooperation built around peace industries boards, concerts of functional interests, and councils of national progress. And as diplomats and foreign policy experts prepared for the coming peace conference, they seemed confident that an association of victors could serve as the instrument for realizing Wilson's international goals.

If the new forms of association rasied hopes, however, they also produced fears, resentments, and disillusionment. Substantial minorities had come to see them not as building blocks of a progressive order but as instruments of monopoly, tyranny, terrorism, injustice, profiteering, or sectional advantage. In the Midwest, in particular, a heritage of isolationism had combined with anger over the wheat program and the loyalty measures to produce a marked revulsion against Wilson and his war managers. And elsewhere, both at home and abroad, the drift of politics in late 1918 did not bode well for the hopeful visions emanating from Wilsonian reconstructionists. Despite Wilson's plea for a Democratic Congress, it was the Republicans who won the congressional elections that fall; and despite his faith that the world's "peoples" were with him, power in Europe was gravitating toward extremists who preached either a peace of nationalistic revenge or one of international social revolution.

The war to end wars was over. But it remained to be seen whether it would achieve its goal or whether the forces it had unleashed would bring greater disorders and eventually a new and greater war.

CHAPTER 3

From War to Peace, 1918–1920

Although the armistice of November 1918 ended the war with Germany, it did not usher in a period of international and domestic tranquillity. The world inherited by the peacemakers was one in which questions of economic and social reconstruction were generating intense political heat and civil strife. And the nation inherited by the demobilizers was one ready to erupt into industrial, social, and political conflict. Both abroad and at home the architects of the war machinery tried to build comparable tools for resolving peacetime conflicts and administering national and international progress. But for the most part, their handiwork either collapsed or was repudiated, and by 1920 they were giving way to toolmakers who were more attuned to the postwar resurgence of individualistic, antistatist, and isolationist values. Eventually, peacetime counterparts for much of the war system would emerge, but they would do so in a different context and take forms that made them less vulnerable to political attack. Failure was to be the fate of the first major efforts to devise and install such counterparts.

THE POLITICS AND DIPLOMACY OF PEACEMAKING

On December 4, 1918, President Wilson, the American Peace Commission, and a large body of technical experts sailed for Europe hoping that the peace envisioned in the Fourteen Points could be translated into reality. Upon arrival Wilson made triumphal tours of the European capitals, and in January 1919, as the Peace Conference assembled in Paris, his hope of integrating a democratized enemy into a new community of power remained high. At home, however, Republican partisans had won control of Congress and were bitter over his exclusion of their leaders from the peace commission, a situation hardly calculated to strengthen his position at the peace table. And in the other victorious nations, supporters of the Wilsonian design were now losing ground to those who called for revenge, heavy reparations, and a permanent reduction of German power. In Britain the elections of December 1918 demonstrated the political potency of such slogans as "Hang the Kaiser" and "Make Germany Pay." In France Premier Georges Clemenceau headed a government bent on retribution and ironclad guarantees of future French security, and in both Italy and Japan emphasis was being put upon obtaining the territories and other concessions that had lured them into the war. Increasingly the pattern seemed to be moving toward a conclave of victors quarreling over the spoils rather than one of disinterested statesmen assuring future world peace.

As the conference met, moreover, the fate of Russia and the impact that Bolshevism might have on the rest of Europe remained huge question marks. German instability, Russian calls for world revolution, and short-lived Communist take-overs in Hungary and Bavaria were all aspects of a larger threat that worried the peacemakers no end. And even as they quarreled over how to rid the world of Kaiserism, they also became involved in running disputes over how best to contain and put an end to the Communist menace. For Wilson and his supporters, the answer was to liquidate the Allied military intervention in Russia, relieve the human misery upon which Bolshevism fed, and build a strong democratic Germany that could act as a stabilizing force. But for other Allied leaders, especially the French, it was military measures to contain and then overthrow Russia's Communist regime. While the United States proceeded to extract its troops from northern Russia and seek stability through large-scale food relief programs, Clemenceau and his supporters urged increased Allied military and economic aid for those Russians and other eastern Europeans who were fighting the Bolsheviks.

As negotiations proceeded, Wilson's opposition limited what the French could do in Eastern Europe. The Allied military interventions did come to an end; and while a series of anti-Communist states emerged along Russia's western border, the new Poland was shaped more by Wilson's designs than by those of the French. In regard to Germany, on the other hand, Wilson yielded much to French demands. Although American and British opposition killed Clemenceau's plan for buffer states in the German Rhineland, the final settlement called for a fifteen-year occupation and permanent demilitarization of the region; for the return of Alsace-Lorraine to France and French acquisition of the coal mines in the German Saarland; and for strict limitations on the future size of Germany's army and navy. In addition, Germany was to lose territory to Belgium, Denmark, and Poland and was not to unite with the remnants of Austria. It was to be stripped of its overseas colonies and forced to pay for its past aggression. And to guard against any future German revival, Britain and the United States were to give guarantees of the future security of France. Wilson's presence undoubtedly prevented an even harsher treaty. But clearly more reliance was being put upon keeping Germany weak than upon integrating a democratic Germany into a new community of democratic power.

On two other key issues, those concerning colonial areas and reparations payments, Wilson also yielded much ground. He agreed, in effect, that Germany's colonial empire and much of the Turkish Empire should be divided up among the Allied nations, their only concession being that the areas should be held as mandates from the League of Nations rather than as outright possessions. He also conceded that the Japanese might take title to the German economic concessions in the Shantung area of China, provided they promised to return political control to the Chinese. And in assessing reparations he gradually gave way to the extreme Allied demands. He acquiesced in a "war guilt" clause under which Germany was forced to acknowledge sole guilt for causing the war and to accept legal responsibility for all losses incurred by the Allied peoples and governments. He agreed to large exactions of reparations in kind, and he did not insist that the reparations be set at a fixed sum payable in a specified time. Eventually a reparations commission would fix Germany's obligations at the astronomical figure of 136,000,000,000 gold marks, approximately $33,000,000,000.

Another major issue at the conference concerned the territories formerly held by an Austro-Hungarian Empire that had now disintegrated. Boundaries had to be set for the successor nations of Austria, Hungary, Czechoslovakia, and Yugoslavia, boundaries that Wilson tried to draw along lines of nationality or ethnicity but which often reflected other considerations. An especially heavy burden for the peacemakers was the clash between Yugoslavian and Italian aspirations, particularly over the city of Fiume at the head of the Adriatic Sea. Italy, as Wilson saw it, had no valid claim to a seaport that was essential to Yugoslavia's economic well-being. He resisted all Italian efforts to acquire it, even going so far as to make a direct appeal to the Italian people over the head of their government. And despite a protest walkout by Premier Vittorio Orlando and Foreign Minister Sidney Sonnino, Wilson remained unwilling to compromise. The issue was finally left for direct negotiations between the Italians and Yugoslavs.

As the peace settlement took shape, Wilson recognized that it contained inequities and defects. Yet these, he believed, were correctable if the right kind of international organization could be established. For him the Covenant of the League of Nations had become the central and redeeming feature of the conference's handiwork, and this he had been able to shape in accordance with his own prescriptions. In early confrontations he had insisted upon an organization open to all nations, not just a league of victors. He had also insisted that the League be an integral part of the peace treaty and the agency for its execution; and subsequently, following a brief return visit to the United States, he had obtained provisions designed to accommodate America's Monroe Doctrine and to exempt domestic issues, allow withdrawal, and permit rejection of a League mandate.

As finally written, the League Covenant called for an organization that would function through two major organs, an Assembly made up of all members, and a Council consisting of the major powers as permanent members and four smaller nations chosen by the Assembly. There would also be an administrative secretariat, an international court, and a variety of technical agencies. And at the heart of the organization, providing the foundation upon which cooperative structures were to be erected, would be a mutual guarantee by all members of each other's independence and territorial integrity. The League would not have its own army or police force. But its decisions would have behind them the force of international law, moral right, and world public opinion, and in cases of aggression it might call upon its members to take appropriate action against the aggressor.

By the end of April 1919, the peacemakers had written a treaty for Germany, and on May 7 it was formally presented to delegates from the new German Republic. They protested strongly, arguing that it was a dictated and punitive peace wholly out of keeping with the one promised in the pre-Armistice negotiations. But there was no alternative to acceptance, and on June 28, in the Hall of Mirrors in Versailles Palace, the formal signing took place. Wilson believed that he had helped to forge a lasting peace structure, but it was certainly not the one envisioned in his Fourteen Points. And critics, then and since, have insisted that, for all the difficulties involved, more of the original design could have been realized. Wilson, they have charged, traded much of it away for the pipe dream of a League of Nations, and as a bargainer he failed to mobilize and use what might have been his most effective weapons. At a time when the Allies were financially dependent on the United States, he made no serious effort to apply the economic pressure that could have brought political concessions.

Whatever the merits of such charges, the big question now was whether the treaty could win approval in the American Senate. At home Wilson faced a Congress controlled by an opposition party anxious to discredit him. He also faced growing sentiment for withdrawing from abroad, isolating America from Europe's "social diseases," and ending arrangements that allegedly allowed Old World politicians to use American resources for their own selfish ends. Furthermore, the treaty as written was satisfactory neither to the advocates of a harsh peace serving narrow national interests nor to those who had shared Wilson's hopes for a new international order. From one side he was accused of serving the interests of the Germans and Bolsheviks; from the other of helping greedy Allied imperialists to hatch an "inhuman monster."

THE PEACE TREATY IN THE SENATE

On July 10, 1919, Wilson formally presented the Treaty of Versailles to the United States Senate. To reject it, he said, would "break the heart of the world," and he left little doubt about his opposition to any amendments or reservations. Equally clear, however, was his opponents' determination not to accept the treaty as written. Their first resort was to lengthy proceedings before the Senate Foreign Relations Committee, a body chaired by Senate Majority Leader Henry Cabot Lodge. And when it became clear that a large majority of the Republican senators favored reservations of varying strength, Senator Lodge placed himself at the head of the "strong rerservationists." The treaty, so his group insisted, must explicitly recognize congressional prerogatives and the nation's autonomy in immigration and tariff matters. It must not commit the United States to preserving such things as the British Empire or Japan's hold on Shantung. And above all, Congress must have the right to evaluate each situation that might possibly require the use of American forces. The League guarantees must not become blank checks for future American participation in collective security measures.

By making a few mild concessions, Wilson might have enlisted the support of a number of the reservationists. His decision instead was to take his case to the people; and for some three weeks in September 1919, as his new speaking tour moved across the country, it seemed that he might indeed check the rising cynicism and force favorable action in the Senate. His health, however, was fragile. He had a long history of cerebral vascular disease, including several earlier episodes that some historians have seen as being partly responsible for his growing intellectual rigidity. And attacks of illness now brought his tour to an end. On September 25, after making an address in Pueblo, Colorado, he became too ill to continue; and on October 2, shortly after his return to Washington, he suffered a severe stroke that paralyzed the left side of his face and body. For two weeks he was close to death, and for six weeks more he remained seriously ill, with his wife and physician shielding him from most matters of government business.

With Wilson virtually out of action, the outcome in the Senate was probably a foregone conclusion. There the "irreconcilables," who opposed the treaty under any circumstances, now joined with the "reservationists" to add some fourteen reservations, twelve of them proposed by Senator Lodge. The choice, it seemed, had become one of a treaty with the Lodge reservations or no treaty at all. Yet Wilson still refused to accept the former or to allow his supporters to do so. On November 19 his followers joined with the "irreconcilables" to defeat the treaty with the reservations included, and immediately thereafter a Democratic resolution to ratify without reservations also failed. As matters stood, neither Wilson nor Lodge could muster the necessary two-thirds majority.

During the next four months a number of individuals and groups tried without success to arrange a compromise. Others pleaded with Wilson to give in, and from the Allied nations came indications that they would welcome ratification on Lodge's terms. But to Wilson this still amounted to nullification; and when a new vote was taken on March 19, 1920, the results were basically similar to the one in 1919. Although twenty-one Democrats broke ranks and voted for the treaty with Lodge's reservations, the number sticking with Wilson was sufficient to prevent ratification. To end the state of hostilities, Congress then adopted a resolution repealing the declarations of war against Germany and Austria-Hungary. But this the President vetoed, thus leaving the nation in a technical state of war. The coming elections, he had declared, would be a "great and solemn referendum" on the League issue, but he was unable to make them so or to alter the Senate in the direction he desired. The United States would not ratify the Treaty of Versailles and would not join the League of Nations.

Whether or not Wilson himself was responsible, his vision of a new international order would remain an unrealized dream. What would take shape instead was two weaker and more national-oriented systems, one built around the Anglo-French alliances and their extension in the League apparatus, the other around a new set of American-sponsored treaties, expert commissions, and cooperative arrangements. The building of a progressive world order, so the policy makers of the 1920s would insist, was taking place without sacrificing the benefits and safeguards of national autonomy. But the structures erected were to prove incapable of preventing a world depression and a second and greater world war.

THE SEARCH FOR DOMESTIC MANAGERIAL TOOLS

At the same time that the peacemakers were laboring to create international order, a number of America's war managers had been trying to adapt wartime structures to the tasks of postwar reconstruction and peacetime management. From mid-1918 on, they had been discussing which features of war collectivism should be retained. As their discussions proceeded, they came to see properly modified war organizations as the tools through which prewar designs for a "new liberalism" might be realized. And by the end of the war they had produced a variety of blueprints for making the necessary modifications. Being planned or discussed were such agencies as a "reconstruction council," a "peace industries board," a "labor relations tribunal," a "peace policies inquiry," and a "living conditions commission."

Just as these designs were being elaborated, however, the obstacles in the way of their realization were becoming insurmountable. Groups that had been critical of the war administration were in no mood to tolerate a peacetime counterpart. Congress was unsympathetic and eager to regain its prewar role in policy making. Private organizational leaders were under increasing pressure to abandon collaboration with class enemies or rival interests. And disintegrating now, as the dollar-a-year men ended their volunteer service, was the administrative elite that had facilitated public-private cooperation and dampened traditional fears of statism, collective action, and monopoly power. Indeed, within the Wilson Administration itself there were strong doubts that such agencies were needed or desirable or that they were politically attainable. Even Bernard Baruch, who had been looked to for leadership, was unwilling to urge extension of the industrial arrangements. Nor had the President been persuaded. On December 2, partly perhaps to placate conservative opposition to his foreign policy, he dissociated himself from reconstruction planning and proposed to leave readjustment problems to the individual efforts of "spirited businessmen and self-reliant laborers."

Not surprisingly, then, early efforts to install postwar substitutes for the war organizations were unsuccessful. They could neither halt liquidation of the key war boards nor establish new agencies of reconstruction. Yet this initial failure did not end the search for domestic managerial tools. As it turned out, a reconversion left to "spirited businessmen and self-reliant laborers" became one punctuated by bitter industrial conflicts and massive fluctuations in employment, demand, and prices. It was one that generated recurring waves of demand for crisis management. And in response to these, a number of the former war managers kept trying to resurrect segments of the war machinery and turn them into tools for resolving and preventing peacetime crises.

In early 1919 the three most urgent crises were those posed by unemployed veterans and war workers, canceled Allied orders for American foodstuffs, and business fears of impending deflation. The great need, given the rapidity of military demobilization, was to find substitutes for the economy's war component. And efforts to do this did involve limited extensions or resurrections of the war apparatus. What remained of the War Labor Administration joined with private and local partners in campaigns to step up expenditures on construction and public works. What remained of the food and war credit machinery became closely linked to relief and rehabilitation activities in Europe, continuing through them to support agricultural and export markets. And in the Commerce Department a group of former dollar-a-year men succeeded in creating an Industrial Board, designed to change business psychology through negotiation and support of "fair prices." From its labors came a steel price schedule, defended by board chairman George Peek as being scientifically determined. But when the Railroad Administration disagreed and the Attorney General threatened antitrust action, the Board's operations came to an end.

In Congress efforts to convert these forms of collective action into continuing stabilizers received little help. There the emphasis was on economy and tax relief, not managerial tools. Yet economic difficulties persisted. By late spring, concern with finding replacements for military demand was giving way to overoptimism and a speculative boom with rapidly rising living costs. By fall the nation was suffering through one of the worst bouts of price inflation and labor turmoil in its history. And while one response was to look for "subversives," another was new attempts to install managerial tools modeled after those of the war period. One new creation was a High Cost of Living Division. Set up in the Justice Department under an extension of the Lever Act, it was charged not only with prosecuting extortionists but also with reestablishing the wartime network of profit restraints, conservation activities, and price interpretation boards. Temporarily the Fuel Administration was also revived. And through two Industrial Conferences, one meeting in October 1919 and the second studying the situation from December 1919 to March 1920, efforts were made to resurrect the wartime system of labor tribunals and labor-management cooperation.

Again, though, the tool designers were unable to surmount the obstacles that blocked implementation of their designs. The Industrial Conferences did not bring forth the contemplated machinery, and the problems of the revived Fuel Administration, the High Cost of Living Division, and what remained of the wartime food organizations were such as to make them more enemies than friends. In 1920 they all expired, their demise signaling another major defeat for those who had hoped to convert the public side of the war apparatus into peacetime managerial tools. When Congress adjourned, the War Finance Corporation was still functioning. But the hope was that new investment cooperatives, to be formed under the Edge Act of December 1919, would soon take its place. And the only other major survivals of the war state were those that had been authorized to continue under the Transportation and Merchant Marine acts of 1920. For railroads and shipping, Congress had rejected nationalization schemes and proposals for national transportation planning. But it had authorized a continuing mix of public aids, regulatory restraints, and government-fostered combination and cooperation, all designed, in theory anyway, to bring rationalized transportation systems.

With the war over, traditional fears of big government had reasserted themselves and been spurred along by taxpayers and regulated interests who believed they stood to gain from shrinking the public sector. Many had come to believe that economic dysfunctions were best corrected by shrinking government rather than by expanding it. And for the time being, this antistatism had blocked not only the advocates of new social programs but also those who would use the state to coordinate and support private organizational elites. Antistatism, however, did not necessarily mean a scrapping of the private side of war organization. Over whether to do this, in whole or in part, other battles were being waged.

ANTIUNIONISM AND NATIONAL PURIFICATION

Two such battles, often interconnected, were over the peacetime roles of labor unions and of loyalty organizations. One involved the fate of war-fostered unionization, specifically whether it should become part of a new organizational order or should be scrapped as something appropriate only for a national emergency. The other involved the fate of the wartime loyalty machinery, specifically whether it should now be abolished as no longer needed or should be retained as a continuing safeguard against subversion and un-Americanism. On each question peace brought a clash of differing expections, which, for a time, made for anything but domestic tranquillity.

Initially, in late 1918 and early 1919, the expectations of unionists and their supporters seemed closer to realization. Workers concerned with maintaining their wartime incomes were joining labor organizations, and through strikes and strike threats were able to expand the area of collective bargaining and defend the real income of union members. For much of the public, however, unions had no rightful place in a peacetime system. They quickly came under attack from a growing antiunion movement, operating both through business associations committed to the "open shop" and through groups urging company unions, corporate welfare programs, and new kinds of personnel management. And by mid-1919 their position was a rapidly weakening one. Unions no longer had government support; they were being blamed for the rising cost of living and lagging productivity; and in a public mind inflamed with anti-Bolshevik hysteria the distinction between good American unions and those bent on social revolution had become increasingly dim. Antiunion activists were charging that all unions tended toward corruption or subversion, and many Americans seemed to agree.

The stage was set for major labor defeats. And in late 1919, as the Communist issue diverted even more attention from legitimate grievances, unionism suffered one setback after another. The great steel strike which began on September 22 was soon crumbling under the weight of massive public disapproval, stern repression of union activities, and armed protection for imported strikebreakers. Intended to achieve union recognition and an eight-hour day, it ended in defeat and obliteration for the new steelworkers' union. In Boston a strike of the police force brought intervention and union busting by Governor Calvin Coolidge. There was, he said, "no right to strike against the public safety by anybody, anywhere, any time." And in November, when the coal miners struck for higher pay, Attorney General A. Mitchell Palmer used the Lever Act to obtain court injuctions ordering them to cease all strike activity. The miners eventually returned to work after receiving a small wage increase and a promise of governmental arbitration.

In the wake of such defeats unionism did not disappear. In 1920 the American Federation of Labor had 3,260,000 members (over 500,000 more than at war's end), and in the early 1920s some unions retained enough power to create major crises. Yet efforts to organize the basic and mass production industries had clearly been thwarted. The dream of converting the war-fostered unions into components of a new organizational system was not to be realized. And as antiunionism gained new impetus during the post-1920 recession, labor organization would soon recede to roughly the same position it had occupied before the war. What the New Era would take from wartime labor developments was not the independent unions. It was rather the management-organized employee associations, the vertical committees in which management exercised leadership, and the new personnel work with its vision of creating a labor force for which unions would have no appeal.

Meanwhile, even as the fate of the wartime labor system was being decided, American society was being rent by conflict of other sorts. Ethnic divisions were being acerbated by ethnic-related quarrels over the peace settlement, new demands for immigration restriction, and new efforts to convert "hyphenated Americans" into "real Americans." Cultural divisions were taking on a new intensity, especially over the war-fostered victories of the prohibitionists and feminists and the new morality and intellectual currents that the war had promoted. Religious conflict was mounting, sparked particularly by a new fundamentalist militancy against modernist error and creeping secularism. And racial tensions now, built up during the war period and exacerbated by clashing postwar expectations, were producing not only racist creeds and organizations but violent and destructive race riots. Between July and December 1919 some twenty cities exploded into orgies of burning, looting, and killing, leaving 120 dead and thousands homeless. Many feared that America was coming apart, the prey of those who hoped to benefit from chaos and anarchy. And it was in the context of such fears that champions of order were busily engaged in finding new uses for the wartime loyalty apparatus.

In particular, it was said, America needed purgatives and antibodies to deal with the social and political poisons now undermining its national life. In the spreaders of such poisons, especially in the newly formed Communist parties and in the anarchists and socialists who were sympathetic to them, it faced a new national enemy too insidious to be tolerated or absorbed into the body politic. It was an enemy that would have to be fought through special agencies and cooperating private bodies, similar to those established during the war. And by late 1919 a new network of such agencies and organizations was in operation. In the Justice Department, Attorney General Palmer had put J. Edgar Hoover in charge of a new antiradical division. Arrayed around it were cooperating federal bureaus and state agencies, and attached as informal or quasi-official extensions were the wartime loyalty organizations plus such newly formed groups as the Allied Loyalty League and the American Legion.

For a time the network's operations enjoyed strong support. In the spring of 1919 a series of terroristic actions, especially the mailing of bombs to prominent officials and the bombing of Palmer's Washington residence, had generated widespread alarm and a growing audience for antiradicalism. When General Leonard Wood called for a policy of "S.O.S.—ship or shoot"—deport or kill the alien radicals supposedly at the root of all political unrest—many Americans seemed to agree. Protest remained minimal as vigilante groups moved into action, state and local officials raided suspected radicals, and federal officials invoked wartime statutes and began dragnet arrests and summary deportations of aliens. Nor were the courts inclined to see such actions as being violations of constitutional liberties. In the Schenck and Abrams cases of 1919, the Supreme Court held that any action constituting a "clear and present danger" to the social order did not enjoy the protection of the First Amendment; and by applying this doctrine, it upheld convictions under the wartime Espionage and Sedition acts.

As hysteria mounted, then, "red scare" justice frequently replaced that grounded in the traditions of Anglo-Saxon jurisprudence. In Centralia, Washington, IWW agitator Wesley Everest was dragged from the town jail, castrated, and hanged from the girders of a railroad bridge. In the coroner's report he was alleged to have "jumped off with a rope around his neck and then shot himself full of holes." In New York thousands cheered as the U.S.S. *Buford*, the so-called Soviet Ark, departed for Hangö, Finland, with a cargo of 249 deportees. Included were not only such notorious "propagandists by deed" as Emma Goldman and Alexander Berkman but also more than two hundred people whose only offense was espousal of anarchist ideas. In Detroit the great majority of some eight hundred people seized and held amid wretched conditions in city buildings turned out to be what a citizens' committee called "plain, ignorant foreigners" rather than "dangerous radicals." And in South Braintree, Massachusetts, police searching for the murderers of a shoe company paymaster arrested Nicola Sacco and Bartolomeo Vanzetti, both Italian aliens and both avowed anarchists. Later the prosecuting attorney would make the defendants' radicalism the cornerstone of his case, and they would be convicted and sentenced to death.

Amid tragedy and moral outrages there was also some comic relief. In Chicago "patriotic" prisoners rioted, taking violent exception to having "reds" put in the same cells with them. "There are some things," one newspaper remarked, "at which even a Chicago crook draws the line." In New Brunswick, New Jersey, the scene of raids on a Socialist club, seized papers that were thought to be plans for "various types of bombs" were finally identified as drawings for an improved phonograph. But such ridiculousness was lost on the great majority of those now caught up in fear, hysteria, and zealotry. It was not until January 1920, when the Labor Department refused to cooperate in holding and deporting the 6,000 victims of the largest raids, that such antiradical measures provoked much concern about civil liberties or denials of due process; and it was several more months before the perceptions used to justify the antiradical operations began to change.

As the "red scare" finally began to recede, loyalty groups had greater difficulty in obtaining governmental support and keeping their quasi-official status. Yet "un-Americanism," as some of them were now defining it, had come, once again, to include more than espousals of radical doctrine. It had become partly a matter of ethnicity, race, religion, and social values, all areas where the true "hundred percent American" must be separated and saved from impure and contaminating elements. And it was as safeguards against and controllers of this "un-Americanism"—as vehicles, in other words, of new nativist, anti-immigrant, and antiurban crusades—that the organizations born of the war and strengthened during the intimidation of 1919 would remain active in the 1920s. Unlike the federal war agencies and the labor unions, they would not only survive but would remain a major political force; and as the decade began, they were already pushing hard for new exclusion, Americanization, and purification measures.

VISIONS OF A NEW INDIVIDUALISM

Running through much of the postwar assault on government, unionization, and "un-Americanism" was a recurring appeal to America's tradition of economic individualism. It was an appeal that could also be used to attack business organization; and for a time, in 1919 and 1920, such attacks did bring a revival of antitrust activities and heightened resistance to organizers of business cooperation. In the face of them, schemes for permanent relaxation of the antitrust laws failed to win legislative approval, schemes for retaining the war service committees lost support and foundered, and business leaders talked less of price and production agreements and more of organizing to promote "intelligent competition." Responding to allegations that business combines were responsible for the economic troubles of the reconversion period, the antitrust agencies stirred from their wartime sleep and began attacking collusion and conspiracy in such areas as foodstuffs, fuels, textiles, and building materials. By early 1920 a number of the prewar antitrust cases had been revived; others were being prepared against war-encouraged associational activities; and some federal and state investigators were hunting "monopolists" almost as zealously as others were hunting "reds."

Unlike labor organizers, however, business organizers were able to erect shields against their antagonists and preserve much of what the war had brought about. Legally they won an expanded "rule of reason," enunciated especially in the U.S. Steel Corporation case of March 1920. Under this no combination seemed too large to be legal, provided it did not unduly restrain competition. And ideologically they managed to cultivate images that distinguished their bureaucracies from other kinds and depicted them as sustainers and improvers of individualism rather than underminers or destroyers of it. Unlike the old "trusts" and "rings," so the argument ran, the new business organizations were service-minded, public-spirited, growth-oriented, technically progressive, and scientifically managed. Their emphasis was upon improving the informational and moral base of economic individualism, not supplanting it. And through them the American people might meet modern social and national needs while retaining business independence and the traditional curbs on big government and monopolistic conspiracies.

Behind such shields corporate consolidators and association builders were active. They formed new holding companies and financial consortia, justifying them as the most effective tools for dealing with national and international problems. They organized expanded informational exchanges, waste elimination programs, and monitors of unethical conduct, all justified as in the public interest and as encouraging healthier competition. And in agriculture, where cooperationists had tough going despite antitrust exemptions, the immediate postwar period brought both a federation of the farm bureaus and continued growth of commodity groups and marketing associations. Much of the war-fostered associational development was sustaining itself now, and it was being argued that actions building on this development could bring the "new individualism" envisioned by some prewar progressives. They could, in the words of the publicist and educator Glenn Frank, bring needed ordering mechanisms and community action while restraining "political government," and could thus save America from "a rampant unsocial individualism on the one hand and an inefficient amateur bureaucracy on the other."

Among such actions, it was also being argued, should be the development of a nonstatist coordinating mechanism, capable of establishing social goals and of ordering associational activities in ways that could achieve them. Numerous collaborative councils, special tribunals, and advisory planning boards, schemes that could allegedly recapture the "truly progressive" features of the war system, were proposed. Offered as well were plans for educational reform, envisioning educators and publicists as promoters of the needed harmony. And especially noticeable were efforts to establish apolitical research institutes, where, it was claimed, objective scientists could generate and disseminate authoritative facts and thereby clear the way for optimal solutions in the interest of all legitimate social groups. By 1920 the business community had brought into being such organizations as the Brookings Institution, the Twentieth Century Fund, the National Bureau of Economic Research, and an adaptation of the wartime National Research Council.

In addition, certain professional groups were offering themselves as having special credentials for the role of social orderers and coordinators. Such could be the role, so Irving Fisher thought, of the American Economic Association. Similar aspirations were voiced by such efficiency groups as the Taylor Society, and the engineering associations were making a particularly strong bid. During the war they had served as quasi-official bodies; pointing now to the untapped social resources created by engineering training, they laid claim to a central role in postwar reconstruction. In 1920 they federated into a national union, elected Herbert Hoover the federation's first president, and began a Waste Survey designed to stimulate and guide associational activities. Out of it and similar surveys, Hoover argued, could come "a plan of individualism and associational activities" that would preserve "the initiative, the inventiveness, the individuality, the character of man" yet would also "enable us to synchronize socially and economically this gigantic machine that we have built out of applied science."

By late 1920 the revulsion against statist activities seemed to be moderating to the point where governmental promotion of a "new individualism" could win limited funding and sustain itself politically. Fears of creating an uncontrollable monster were receding. Demands for economic aids were growing again, reflecting the collapse of the inflationary boom and the onset of a severe recession. And exploiting the situation were promoters of governmental services that would allegedly advance scientific understanding and assist in developing the new system of associational activities. In essence they were calling for departments of Commerce, Labor, Agriculture, Interior, and Social Welfare that would function as carefully delimited and therefore safe and productive extensions of private associational networks, and as the year ended their proposals were intermixed with those calling for greater economy, less government, and more tax relief.

THE SELECTION OF A NEW PRESIDENT

For promoters of the "new individualism" the ideal President would have been Herbert Hoover, and in early 1920 a short-lived Hoover boomlet did develop. Among those who controlled the Republican party machinery, however, Hoover had relatively little support. On June 8, when the convention gathered in Chicago, the leading contenders were General Leonard Wood, Governor Frank Lowden of Illinois, and Senator Hiram Johnson of California. None of them, as it turned out, could put together a majority, and in this situation the initiative passed to a small group of senatorial and business leaders who hoped to nominate a dependable and controllable party regular. On the evening of June 11, with the convention adjourned overnight, the group decided to support Senator Warren G. Harding of Ohio. And it was Harding, a man whose chief qualification seemed to be his good relationships with all party factions, who now became the compromise candidate. When balloting resumed he became a prominent contender, and on the tenth ballot he received the nomination. For Vice-President, Harding's supporters had picked Senator Irvine Lenroot of Wisconsin. But on this the convention refused to go along. It chose instead Governor Calvin Coolidge of Massachusetts, the man who had won public fame and widespread acclamation for crushing the Boston police strike.

The Democrats met in San Francisco on June 28, and their convention too turned into a deadlock. The two leading contenders were former Secretary of the Treasury William Gibbs McAdoo and Attorney General A. Mitchell Palmer. After a protracted struggle, Palmer released his delegates. But most of them went to candidates other than McAdoo, and eventually the Democrats followed the Republican example and looked to Ohio for a nominee. On the forty-fourth ballot they nominated James M. Cox, the state's governor and the candidate with the closest ties to the party's urban and antiprohibition elements. As Cox's running mate the convention chose Franklin D. Roosevelt of New York, who was serving at the time as Assistant Secretary of the Navy and was a strong League of Nations supporter.

During the campaign Cox and Roosevelt urged ratification of the Versailles Treaty and warned that a victory for Harding would mean the end of progressivism in domestic politics. Harding, on the other hand, straddled the League issue, encouraging both "irreconcilables" and "reservationists" to believe that his victory could serve their cause. He also appealed to the longing for domestic peace, for "normalcy," as he put it, rather than "nostrums." And campaigning against Wilson rather than Cox, he won over a number of groups that had come to blame Wilson and his works for their difficulties. In particular, the Democrats lost the support of the ethnic, independent, and western farm blocs that had enabled them to reelect Wilson in 1916, and when the votes were counted Harding had won the most lopsided electoral triumph since the reelection of James Monroe a century earlier. In the electoral college Cox carried only eleven states—the Democratic "solid South"—for an electoral count of 127 to Harding's 404. In the popular vote Harding received 16,152,200 votes, some 61 percent of the total. Cox got only 9,147,353, while Eugene Debs, running on the Socialist party ticket even though he was still in federal prison for obstructing the war effort, polled a surprising 919,799. In the congressional races the Republicans ended up with a majority of 309 to 132 in the House of Representatives and 59 to 37 in the Senate.

Hopes of reestablishing a reform coalition, obtaining ratification of the Versailles Treaty, and installing the peacetime management envisioned in 1918 had all been shattered. Yet the victorious political coalition was hardly a monolith rigidly committed to laissez faire and hypernationalism. Nor were the economic interests supporting it all rigid adherents of old-style business fundamentalism. Within it were substantial elements of the organizational elite that had built and administered the war system, those who shared much of the perception that lay behind the organizational initiatives that were defeated in the immediate postwar period. And under the auspices of such administrators as Herbert Hoover, Henry C. Wallace, and Charles Evans Hughes, all preaching versions of a "new individualism," this elite would mount its own quest for resurrecting and perpetuating what it regarded as the "progressive features" of the war apparatus.

CHAPTER 4

In Search of Peace and Prosperity, 1921–1924

Historians have long looked upon the presidency of Warren G. Harding as a major debacle. "Normalcy," they have explained in great detail, really meant the transfer of government to corruptionists, incompetents, and rapacious special interests. Often missing from their accounts is the fact that the Harding era also came close to combining full employment and rising living standards with stable prices and international peace. For all the scandals, the new administration presided over a series of developments that made the American economy the envy of much of the world; and for all its commitments to small government and national protectionism, it offered a base for those seeking to reestablish major features of the war system and to organize a Republican alternative to Wilsonian internationalism. In part, the story of America from 1921 to 1924 was one of political pilfering and continuing xenophobia accompanied by retreats into weaker government, a narrower interest consciousness, and a diminished sense of international obligation. But it was one as well of new managerial designs reflecting the continuing search for a "new liberalism" and foreshadowing the "modern capitalism" of a later era.

THE PRESIDENT AND THE POLICY MAKERS

The new President, of course, was not among those who had helped to build the war organizations or enunciate managerial goals and values. Born in Blooming Grove, Ohio, in 1865, Harding had risen in life as

owner and editor of the *Marion Star* and as an effective practitioner of
local politics and small-town amenities. In a career that carried him
from the state legislature to the United States Senate to the White
House, he had become noted chiefly for his affability and party
loyalty, his knack for promoting harmony, and his capacity for saying
little yet impressing people with how he said it. His understanding of
the world outside Ohio politics was minimal, and in the White House
he continued to operate as an Ohio politician and small-town
socializer. "God, I can't be an ingrate," he is supposed to have said.
And in practice, the friends, associates, and supporters to whom he felt
grateful received ample rewards. Men from his circle in Marion were
appointed to such positions as Comptroller of the Currency, Director
of the Mint, and Superintendent of Federal Prisons. Men to whom he
had taken a liking were responsible for subsequent scandals in the
Veterans' Bureau and the Alien Property Office, and in what turned
out to be two of his most disastrous appointments he elevated close
personal friends to cabinet positions. For Attorney General he chose
his long-time political manager, Harry M. Daugherty, and for
Secretary of the Interior his closest friend in the Senate, Albert B. Fall
of New Mexico.

Having taken care of friends and supporters, however, Harding was
willing to delegate economic and diplomatic policy making to the
"superior minds" who understood such matters. Thus his cabinet
came to include not only Daugherty and Fall but four of the strongest
cabinet-level officers in the nation's history. Andrew Mellon, wealthy
head of a financial empire and master of corporate finance, now
became Secretary of the Treasury and the man responsible for making
fiscal policy and bringing business methods to public finance. Charles
Evans Hughes, the Republican presidential nominee in 1916 and the
nation's most eminent lawyer, became Secretary of State. Henry C.
Wallace, Iowa farm editor and a major figure in farm politics, became
Secretary of Agriculture and took charge of efforts to aid agricultural
readjustment. And Herbert Hoover, the wartime food administrator
and the nation's most eminent engineer, became Secretary of Commerce and set out to turn that department into a vast research and
consulting service for economic decision makers.

Three of this "big four" had ties to Republican progressivism and
had shared some of the earlier hopes for developing cooperative

harmony under expert leadership. Hughes, Wallace, and Hoover had all been appointed in the face of opposition from party conservatives, and as administrators they envisioned a positive role for government going beyond that prescribed in business fundamentalism or Republican orthodoxy. Properly staffed and delimited, they argued, government could serve as a catalyzer and coordinator of cooperative endeavors, a gatherer and clearing house of needed information, and a consulting service for those in need of organizational and technical expertise. It was, to be sure, a poor instrument for making economic decisions or delivering social services. But it could act constructively to improve the private institutions responsible for economic and social welfare and to help institutional leaders see the larger picture and their particular role in an integrated and harmonious whole.

As constituted, then, the new administration contained influential spokesmen for a view of government drawn from the war experience and certain elements of prewar progressivism. Yet limiting what the new administrators could do were a number of constraints and obstacles. They could not ignore the pressures for tax reduction, government shrinking, and old-style protectionism. They faced uncooperative economic blocs and powerful administrative agencies. Power systems abroad, especially in Japan, Russia, and France, were annoyingly resistant to their designs for world order. And their positions depended upon a president who was inclined to defer to the "best minds" yet reluctant to accept measures that were politically damaging or did too much violence to his small-town value system.

Policy was based on the balances struck between these opposing forces; and not surprisingly it contained a number of inconsistencies. Government shrinking advanced hand in hand with national protectionism, new programs of internal improvement, and new measures of farm relief. And there was movement toward the kind of managerial tools and aids that Hoover, Hughes, and Wallace envisioned—enough movement, indeed, to lend credibility to claims that permanent peace and prosperity were in train and that ways had been found to realize the dreams of the progressive era while avoiding the evils feared by conservatives. In part the continued weakness of reform statism can be explained in terms of weariness, disillusionment, popular diversions, and political fragmentation. But also involved was a widespread belief that the "best minds" of the time were committed to progressive ends and were successfully developing superior tools for attaining them.

THE SEARCH FOR INTERNATIONAL STABILITY

As Americans looked out upon the world in 1921, they tended to see a compound of error and depravity that was partly responsible for worsening economic conditions in the United States. Europe, in particular, was accused of misusing America's postwar aid and now seeking to avoid the consequences through emigration, export dumping, and debt cancellation. The nation, many were persuaded, had to defend itself. And the result, when Congress met in special session, was quick action on two measures previously vetoed by President Wilson. In May, Harding signed both an Emergency Quota Act cutting immigration some 60 percent and an Emergency Tariff raising agricultural duties, embargoing other products, and providing new protection against foreign dumping. In addition, government leaders promised that taxpayers would be protected from Europeans' efforts to escape just debts or to bail themselves out through new raids on the American treasury.

Within the new administration, however, these protectionist impulses collided with a business internationalism seeking export expansion, wider opportunities abroad, and reduced political and military burdens. America, it was argued, could not prosper if denied access to world markets and resources or if forced to wall itself off from an unstable and unprosperous world. And America did have the capacity to change things. Properly organized and assisted, its financial, industrial, and technical communities could form links with similar groups abroad, reduce the economic "politicization" that lay at the root of the difficulty, and put idle resources to productive use. The need was for a diplomacy that would help American business do these things, and it was this kind of diplomacy that Hughes and Hoover sought to provide. Through conferences and negotiations they set out to reduce political obstacles to enlightened private development.

Through fact-gathering agencies and commissions of experts they sought to create shared values and keep decision makers enlightened. And through other conferences and consultations they promoted new units of public-private collaboration, at both the national and the multinational level. The world they hoped to create was much like that envisioned in progressive and Wilsonian diplomacy. But their perceptions of how it could be created and the kinds of tools that would be most effective were not the same.

In 1920 both Hughes and Hoover had urged American membership in a delimited version of the League of Nations. But this, they now concluded, had become politically impossible. The most that could be hoped for was a series of separate measures linking the United States to the best features of the Versailles system, and in a series of skillful diplomatic moves Hughes successfully forged such links. The Treaty of Berlin, ratified in October 1921, normalized German-American relations on the basis of the Versailles settlement. Similar treaties did the same for relations with Austria and Hungary. And beginning in 1922 the United States moved, through unofficial observers and conduits, to develop a system of cooperation and consultation with League agencies. In addition, Hughes pushed for American entry into the World Court, but this failed to win Senate approval.

While forging links to the Versailles system, Hughes also moved to "depoliticize" the Far East and reduce what the President called "the crushing burdens of military and naval establishments." In July of 1921 the United States took the initiative in inviting the major powers and such other nations as had interests in the Far East to a conference in Washington. And there on November 12, in a keynote address that made banner headlines, Hughes not only discussed the need for transforming rivalry into cooperation but set forth specific proposals for scrapping ships and maintaining fixed naval ratios. In thirty-five minutes, as one observer noted, the Secretary of State sank "more ships than all the admirals of the world have sunk in a cycle of centuries."

And Hughes's proposals bore fruit. By the time the conference adjourned in February 1922, it had produced three major treaties and several lesser ones. There was, first of all, a naval limitations treaty pledging the five leading naval powers to halt the construction of capital ships (battleships over 10,000 tons) for ten years and to bring their holdings of such ships into a fixed ratio of 5 : 5 : 3 : 1.67 : 1.67. This would mean 525,000 tons each for Britain and the United States, 315,000 for Japan, and 175,000 each for France and Italy. At French insistence the provisions would not apply to smaller vessels, and at Japanese insistence the United States and Britain promised not to fortify their outlying island possessions in the Western Pacific. Second, there was a Four Power Treaty ending the existing Anglo-Japanese alliance and substituting an agreement under which the British, Japanese, French, and Americans pledged themselves to respect each other's Pacific possessions and to consult in case of controversy. Third, there was a Nine Power Treaty pledging all the nations at the conference to respect Chinese sovereignty and refrain from seeking special privileges in China. And finally, in a series of supplementary treaties, agreements were reached on limiting the use of submarines and poison gas, on cable rights and Chinese tariffs, and on the withdrawal of Japanese forces from Siberia and Shantung. In Hughes's eyes the new treaty system provided a framework for peaceful relations and economic cooperation in the Far East, and for a time it seemed that Japan might indeed become a cooperative partner in Far Eastern development.

While building the new treaty system, American policy makers worked to remove other political obstacles to enlightened private development. Another series of negotiations was aimed at isolating and ostracizing Soviet Russia, the assumption being that the Communist system there must soon collapse. Another attacked and sought to reduce British restrictionism in the Near East. And in Latin America they attempted to replace military interventionism and gunboat diplomacy with a subtler management designed to install and sustain cooperative governments. For Santo Domingo this meant the ending of military government and the gradual withdrawal of American marines—the last of whom left in 1924. For Cuba it meant the withdrawal of a military mission that had overseen new elections in early 1921. For Nicaragua it meant preparations for ending still another military mission, and for Colombia it meant ratification of a treaty under which the country received compensation for its loss of Panama. The year 1923 also brought recognition of Mexico's revolutionary government, after the Mexicans had agreed to settle American claims and respect previous land grants. And out of protracted negotiations in 1922 and 1923 came an American-supported system for stabilizing Central America, primarily through arms limitations, international tribunals, and economic development programs. The hemispheric goal of the United States, so Hughes declared, was a framework within which the American republics could work together to build a common prosperity, and by 1924 he believed that major segments of that framework had been created.

Meanwhile, in conjunction with the creation of such frameworks, Hughes and Hoover were also organizing and seeking to use new units of public-private collaboration. Through their initiatives, the nation's export industries were now organized and linked to expanding governmental services; an interdepartmental committee on foreign loans began working with banking leaders to guide the movement of American capital abroad; and a revitalized banking consortium became the vehicle through which foreign investments were expected to modernize China. In addition, Hoover sought to deal with the abuses of foreign cartels and combines by mobilizing and working through consortia of oil producers, rubber and coffee importers, and communications developers. He sought to implement his vision of a Pan-American economic community by organizing still other groups. And hoping that famine relief would serve not only humanitarian but antidepression and anti-Bolshevist ends as well, he resurrected his postwar relief organization and used it to conduct a private and ostensibly "apolitical" program that fed approximately 10,000,000 starving Russians.

Such initiatives, moreover, were accompanied by continuing efforts to organize an "apolitical" revival of the European economy. The key to this, it was believed, lay in reparations revision and other reforms that would allow American capital to rebuild Germany. By 1922 both Hughes and Hoover were proposing a committee of private financial experts to determine Germany's "capacity to pay" and the conditions necessary to attract a large foreign loan. At first, the French blocked this kind of solution. They proceeded instead to occupy the Ruhr industrial district and attempt to collect reparations by force. But when the Germans reacted with passive resistance based on their runaway currency inflation, France yielded to American and British pressures and acquiesced in the appointment of two expert committees, the most important of which was headed by the American banker Charles G. Dawes. Out of this, in 1924, came the Dawes Plan, adjusting reparations to accord with economic conditions and arranging for an infusion of capital, mostly from American investors, to restabilize Germany's currency. Hailed at the time as both a "scientific" and a "business" solution, the plan laid the foundation for the American-financed German boom of the middle and late 1920s.

As American policy makers moved to solve the German problem, they were also seeking to "depoliticize" and thus reduce the irrational features of America's debt, tariff, and immigration policies. In 1922 Hoover, Hughes, and Mellon became the key members of a World War Foreign Debt Commission. And while the law creating the agency narrowly restricted its powers, Congress later acceded to a series of funding agreements that disregarded such restrictions and attempted to adjust interest rates and terms according to a scientific capacity-to-pay principle. Similarly, the Tariff of 1922 combined higher schedules with a flexibility provision under which the President, assisted by informed experts, could adjust rates to meet changing economic conditions. At the time it was not foreseen that virtually all such adjustments, except for inconsequential items, would be upward. In 1924 Hughes attempted, without success, to prevent a racist ban on immigration by Asians. The unnecessary insult to Japan, he argued, would undo much of the work of the Washington Conference. But in this field Congress was unwilling to delegate policy making to administrative experts. Its only concession was to allow another expert commission, again with Hoover as a member, to work out the details of a new quota system that was to reflect the "national origins" of the American people.

As Republican diplomacy took shape, then, it made important concessions to the resurgent demands for withdrawal, protection, and unilateralism. These were too powerful to be ignored or overcome. And further restraining the major policy makers were their own attitudes toward political tools, military interventions, and entangling commitments. Yet these same policy makers also believed that American prosperity required a stable and prosperous world. Their search, like that of the Wilsonians, was for new ordering mechanisms in the international arena, and between 1921 and 1924 they set out to build structures through which enlightened international managers could move the world in desirable directions. It remained to be seen whether their handiwork could actually bring the peace and prosperity envisioned.

THE OLD INDIVIDUALISM AND THE NEW

If Republican foreign policy was a curious mixture of the old and the new, the same was also true of Republican economic policy. In this field the Harding Administration inherited a worsening recession characterized by mounting unemployment, bankruptcies, and farm distress. And conflicting impulses in domestic policy affected the debate over how the recession was related to foreign developments. For some the proper response of government was the classic one of retrenchment and property protection, on the theory that this would allow natural economic processes to liquidate past errors and create the conditions required for further growth. Others thought the government could and should play a positive role. It should help to build structures which enlightened managers would use to expedite the readjustment process and avoid much of the suffering, waste, and disorder that had accompanied the workings of the business cycle in the past.

For those stressing governmental retrenchment Andrew Mellon emerged as the chief spokesmen. It was Mellon who supervised the installation of a new budget and accounting system ordering federal expenditures. And under the nation's first budget directors, Charles G. Dawes and Herbert Lord, economy measures did reduce federal spending by more than 20 percent. This allowed Mellon to argue for tax cuts, and in the revenue measures of 1921 and 1924 he succeeded in securing the kinds of reductions he believed capable of stimulating new business growth. Although defenders of the graduated income tax blocked parts of his program, the surtax applicable to the highest income bracket was reduced from 65 to 40 percent.

In addition, efforts were made to reduce areas of public enterprise that had developed during the war. Government ships were offered to private companies on generous terms, and when there were few takers Harding tried unsuccessfully to get Congress to provide still greater incentives. Attempts were made to dispose of the governmental power and nitrate facilities at Muscle Shoals on the Tennessee River though they failed when an offer by Henry Ford encountered unexpectedly strong resistance from public power advocates and rival business interests. And while the War Finance Corporation received a new lease on life in 1921, its functions were largely confined to aiding rural banks and helping to mobilize farm credit.

When men like Mellon, Dawes, and Attorney General Daugherty could make policy, the Harding administration also leaned toward crushing labor efforts to block what were perceived as natural economic readjustments. In 1921 it used federal troops to restore order in the coal fields of West Virginia. A year later it encouraged state action to break a national coal strike. And when government-backed wage cuts produced the national railway strike of 1922, Attorney General Daugherty obtained a sweeping court injunction prohibiting all strike activity on the ground that it violated both the Sherman Antitrust Act and the transportation law of 1920. At times the administration also lent encouragement to the resurgent open-shop movement; and when the courts narrowly restricted organizational rights and labor weapons, it opposed the legislative relief sought by labor leaders. Repeatedly, when union action was the issue, administration spokesmen talked of recovery and progress through the restoration of traditional individualism, the underlying assumption being that this restoration was most needed in the labor field.

Even as these actions were taken, however, such administrators as Hoover and Wallace were seeking to revive major features of the war system and thus provide frameworks for constructive group action and a new and more cooperative individualism. The economic difficulties, as they perceived them, were due less to swollen government or violated property rights than to misinformation, inadequate foresight, and poor organization. The remedy lay in cooperative structures that would correct these weaknesses. And with Harding's acquiescence and occasional support, both Hoover and Wallace moved to transform their departments into agencies chiefly concerned with building and servicing such structures.

Hoover, in particular, proceeded to reestablish major elements of the wartime standardization, statistical, and conservation programs, again relying upon industrial agreements and entrusting much of the administration to trade associations. Such programs, he argued now, would allow industry to reduce costs and stimulate new investment without putting workers through an economic wringer. He also organized a program of managerial reform linked to the engineering studies that he had helped to launch in 1920 and promoted through ties to the trade press and other publicity channels. He established new agencies to help organize such troubled areas as housing, transportation, radio, agriculture, and bituminous coal. Moving into the labor and welfare fields, he became not only a promoter of labor-management collaboration and private welfare programs but also a key figure in devising new mediation machinery, pressuring the steel industry into adopting an eight-hour day, and organizing the first federal efforts to deal with unemployment. Out of the Unemployment Conference of late 1921 came both an organization for mobilizing local and private relief and agencies that attempted to expand construction activities and develop the kind of business planning that would bring future stability. Recommended as well was a program of public works planning designed to offset private fluctuations, but this failed to win congressional approval.

Meanwhile, sometimes in the face of Hoover's opposition, Wallace was establishing similar agencies in the Department of Agriculture. There a new Bureau of Agricultural Economics under Henry C. Taylor became the tool that was to provide agribusinessmen with better information, greater foresight, and needed organizational expertise. Also convened, in January 1922, was an Agricultural Conference designed to link public and private action and commit both to "sane solutions." And drawing support from both the Harding Administration and a congressional farm bloc, Wallace pressed for new farm legislation. Between 1921 and 1923 measures were passed empowering his department to regulate various kinds of agricultural middlemen, exempting farm marketing associations from the antitrust laws, and establishing new farm credit institutions. When he moved toward solutions with a larger governmental component, however, he was unable to carry either the administration or the Congress with him. In 1924, as farm distress persisted, he endorsed the controversial McNary-Haugen bill, a measure calling for federal price supports and the dumping of agricultural surpluses abroad, but his endorsement was not enough to overcome congressional opposition.

What Hoover and Wallace accomplished was also attempted by other administrators, some of whom had a degree of success. Under William B. Greeley, for example, the Forest Service initiated an extensive array of cooperative action programs. Under Stephen Mather the Park Service formed a close alliance with transportation and recreational groups and continued to expand its domain. And under H. Foster Bain the Bureau of Mines became a promoter of cooperative conservation and safety programs. Plans for a department that would work with personnel managers and labor associations, on the other hand, failed to win sufficient support, and so did proposals for a welfare department that might help the providers of social services to order and rationalize their activities. Not all was retrenchment in this sphere. There were additions like the new grant-in-aid programs for vocational rehabilitation and maternal and child health care. But there was nothing to compare with the Hoover and Wallace operations.

What was happening at the federal level had its counterparts at the state and municipal levels. It was the states and cities that were still doing about 75 percent of all public spending. And alongside their rapidly expanding highway, educational, and civic improvement programs, they too were spawning cooperative structures and administrative networks that linked their services to the bureaucracies and associations of the private sector. To a greater extent than the federal government they were expanding their activities in the social welfare field, both in providing new public services or controls and as would-be rationalizers of the services and controls provided by private agencies. This was especially true of welfare activities that were seen as aspects of the quest for scientific efficiency and rational resource use, as extensions of enlightened management, and as promoters of social cohesion and harmony.

There were exceptions to these patterns, of course—governments that remained locked in a politics of rural nostalgia, antimodernism, or venal bossism; and governments, on the other hand, that were occasionally more responsive to antiestablishment rebels or humanitarian reformers than to modernizing organizational elites. But the central direction at the state and local levels, a direction the new federal administrators sought to encourage, was toward structures resembling those being built by Hoover and Wallace at the national level. For both state and municipal government the 1920s were a period of expanding services to managerial institutions; of increasing influence on the part of administrators, planners, and rationalizers; and of a developing organizational base upon which the bureaucracies of the next decade would rise. In the postwar era "good government" had come to be equated not only with honesty and economy but with the provision of managerial and technical aids and the creation of modern ordering mechanisms. Nor was this merely theory. The impetus toward realizing this form of "good government" was such as to produce what a subsequent scholarly survey would call "a decade of administrative improvement, perhaps the most effective and promising in the history of the United States."

As the New Era organization builders proceeded, they insisted that their programs were making "individualism" workable under modern conditions and thereby reducing irrational pressures for big government and other forms of collectivism. But they were sometimes challenged. Some conservatives grumbled that an administration elected to get the government out of business was now "doing more interfering with business than any other administration that we have had in peace times." Some liberals saw new exercises in trust building and government-supported exploitation. And within the government, the organization builders encountered opposition not only from economizers and stand-patters but also from defenders of the antitrust laws and the agencies entrusted with their enforcement. Hoover, in particular, became involved in a running conflict with the Justice Department and the Federal Trade Commission and as a result of antitrust decisions was forced to back away from certain kinds of informational exchange and business collaboration. It was not until 1925 that the Supreme Court upheld his interpretation of the law as being the correct one.

Had economic distress persisted, the programs of Hoover and like-minded administrators might well have been discredited and the way paved for larger elements of governmental coercion. Indeed, where distress did persist, as in agriculture and some "sick" industries, the drift by 1924 was already toward solutions featuring some form of government-backed cartelization. But through most areas of the economy the years 1922 and 1923 brought rapid recovery. Unemployment, which had reached an estimated 12 percent in 1921, dwindled to less than 4 percent. Output climbed nearly 50 percent, and from 1923 on the nation experienced a happy combination of rising productivity and income, stable prices, and nearly full utilization of resources. These developments supported claims that the "best minds" had indeed organized recovery and were in the process of organizing permanent prosperity. They undercut much of what the critics of such organizational activities were saying, and the result was to be not only a further growth of Hooverian programs but the subsequent elevation of the "Great Engineer" to the White House.

THE HANDLING OF ETHNOCULTURAL ISSUES

As Harding's "best minds" sought to organize peace and prosperity, his administration faced new political disturbances generated by ethnocultural conflict. Emerging from the wartime loyalty organizations and the postwar crusades against "un-Americanism" was a set of pressure groups bent upon restoring an older status system and erecting defenses against contaminants of the national life. In effect, nativism, racism, and social reaction had managed to cloak themselves in the garb of nationalism. And around the political efforts of these "hundred percent Americans" and the counterefforts of their opponents much of the period's political activity revolved. At the national level the central issues were immigration controls, minority rights, freedom of expression, and the extent to which national prohibition should be retained and enforced.

In part the impetus behind immigration control was pressure for economic protection. Yet by itself this could not have produced the legislation of the period; nor could it account for the type of quota system established. Also involved were heightened concerns about an America being undermined by alien cultures, races, and ideologies. And it was the two together that swept aside business efforts to maintain a flow of cheap labor and overcame the objections of those concerned with America's respect abroad. In 1924 Congress passed and the President signed the Johnson-Reed Act, replacing emergency curbs with permanent legislation aimed primarily at drastically reducing immigration from southern and eastern Europe. Under it Asians were to be excluded completely, and immigration from other areas (with the exception of the Western Hemisphere) was not to exceed fixed annual quotas for each nationality. Initially these were set at 2 percent of the foreign born of such nationality resident in the United States in 1890. But in permanent form, as finally calculated and implemented in 1929, the quotas were to apportion an annual maximum of 150,000, so as to reflect proportionately the national derivations of America's population in 1920. Their basis would be foreign ancestry or "national origins" rather than foreign birth, and in theory this would prevent any change in America's ethnic and racial make-up.

The triumph of immigration restriction, however, did not mean administration support for all the causes being pushed by "hundred percent Americans." Harding showed no interest, for example, in reviving the red hunt, as some of his political associates were urging him to do. He gave no encouragement to proposals for peacetime sedition laws, but proceeded instead to pardon Eugene Debs and other victims of the earlier repression. He also refused to support "lily-white" politics or the reaction against feminism, going out of his way instead to chide southerners for their discriminatory practices, urge passage of a federal antilynching law, and appoint women to federal positions. During his administration, Mabel Willebrandt became Assistant Attorney General; Mary Anderson, Grace Abbott, and Louise Stanley were appointed to head federal bureaus; and Lucille Anderson became the first woman to enter the diplomatic service. Nor were the prohibitionists satisfied. They complained constantly about the lack of enforcement zeal on the part of the President and such cabinet members as Andrew Mellon and Secretary of War John Weeks.

On the other hand, it is difficult to see Harding and his associates as ardent champions of minority rights or cultural pluralism. Their disagreement was mostly with the extremist elements of the new "Americanizers," not with the underlying assumptions. And along with their refusal to support such elements went reassurances to Americanizers of more moderate temperament. The freeing of political prisoners, for example, was accompanied by new calls for alien registration and more Americanization and by continued efforts to depict anticapitalist ideologies as alien, un-American, and psychopathic. The defense of minority rights was accompanied by toleration for lily-white operations, refusal to move against the terrorism of the Ku Klux Klan, and advice to blacks not to seek an unattainable social equality. The support for women's causes did not extend to such things as the proposed Equal Rights Amendment, and the skepticism about prohibition did not mean that the "dry" organizations lacked influence in the Harding Administration. Indeed, the Prohibition Unit under Roy Haynes seemed to function more as an extension of the Anti-Saloon League than as an arm of the presidency.

Neither the "hundred percent Americans" nor their opponents were fully satisfied with this mixture of policies. Yet it did placate those of moderate temperament, and given the nature of America's party structure it was difficult for the unplacated to challenge such policies in the electoral arena. Third parties seemed exercises in futility. And when the two opposing groups both sought to capture the Democratic party and use it for their purposes, the result was intraparty warfare that virtually assured continued Republican ascendancy.

POLITICAL ALIGNMENTS AND NATIONAL SCANDALS

By 1923 a mixture of political skill and good fortune seemed well on the way to converting the anti-Wilson coalition of 1920 into continuing support for Republican rule. For a time, to be sure, it had appeared doubtful that such a conversion would take place. In early 1922 a number of discontented farm, labor, and reform elements had organized the Conference for Progressive Political Action, a move that seemed to foreshadow the kind of Republican party split that had enabled Wilson to win the election of 1912. And in the congressional and state elections of 1922 the Republicans suffered heavy reverses. But what appeared possible never occurred. After the elections of 1922, economic protest rapidly faded, defused, so it seemed, by a combination of returning prosperity, antiradical rhetoric, and public acceptance of the claims of Hooverian administrators and their business allies. And while ethnocultural conflict remained intense, most of its potential for political mischief was being successfully shunted into the Democratic party. Politically, the policy mix of the Harding Administration had become a going concern, and it would remain so for the rest of the decade.

What threatened to make Harding a political liability and led some Republicans to regard his death as rather timely was not discontent with his policies. It was the famous "Harding scandals," involving corrupt activities by a number of his appointees and associates. As revealed by investigations in 1923 and 1924, this corruption had become particularly pronounced in the administration of veterans' benefits, oil reserves, alien property, and law enforcement. And for a time it was not clear that the President's death in August of 1923 would be sufficient to save his party from the feared political consequences.

One major set of scandals involved the Veterans' Bureau, the agency that Harding had entrusted to the political adventurer Charles R. Forbes. Between 1921 and 1923, so subsequent investigations revealed, Forbes and his associates were engaged in systematically defrauding the government, primarily through accepting payments to approve padded construction contracts and arrange sales of government property at a fraction of its cost. In all, it was estimated, their activities cost the taxpayers some $200,000,000. Yet when Harding learned part of what was going on, his anger quickly gave way to concern that the activities not be disclosed. After confronting Forbes and allegedly choking a confession out of him, he agreed that the miscreant should go abroad and resign. It was not until later, after Harding's death and after the Senate had investigated, that Forbes was finally prosecuted and sent to prison.

A second major set of scandals involved the Justice Department and its law enforcement agencies. There Attorney General Daugherty allowed his close friend and confidant, Jesse Smith, to drift into extensive influence peddling, selling not only jobs, pardons, and permits, but protection for bootleggers, wartime profiteers, and tax evaders. In May of 1923, when the President learned something of these activities and exposure seemed imminent, Smith committed suicide in Daugherty's Washington apartment. Nothing further came out at the time. But later, after Harding's death, an investigation uncovered much of the story. In March 1924, President Coolidge demanded and got Daugherty's resignation.

The third major agency involved was the Office of Alien Property Custodian, headed by the former congressman and war hero Thomas W. Miller. At the time of his appointment Miller seemed the epitome of rectitude. But when approached by Jesse Smith and other political fixers, he proved to be corruptible. In September 1921, in return for a payment of $50,000, he decided that German shares in the American Metal Company had been wrongly confiscated and transferred the property to a bogus claimant. For this he was eventually sent to jail. And when it was found that $50,000 of the sum paid to Smith had been deposited in a bank account shared by Daugherty, the former Attorney General was also indicted. At the trial Daugherty declined to testify on the ground that his personal relations with the President had been such as to make it impossible for him to do so. He was commonly considered as guilty as Miller, but after two juries had failed to convict, the charges were dropped.

Finally, there was the Teapot Dome scandal, which involved Secretary of the Interior Albert Fall. This had its beginnings in May of 1921, when Fall succeeded in getting responsibility for the naval oil reserves, at Elk Hills in California and Teapot Dome in Wyoming, transferred from the Navy Department to the Interior. He then proceeded, secretly and without competitive bids, to lease the reserves to Edward Doheny of the Pan-American Oil Company and Harry Sinclair of the Sinclair Consolidated Oil Corporation. This was necessary, he would later argue, to prevent the loss of oil to adjacent wells and to secure storage facilities necessary for national security. His anticonservation attitudes and designs, however, had already aroused the ire of such conservationists as Gifford Pinchot and Harry Slattery. Out of their probings had come the launching of a senatorial investigation headed by Senator Thomas J. Walsh, and from this would come revelations that Fall received extensive favors at the time the leases were made. In conjunction with the lease on Elk Hills, Doheny had given him $100,000, allegedly as a "loan" but without security or specifications for repayment. And in conjunction with the lease on Teapot Dome, Sinclair had given him $223,000 in government bonds, $85,000 in cash, and some livestock for his New Mexico ranch. Eventually the government would win its suit to cancel the leases, and Fall would finally be convicted and sentenced to a year in prison and a fine of $100,000.

That Harding knew of Fall's activities seems doubtful. But clearly he knew enough about other acts of corruption to make his last days in office a time of deep worry and concern. Being President, he told Senator Frank Brandegee, was "hell." There was no other word to describe it. And to the newspaperman William Allen White he expressed similar sentiments. "I have no trouble with my enemies," he declared. "But my damn friends, my God-damn friends, White, they're the ones that keep me walking the floor nights."

In July of 1923, then, as he set out on a trip to Alaska, the President was already deeply depressed and worried. In Alaska the depression deepened; and in Seattle, where he stopped on his return trip, there was a near collapse on the platform. He then went on to San Francisco, where he went to bed with what was diagnosed as bronchial pneumonia. And there, on August 2, 1923, he suffered a coronary thrombosis and died. At the time the nation was shocked and grieved but the revelations that followed quickly deflated Harding's reputation. Rumors spread that he had committed suicide or had been poisoned by his wife or his doctor, and in a flood of exposés the public learned about his drinking, gambling, and sexual peccadilloes. In one of the more sensational of these, his former mistress offered details about how he made love to her in a White House clothes closet and had fathered her illegitimate child.

As Harding's reputation declined, Republican politicians worked actively to dissociate themselves from Harding the man and to blame him rather than the party for the misbehavior that had occurred. Their goal was to retain power and continue the policies of the Harding Administration while escaping political punishment for the scandals. And while their success in doing this can be attributed partly to public apathy and marginal involvement of Democrats in the oil scandals, it is perhaps most explained by the fact that Harding's successor was Calvin Coolidge. Not only did the new President move to take the scandals out of partisan politics, primarily by appointing special prosecutors from each party and guaranteeing them a free hand. He was also able, through his personality and demeanor, to provide a reassuring sense of austerity, rectitude, and fundamental morality. In what one historian has called "an amazingly short time," he was able to repair whatever damage the Republican party had suffered.

THE CONSOLIDATION OF REPUBLICAN ASCENDANCY

Although Harding and Coolidge were both from rural villages, the two men were hardly of the same type. Where Harding had been affable, extroverted, and easygoing, Coolidge was almost a caricature of rural New England reserve. Born and reared in the farming village of Plymouth Notch, Vermont, he had risen in Massachusetts politics through shrewd appeals to such virtues as thrift, caution, honesty, and taciturnity. And once in the White House, he became a symbol of integrity and simplicity in an age of organization, extravagance, and threatening change. Sophisticated urbanites might poke fun at his dour sobriety and eccentric mannerisms. But for many he became a reassuring presence and almost a folk hero.

In political outlook Coolidge tended toward what Herbert Hoover called "real conservatism." His major concerns were with reducing federal expenditures, lowering taxes, and blocking legislative initiatives. And not surprisingly, Mellon's influence on public policy tended to increase now, while that of the more activist administrators tended to diminish. The change, however, was essentially an adjustment within an ongoing set of policies and programs, not a change in direction. Nor were dissident groups in Congress able to force any major policy alterations. Their only significant success in 1924 was in passing a veterans' benefit measure over the President's veto. Under it veterans of World War I were to receive "deferred compensation" in the form of paid-up life insurance maturing in twenty years.

Coolidge's major worry, once the scandals had been "depoliticized," was the mobilization of a political base for the coming presidential election. While his secretary, C. Bascom Slemp, rounded up southern delegates, the President used his New England connections to good advantage and was successful at the same time in improving relations with western Republicans and developing substantial business support. Symptomatic of the Coolidge take-over of the party machinery was the elevation of the Boston industrialist William M. Butler to the post of national chairman. And as the take-over proceeded it became apparent that the Coolidge forces would dominate the Republican convention that met in Cleveland on June 10, 1924. There, on the first and only ballot, Coolidge received 1,065 of the 1,109 votes cast. As his running mate the Republicans finally decided upon Charles G. Dawes, implementer of the federal budget system and author of the Dawes Plan.

On June 24 the Democrats gathered in New York's Madison Square Garden for what would be their most divisive convention since 1896. Arrayed on one side were elements of the party controlled by defenders of rural values, national prohibition, and hundred percent Americanism. Their candidate was the former Secretary of the Treasury and war administrator, William Gibbs McAdoo. Arrayed on the other were elements controlled by urban political machines and ethnic groups, opponents of the liquor law, and defenders of a heterogeneous America. To oppose McAdoo these groups offered Governor Alfred E. Smith of New York, a man who had risen from the city slums through the Tammany Hall organization. For sixteen days, amid fierce and bitter platform fights and ballot after ballot, the convention provided evidence of how deep ethnocultural conflict could run. Finally both Smith and McAdoo agreed to withdraw, and on the 103rd ballot the weary, exasperated delegates nominated John W. Davis, a conservative corporation lawyer who had served as Solicitor General during Wilson's administration. To assuage rural elements, the convention then chose Governor Charles W. Bryan of Nebraska, brother of William Jennings Bryan, as Davis's running mate.

Also in the field in 1924 was a third party, including Republican insurgents and the groups that had formed the Conference for Progressive Political Action in 1922. Meeting in Cleveland on July 4, these groups formed the Progressive party, nominated Senator Robert

M. La Follette of Wisconsin, and adopted a platform calling for nationalization of key industries and a variety of political reforms. Some hoped that the new party could become the American counterpart of the Labour party in Britain; others that it could at least prevent the consolidation of Republican ascendancy. But in operation it was to do neither. It proved short-lived, and its ability to pull Republicans away from Coolidge was more than offset by the repellent effects of its "un-American" image.

Indeed, Republican campaign strategy seemed chiefly aimed at promoting this image and spelling out the dire consequences that could stem from votes for La Follette. The choice, so Republican oratory declared, was "Coolidge or chaos." And as the campaign progressed, it became clear that most of the defections to La Follette were coming from Democratic rather than Republican ranks. On November 4 Coolidge polled 15,725,016 votes to only 8,385,586 for Davis and 4,822,856 for La Follette. In the electoral college this translated into 382 for Coolidge, 136 for Davis, and 13 for La Follette. The President had scored a solid victory, and in Congress the Republicans reestablished large majorities. In the new Congress they would control 56 seats in the Senate and 247 in the House of Representatives.

In part, Coolidge's victory can be attributed to the divisions among his opponents and their inability to mobilize the kind of mass discontent that could have challenged Republican rule. Yet these divisions and inabilities were related not only to improving economic conditions but also to Republican success in coopting the political center, defusing the kinds of tensions that tore the Democrats apart, and fusing traditional Republicanism with a managerial ideology especially attractive to America's expanding organizational elites. The victorious coalition of 1920 had become a going concern well attuned to political survival. The substitution of Coolidge for Harding had neutralized a major threat to the enterprise and facilitated the consolidation of its ascendancy. And continued peace and prosperity lent growing credibility to its claims of organizational success. Although opponents would still be able to mobilize occasional bursts of insurgency, it would take major changes in the political and economic environment and major exercises in political mismanagement to shatter the pattern of loyalties that had been established by 1924.

CHAPTER 5

Toward a New Economy and a Higher Self-Government

As the American economy recovered from the recession of 1921, it entered upon a pattern of development that made it the envy of much of the civilized world. In essence, it became the first industrial economy geared to the production of consumer durables and cultural fare for the masses, and as such it was widely hailed as a new kind of economy, a "people's capitalism" seeking profits through volume production and in the process healing social divisions and creating an uplifting abundance. In America, it was said, men had learned how to build a technically advanced economy that was both increasingly efficient and increasingly attuned to popular needs. They had learned how to link the great functional groups of society—workers, investors, and consumers—into an interdependent community in which each was concerned with the interests of all. And marvel of marvels, they had been able to do these things while retaining the benefits of a private property system, individual initiative, and a carefully delimited government.

It was, of course, too good to be true. The self-disciplining arrangements believed capable of accomplishing such feats proved unable to check the massive economic contraction that got under way after 1929, and the impact of frustrated expectations was quickly felt in the political arena. Yet the failures should not obscure the considerable economic achievements of the 1920s. Nor should they obscure the extent to which the arrangements and designs of the era foreshadowed the kind of modern capitalism that would be hailed as successful in the 1950s. Long depicted as the Indian summer of an outmoded and passing economic order, the period from 1922 through 1928 really stands as a kind of premature spring for the capitalist adaptations of our own time.

TECHNOLOGY AND MANAGEMENT

Taken as a whole, the industrial statistics for the 1920s tell a story of amazing success. From 1922 to 1928 the index of industrial production climbed some 70 percent. Gross national product, measured in constant dollars, rose nearly 40 percent and per capita income about 30 percent. Unemployment largely disappeared while wholesale and retail price levels remained stable; and as the tools of production became increasingly efficient, output per factory man-hour climbed nearly 75 percent. The expanded product, to be sure, was being allocated in such a way as to widen the gap between rich and poor. But the share going to blue- and white-collar workers was enough to produce the world's first excursion into mass affluence. The real earnings of employed wage earners increased about 22 percent, this at a time when the average work week was shrinking about 4 percent. And for the first time in world history, mass man was able to acquire complicated pieces of power machinery and electronic apparatus, afford higher education and extended leisure for his children, and participate in experiences once reserved for a wealthy few.

Behind this unheard of mass affluence lay a new capacity to produce standardized goods at low per-unit costs. The period witnessed the rapid spread of the manufacturing techniques pioneered by Henry Ford and then used in war production. It saw, in other words, the marriage of machine-produced interchangeable parts with a moving assembly line that coordinated the efficient performance of numerous simplified tasks. It also saw the rapid introduction of scientific work management as pioneered by Frederick W. Taylor and his disciples.

Their systems of shop organization, task analysis, worker motivation, and engineering control were now bringing gains in efficiency to numerous work sites. The 1920s witnessed as well the first major growth of systematic research into industrial methods. And as still another part of what was being called the "technological revolution," the period witnessed a phenomenal growth in the use of mechanical power as a substitute for human or animal muscle. Along with improvements in steam-powered machinery came the extensive introduction of electric motors and internal combustion engines.

Also contributing to the new productive ability was the rapid growth of personnel work aimed at creating cooperative and production-oriented work forces. From the war experience had come a faith in personnel management, both as a way to curb undesirable labor organization and as a tool for increasing productivity. Contented, right-thinking, and relatively secure workers, so a new group of managerial specialists had come to believe, were not only socially desirable but essential to mass production systems using modern techniques. And operating now through expanding corporate personnel departments, these specialists were busy with efforts to engineer the kind of labor that was needed. They were developing scientific selection and motivation procedures, initiating new kinds of educational activity, and setting up programs aimed at giving workers a sense of participation and a stake in company welfare. As they saw it, these specialists were doing even more to spur progress than the designers of new machines and assembly systems.

Along with revolutionary technologies and willing workers the kind of economy being developed in the 1920s also required willing and able consumers. Sustained operation of the new factories required a sustained demand for the goods they were producing. And to some extent, this too was being engineered through the operations of a new group of business specialists. Advertising, its power greatly enhanced by new means of mass communication, was being used to change spending habits and create new wants. Marketing organizations were being reformed to stress the rapid turnover of a limited stock of items. Frequent style and model changes were being used to render inherently durable goods obsolete. Business leaders were accepting and pronouncing desirable the increased income of wage earners, and the rapid development of consumer credit was helping to supplement mass purchasing power. A relative rarity before the 1920s, consumer credit became a major new form of financial activity that allowed consumers to mortgage their future earnings, buy expensive durables for which they would never have the full purchase price at one time, and hope that continuing economic growth would take care of the debt burden.

Structural changes in the mass labor market also contributed to the new mass consumption. A growing number of jobs left more time and energy for leisure and for the consumption that could accompany it. A growing number offered little challenge and few satisfactions, leading their holders to seek status and recompense through consumption. And the new family, with more women employed outside the home and more of these holding white-collar and quasi-professional jobs, became a prime customer for household appliances, new forms of nonfamily child care, and expanded educational, cultural, and recreational facilities.

Through various actions, then, Americans were creating an acceptable substitute for war consumption and reassembling major components of the war economy. Organizationally they were moving toward a new kind of peacetime economy; and while profit seeking was a major motive force, it was hardly the whole story. Also involved was a value system that regarded profits made through such operations to be of greater merit and more social value than profits made by other means. It seems at least possible that the power of American business might have yielded even greater profits had it been used to reduce wages, suppress invention, or sustain high profit margins on limited flows of luxury goods—all techniques that were widely adopted in Europe. But the power was difficult to mobilize for such purposes, chiefly, it seems, because a growing segment of America's corporate managers regarded them as antisocial or self-defeating and believed profits could be made in socially beneficial ways. While America was not without its wage reducers, invention suppressors, and high-profit-margin monopolists, these groups tended to be seen not as saviors of their class but as remnants of an unenlightened past or abusers of the social trusteeship that property management was becoming.

In part this set of managerial attitudes had been fostered by prewar progressivism and the war experience. For a time profit making of a certain kind had been identified with social service, much as the prewar business clubs and professionalizers of business had insisted that it could be. And it was perhaps natural for those who had reaped this double reward to seek arrangements that would continue to provide it. There was more involved, however. There were not only changes in the attitudes of individuals but changes in the kind of person who was directing corporate enterprise and making business policy. Coming into management was a growing number of people who had acquired the vision of a new capitalism at business or professional schools, and allowing such people to take charge were structural changes that reduced the policy input of shareholders and bankers. As the ownership of large corporations became increasingly diluted, the accountability of management to the stockholders became more myth than reality. While stockholder representation continued, it consisted in large part of people chosen by management to ratify managerial decisions. And once managers had acquired the ability to generate new capital internally, through the withholding of corporate profits, their dependence upon the great investment banks that had dominated an earlier period was substantially reduced. Increasingly, managerial accountability was to other managers rather than to owners or financiers, and it was managerial perceptions and ideals that shaped the use of corporate property and the purposes for which corporate power could be mobilized.

This is not to say that all managers behaved according to the ideal. Behind the mask of the socially responsible manager there also appeared a new breed of corporate plunderers intent upon enriching themselves through raids on company treasuries and misrepresentation of business prospects. Professional accountability, such as it was, could not prevent this, and as subsequently magnified through investigations born of the Great Depression, it would do much to discredit the managerial images of the 1920s. But if there was a gap between ideal and reality, the two were hardly polar opposites. The American economy was the first to reassemble much of the war system and gear it to the mass consumption of durable goods and cultural artifacts. And while this can be partly explained by the peculiarities of American technologies, markets, and resources, a key factor may well have been the value system of those making business policy.

GROWTH AREAS AND NEW MALADJUSTMENTS

Of the new industries being developed in the 1920s, the most spectacular was automobiles. The breakthrough here had come with Henry Ford's mass-produced, inexpensive Model T, and through elaborations and improvements on the Ford system the industry continued to combine extraordinary gains in productivity with steadily mounting sales and more and more customers. Hours per unit of output declined steadily, falling on the average more than 7 percent a year. Sales rose from about 1,500,000 vehicles in 1921 to over 5,000,000 in 1929, and automobile ownership was now rapidly extended to include nearly 60 percent of all American families. More than any other, the industry became the showpiece of the new capitalism. And although some historians now question whether the new "automobility" really improved the quality of mass life, there were few questioners at the time. The industry was widely regarded as a progressive social force, engaged in fulfilling a long-standing popular dream and helping in the process to heal social divisions, stimulate social improvements, and satisfy social needs.

Growth in this area also brought growth in a number of ancillary areas. An expanding automobile industry meant rapidly expanding demands for steel, petroleum, glass, rubber, lacquers, and machine tools. It meant rapid growth for new service industries catering to automobile users and travelers. It meant, less directly, an increase in building and real estate development, especially in suburban and vacation areas. And since governmental bodies were generally responsive to the industry and its customers—a fact reflected both in state appropriations and in generous grants-in-aid for federal highways—there were rapid increases as well in expenditures on roads, traffic control, and highway amenities. America was not only producing automobiles for the masses but reshaping its economy and society to accommodate mass usage, and the latter involved immense new capital expenditures.

Although the coming of mass "automobility" was the greatest generator of new growth, it was by no means the only one. Another was the rapidly expanding use of electrical power and equipment, both by industry and by the growing number of families who were now acquiring electricity in their homes. In 1928 this did not include many farm families, but it did encompass approximately two-thirds of all families in the nation, and many of these had gone on to acquire electric irons, vacuum cleaners, washing machines, and other appliances. By that time approximately 70 percent of all factory machine equipment was also being run by electric power. Together these developments had brought sales of power and equipment that were nearly three times as large as in 1919. Both the electrical power industry and that of electrical manufacturing became major new areas of capital investment and resource use.

Two other growth areas of major significance were motion pictures and radio. These now became the great purveyors of commercialized mass entertainment, and the demand for this proved exceptionally expansive. In 1922 some forty million movie tickets were being sold weekly. Seven years later, after the development of the "star system" and the introduction of sound, weekly attendance at the nation's twenty-three thousand movie theaters had climbed to something approaching a hundred million. And the saga of radio was even more impressive. Bursting on the scene in 1920, when Station KDKA began operating in Pittsburgh, it quickly developed into a new industry with far-reaching effects on popular life. By 1929 about 40 percent of all American families had acquired receiving sets, and by then there were nearly eight hundred broadcasting stations organized into two major and two minor networks. A telephone polling system had been developed to measure the audiences being reached, and to a large extent this system determined the value of the time and programs sold to commercial sponsors.

Nor did these developments exhaust the areas that were expanding. Americans in the 1920s were making major additions to their educational plant, especially at the high-school and college levels. They were expanding their health-care and social service system, especially the private-sector portion of it. They were altering their habits in ways that meant prosperity for the tobacco, cosmetics, soft drink, synthetic fiber, and commercial recreation industries. And for a time their demand for new or better housing, enhanced somewhat by new methods of mortgage financing, produced rapid growth in construction activities and the building materials industries. Part of the expansion too was the new aviation industry, a development of the war that continued to depend upon various kinds of governmental subsidies. Although its expansion was limited, the feats of aviators and airplane builders were much publicized; and by 1929 the nation had a new air mail system and the beginnings of air passenger and transport services.

To some extent such growth industries merely absorbed resources that were being freed by increasing efficiency elsewhere. But to some extent as well they grew by displacing older industries. The result for such fields as bituminous coal, cotton textiles, railroads and railroad equipment, horse-drawn conveyances, and the older agricultural staples was shrinking demand and all the problems involved in reducing capacity. Some of these industries, moreover, had great difficulty in solving their problems. Alongside the growth industries of the period there also appeared a number of "sick" industries characterized by continuing overcapacity, low returns, irrational economic behavior, and bitter confrontations between management and labor.

Four industries stand out as the most prominent of those on the sick list. One was the mining of bituminous coal, an industry that suffered now from a combination of shrinking demand, wartime overexpansion, technological backwardness, and bitter but unsuccessful struggles to maintain wartime wage rates. During the decade it became the subject of numerous investigations and much legislative and engineering consideration, but solutions for its problems never seemed to emerge. A second industry in much the same trouble was cotton textiles. In it shrinking demand and overcapacity put strong pressures on profit and wage rates. Excursions into cooperative advertising, export promotion, and production restraints seemed unable to relieve these; and the result was accelerated movement of textile manufacturers from the Northeast to the South, bitter resistance to all efforts to unionize southern workers, and the persistence of substandard wages and

meager or nonexistent profit margins. In railroading a heritage of
overcapitalization and mismanagement, unimaginative regulation, and
relatively powerful labor unions made it difficult either to meet the
competition from newer forms of transportation or to adjust capacity
to shrinking demand. And finally, there was the depressed shipping
industry, losing out not to a newer form of transportation but to more
efficient or more heavily subsidized foreign fleets. A few shipping
operators grew wealthy on government money, but most workers in
the industry were not participants in the upward movement of income
and living standards.

Also exhibiting many of the characteristics of the "sick" industries
was the nation's agricultural sector. In some ways, to be sure, it was
another major participant in the "technological revolution" and in
developments that foreshadowed the post-1945 economic order, including a new machine technology built around tractors and trucks, striking advances in managerial practices and plant productivity, the growing utilization of systematic research and capital-intensive methods,
and the disintegration of traditional wisdom and folkways. In some
areas of agriculture exploiters of new technologies and markets pros-
pered. This was true, by and large, of citrus, dairy, and truck farming,
and of the large corporate enterprises that farmed the new wheat lands
on the high plains. But for most agricultural products the markets
proved unexpandable, at least with the tools that farmers were able to
develop. They could neither recapture the markets they had once had
in Europe nor expand domestic markets enough to compensate for the
loss. And since the population movement out of this increasingly
mechanized and efficient sector was not large or rapid enough to
reduce its productive capacity, most of the country's farmers continued
to suffer from market gluts, prices that did not cover fixed costs, and
intensified exploitation by each other and by various business groups.

Economic rationality seemed to call for massive agricultural disin-
vestment and for a greatly enlarged exodus of marginal producers. But
hopes of market revival, attachments to farming as a way of life, and
the quasi-peonage that still existed in much of the rural South made
the lot of would-be rationalizers an exceedingly frustrating one. Net
farm income rose from about $6,000,000,000 in 1922 to about
$8,000,000,000 in 1929, but per capita income remained substantially

below what it had been in 1919, and the disparity between farm and nonfarm incomes continued to grow. In 1929 the average income per person on farms was $223 as against an average of $870 for those not on farms.

There were also sectors of industrial labor that did not share in the growing affluence. In the first place, there was a large pool of unskilled or casual workers that was now being constantly replenished by displaced husbandmen and blacks leaving the rural South. Such workers were in weak bargaining positions and were largely unaffected by the new company welfare and employee management programs. They filled low-paying jobs, especially in industries with high intermittency and seasonality; and for them wages and working conditions showed little improvement. They remained at the fixed lower end of a wage-and-condition scale that was characterized by increasingly large differentials. And second, there were the workers suffering from displacement and market pressures in the "sick" industries. For irregularly employed coal miners, for textile workers stranded in New England towns, for victims of cost cutting focused on wage reduction, and for other similar groups, conditions tended to deteriorate rather than improve.

Finally, the kind of growth taking place was not without its costs in resource despoliation and community destruction, declining business independence and worker autonomy, and the reduction of skilled craftsmen to machine tenders and service employees. Many Americans were worse off in terms of the air they breathed, the water they used, the outdoors they enjoyed, and the communal relationships that gave their lives meaning. Many were compelled to purchase their places in the consumer culture at the expense of declining work satisfactions and less control over their labor. And many were shunted into jobs offering neither material nor other rewards. The notion, moreover, that poverty was about to disappear was clearly an erroneous one. In 1929 some six million families had incomes lower than $1000 a year, and neither the growth nor the social action of the period had done much to alter the pattern of rewards and barriers that kept them at this level.

In places, then, the new economy exhibited glaring gaps between promise and reality, gaps that could potentially lead to mass protest and political upheaval. Perhaps the remarkable thing about the period was how little of this potential became actuality. For some an older rationale for inaction took on new life: the gaps were attributed to individual failures and became the fault of the sufferers themselves. And for others there was the new faith that problems could be resolved by widening the area of professional management. They sought not to overthrow the organizers and administrators of growth but rather to borrow their methods and secure their cooperation in reorganizing poorly functioning areas and reducing social costs.

PRIVATE BUREAUCRACIES AND ASSOCIATIONAL ACTIVITIES

Since the turn of the century social theorists, both in the United States and abroad, had drawn distinctions between the trusts and combines of a monopoly capitalism and the modern managerial corporations that could evolve into a neutral technocracy administering orderly growth and progress. Such conceptions formed one variant of the "new liberalism" advanced in the prewar period and the postwar debates, and during the 1920s they were widely accepted in both academic and governmental circles. The direction of the great corporation, it was noted, was passing to growth-minded and system-conscious professional managers. And so directed, the argument ran, such organizations no longer threatened liberal and democratic values. On the contrary, their productive and marketing power became a great liberating force. Their leadership in their respective industries worked to socialize and professionalize business behavior, and their responsiveness to popular and national needs was really greater than that shown by political parties or governmental bureaucracies. The leaders recognized their dependence on and obligations to the various functional groups of the national community—to laborers, customers, and the public as well as to investors; and they were developing institutions through which they could remain responsive to all these constituencies.

Such images did not bring repeal of the antitrust laws, but they were undoubtedly a major factor in bringing reinterpretations that turned their antimerger and anticoncentration provisions into little more than dead letters. Under the court rulings of the period a new merger and consolidation movement became legal; and since this was widely accepted as socially beneficial, legislators made little effort to halt it. Between 1920 and 1928, approximately 1200 manufacturing and mining mergers took place, accounting for the disappearance of nearly 6000 firms. In utilities a similar process accounted for the disappearance of over 4000 firms, and in distribution and finance there was a rapid growth of chain and branch systems. Vertical combination also made great strides, creating large, integrated firms that produced their own raw materials and operated their own distributive outlets. And such "weeding out" as occurred had the effect of leaving more and more of the major industries in fewer and fewer hands. Alongside the corporate giants inherited from the earlier consolidation movement there now appeared a new array of gigantic automobile, electrical, radio, motion picture, and mass distribution firms.

To administer these operations the new managers were developing elaborate private bureaucracies. Under central offices engaged in planning and appraisal, they were grouping a wide array of managerial specialists into functional departments concerned not only with production and marketing but with personnel work, public and political relations, and future product development. Some units also amounted to federations of enterprises, centrally coordinated yet including quasi-autonomous product and territorial subunits. And being developed as extensions of the corporate structures were a variety of company labor associations, educational institutes, better-business bodies, and social action programs.

That this expanding private bureaucracy was adequately constrained and operating in the public interest was a central theme in business advertising and promotion at the time. Americans, it was said, owed their prosperity and progressiveness to a system that had avoided the pitfalls of statist control and developed ordering mechanisms and stimulants to progress in the private sector. What this promotion did not focus on and what apologists for the growing bureaucracy found increasingly difficult to defend was the failure of existing constraints to prevent monopolistic exploitation, capricious acts by industrial tyrants, and organized defrauding of investors. Critics continued to uncover cases in which high profit margins and gross inefficiencies were being sustained through price fixing. They uncovered other cases in which corporate power was being used to deny or suppress civil liberties, and by 1928 they were finding much to criticize in the organizational arrangements of the electric power industry. There corporate organizers had created complex pyramids of holding companies, occasionally to insure better coordination or greater efficiency but much more often as devices for bleeding the operating companies, evading the control of public utilities commissions, and defrauding investors.

Meanwhile, as corporate bureaucracies expanded, those administering trade and industrial associations also underwent rapid growth and development. Here, to be sure, the antitrust laws continued to be more of an obstacle. There was as yet no "rule of reason" for cartel agreements. But new court rulings did sanction a kind of "cooperative competition," and "cooperative competitors" were being organized to oppose common enemies, mitigate "destructive competition" among themselves, and provide a common informational and moral base for decision making. By 1929 there were about two thousand national trade associations, spanning nearly every industry and trade and engaged in activities that ranged from annual conventions and trade publications to elaborate programs of statistical dissemination, trade promotion, political lobbying, labor management, waste elimination, and trade practice control. Especially elaborate were the programs of the new "institutes" formed in the late 1920s. And while the full-fledged war system failed to reappear, the new bureaucracy did include many of the former war administrators; it was linked to government through a committee system resembling that of the war years; and it worked with government officials, as during the war, to formulate publicly approved industrial codes and agreements. As an association of associations, moreover, the Chamber of Commerce continued to serve as a harmonizer and an informational clearing house, and to provide a mechanism through which associational cooperation could be mobilized and deployed.

In a few areas these organizational leaders preached the kind of antimodernism that characterized small-business and artisan associations in various European countries. But generally they saw themselves as advancers of a superior kind of modernization, one that could bring the advantages of corporate consolidation and scientific management without sacrificing the advantages of entrepreneurial independence. It was this vision that they articulated through association organs, governmental supporters, and their professional organizations. And it served both as camouflage for associations that were really extensions of the corporate bureaucracy and as an impetus to organization in industries that were unable or reluctant to participate in the consolidation movement. The coal, textile, and construction industries all tried to solve their problems through new excursions into association building, but most of these associations delivered far less than they promised. And under the auspices of the American Farm Bureau Federation and allied groups, agribusinessmen tried to develop cooperative marketing associations that could restore order and prosperity to the agricultural sector. In 1922 they obtained antitrust exemptions for such marketing combines; and while many quickly became disillusioned and turned to governmental relief schemes, others kept trying to work out a form of the "association idea" that would allow use of corporate methods for agrarian ends.

Still another extension of this associational bureaucracy also took shape in the troubled labor sector. There unionism and collective bargaining continued to suffer major setbacks. They were under attack both by organized advocates of "individual bargaining" and by corporate administrators seeking to engineer cooperative work forces; and as one defeat followed another, total union membership declined from about 5,000,000 to less than 3,500,000. Yet even as this occurred, other organizers moved in and sought with some success to build labor associations imbued with managerial values and receptive to the new kind of managerial leadership. By 1929 such organizers had installed about five hundred employee representation plans, each involving the creation of one or more company labor associations. And by the same date, corporate-minded men had taken over large sections of the remaining union apparatus and were using it to advance the idea of "copartnership" and to administer joint productivity and waste elimination programs.

At the time, many observers hailed such developments as constituting a truly progressive system destined to supplant both the adversary proceedings of collective bargaining and the atomism of individual action. At last, they argued, the associative impulses of workers were being guided into constructive as opposed to antisocial channels. But subsequent developments would reveal that the foundations beneath these forms of association were exceedingly shaky. In too many cases what purported to be a productive "partnership" generating and sharing new wealth was in reality a device for denying associative rights, extracting more work for the same pay, allowing union bureaucrats to keep their jobs, or enlisting labor support for market-rigging operations. Too much of the structure had been put together for these ends, and when so used tended to discredit the portion that had not. Unlike some segments of the expanding private bureaucracy, that in the labor field would be largely supplanted by a new and different kind of growth in the 1930s.

THE QUEST FOR MACROECONOMIC TOOLS

As corporate and associational bureaucracies grew in the 1920s, some thought was also given to the overall coordination of their economic decisions. The painful fluctuations and dysfunctions of the immediate postwar period had left vivid memories, and from 1921 on a number of economic leaders and former war administrators continued to question whether the suffering and waste had been necessary to restore economic health, and whether the new organizational arrangements and growing professionalization of management could, in and of themselves, prevent worse breakdowns and dysfunctions in the future. The new economy, some argued, required forms of business and labor security that weakened or destroyed its capacity for automatic self-adjustment. But this did not mean that such an economy was doomed to ever more destructive breakdowns and purges. Nor did it mean that avoiding this fate required ever increasing areas of statist control and management. It was possible to devise nonstatist machinery through which private organizational leaders and private groups of professionals could keep the economy in balance and correct such imbalances and problems as did develop.

One kind of machinery that continued to have its advocates was an economic council system through which the leaders of the major industries and functional blocs would coordinate their activities, discern developing problems, and organize remedial action. As some saw it, the American economy could benefit from a less formal equivalent of the industrial council and functional representation systems being organized or advocated in Europe. But for most the more relevant model was the wartime Council of National Defense with its functional representatives, its public-private collaboration, and its capacity to organize new action agencies as new problems arose. It was a voluntaristic counterpart of the council that those associated with the National Civic Federation, the Chamber of Commerce, the American Federation of Labor, and the Department of Commerce continued to advocate. And on several occasions some form of economic advisory council, either attached to the Commerce Department or established as a private institution, seemed on the verge of taking shape. That it did not testified less to an absence of formative efforts than to persisting conflict among private leaders, continued subscription to competitive ideals, and enduring commitments to class action.

What did develop, serving as a kind of substitute for the envisioned council system, was a series of quasi-official "advisories" endorsed by committees of functional representatives and offered as guides and stimulants to organizational action. Out of the Unemployment Conference in 1921 came an organizing committee for such operations, acting both to arrange scientific surveys of the situation and to form the representative bodies that would endorse the findings and stimulate remedial action. A number of the committee's efforts were stillborn, but it did arrange two major and several minor productions. In 1923 its Business Cycle Committee, chaired by Owen D. Young of General Electric, endorsed the latest scientific wisdom on business fluctuations and urged stabilizing actions, especially programs to improve the informational base of decision makers and reduce their susceptibility to speculative enthusiasm and panicky retrenchment. Lesser "advisories" followed, and in 1927 the machinery of the 1923 study was reassembled to survey recent developments and stimulate a new round of corrective action. Under the direction of the economist Wesley C. Mitchell, it eventually produced a voluminous report entitled *Recent Economic Changes in the United States*.

The Business Cycle Committee and its supporters also recommended special stabilizers to head off incipient booms and busts. Unemployment insurance and wage maintenance, it was recognized, might prevent unbalancing swings in consumer spending. Countercyclical monetary actions might correct irrational demands for capital. Proper management of exports might offset market disturbances at home, and construction "reserves" might be built up and released in ways that would maintain a stable flow of investment expenditures. Where the recommenders drew the line, however, was against any proposal for erecting such stabilizers in the public sector. Governmental spenders and managers, they insisted, tended inherently toward irrationality and wastefulness. Their sphere must be kept to a minimum; and while this minimum should be managed with a view toward preserving economic equilibrium, the major stabilizing responsibility must be lodged with private organizations. The answer, in other words, lay not in a managerial state but in appropriate extensions of the "higher self-government" that was taking shape outside the state. It lay, more precisely, in a cooperative system of unemployment insurance, private mechanisms for triggering cooperative wage and job maintenance, private banking and export fraternities organized to act cooperatively in the public interest, and quasi-private councils through which construction expenditures could be shaped into a countercyclical tool.

Viewed through the experience of the 1930s, such stabilizers as were actually developed seemed weak indeed. The great majority of business firms did not install unemployment insurance or other forms of employment stabilization. The cooperative mechanisms through which organized wage payers, bankers, and exporters were to act as macroeconomic stabilizers proved extremely fragile when put to the test. And the prime instrument through which construction activities were to be converted into an economic balance wheel, the Hoover-sponsored American Construction Council that Franklin D. Roosevelt helped to found in 1922 and continued to head for the next six years, proved to be little more than a paper organization. Yet as of 1928 the strength of the tools needed was not readily apparent. Advances at the firm and industrial levels, it was widely believed, were creating a new economy less susceptible to booms and busts, more sensitive to danger signals, and more amenable, should it become necessary, to the kind of corrective action taken by the Unemployment Conference in 1921. Although hope continued for a council system, improved "advisories," and stronger stabilizing mechanisms, a number of those involved in the quest for macroeconomic tools seemed to think that their search had been successful.

ROOTS OF THE COMING CRISIS

Beneath the surface indications of stability, however, the economy of 1928 was already in deep trouble. Markets for the new mass production industries were already becoming saturated. The call for capital in the new industries and ancillary fields was slackening. And new areas of spending that could take up the slack were failing to develop. Investors were not moving to develop large new growth industries, partly perhaps because the pattern of income distribution and consumer debt was now such as to make market creation difficult. Exports, too, were not readily expandable with the tools at hand; construction demand had not been deferred as the proponents of "reserves" had advocated; and the compensation that could come from public sector expansion was narrowly limited by taxpayer resistance and commitments to retiring public debts and holding governmental activities to a minimum. The new economy, in short, had not really developed the mechanisms that could turn the new kind of growth into a continuing process, and its failure to do so would soon become apparent.

Nor was the economy, should it stop growing, really resistant to major contractions. The "balance wheels" that were supposed to prevent this were not equal to the task and were indeed more than offset by potential depressants that relatively minor declines in demand could trigger into action. The banking system, despite some reforms, still contained many weak and overextended units and still lacked the means to keep the failure of such units from causing irrational bank runs and a general monetary contraction. In a large segment of the corporate structure, especially the public utilities field, even slight shocks could mean enormous losses for investors and further contractions in investment spending. Much of the market for consumer durables rested on spending and lending behavior that could be thrown into reverse with relative ease. And much of the new organizational machinery, once its operators became convinced that it lacked the power to regulate demand, could be turned into engines for idling resources and making old-style liquidation exceedingly difficult if not impossible. The economy was such that blows of a relatively limited sort might turn a slowing of growth into an economic breakdown, and three developments were already under way that would eventually deliver such blows.

The first blow would be the bursting of a massive speculative bubble that was already out of control by the end of 1928. New informational services, it became clear, had not made the system immune to speculative fever. An early bout of it had produced a boom in Florida real estate. And while the collapse of this in 1926 did not seem to affect general growth trends, the new fever that was spreading in 1927 and 1928 would prove much more damaging. More and more Americans seemed willing to credit the unrealistic optimism of securities promoters, ignore traditional measures of value, and bid against each other for shares in corporate growth. Many were willing to finance such acquisitions by borrowing money at high rates of interest; and the monetary authorities, more concerned with international gold movements than with domestic credit uses, were slow to move and ineffective when they did. By the end of the year the economy seemed destined to suffer the consequences of a major exercise in speculative folly.

The two other blows that would follow the stock market crash were being prepared abroad, the consequences of unsolved international problems. One was to come from the dumping of agricultural surpluses that were being accumulated by national price-maintenance agencies. By 1928 such programs had become the typical response to continuing market gluts in agricultural goods. A number of nations had adopted them; and when they reached their limits, as most would do in 1930, the result would be a second major blow to American economic expectations. The third would come from the collapse of the international exchange system erected under the Dawes Plan and the war debt settlements. This system depended upon a continued outpouring of American capital to help Europeans meet their trade deficits and debt obligations. And when the mechanisms that produced this outpouring failed, as they did after 1929, the result would be a proliferation of trade barriers, a rapid shrinkage of world trade, and a European panic that would trigger further contractions in the United States.

The movement toward a new economy, then, was about to encounter major obstacles that would make a temporary mockery of its formulas for a people's capitalism and a higher self-government. The New Era system would soon be an economy in crisis, with a quarter of its work force unemployed and much of its plant idle. Yet the crisis, it now seems clear, was less the product of outmoded ideas and institutions than of institutions that foreshadowed the future but could not bear the weight being put on them. Although badly discredited for a time, much of the organizational apparatus would survive. And what would follow, at least in its major outlines, was alteration aimed not at scrapping this apparatus but at filling organizational gaps, reinforcing it with the power of the state, and organizing governmental balance wheels to replace the private ones that had failed.

CHAPTER 6

The Associative Vision at Home and Abroad, 1925–1928

In June 1925, three months after Calvin Coolidge's second inaugural, Herbert Hoover journeyed to Oskaloosa, Iowa, and spoke to the graduating class of William Penn College. It was a ritual that might have been given over to the usual platitudes. But Hoover chose instead to expound a theory of national progress and of how governmental activity could foster it. America, he said, had long shown an instinct for the kind of community action that could resolve social problems and prevent the growth of stultifying bureaucratization. This peculiar genius had enabled it to conquer a continent and become the world's leading industrial nation, and this same genius was now developing forms of "associational action" that would allow progress to continue along a "new scientific and economic frontier." The great concern of true progressives was that this development might be halted. It might succumb to unenlightened selfishness, to destructive forms of statist intervention, or to a "vast syndicalism" that captured the state and utilized it for class purposes. The job of progressive government, he continued, was both to guard against these eventualities and to stimulate progressive forms of cooperative organization. Its ultimate aim should be a "partnership" of responsible and interdependent social groups acting together to stretch "an enlarged vision of neighborly relations" over "the nation as a whole."

Hoover, of course, spoke for only one segment of the Republican administration. His vision of governmental activism was not shared by such conservatives as Andrew Mellon and Calvin Coolidge. Nor did his perceptions of progressive organization agree with those of critics in the antitrust agencies and conflict-oriented areas of the federal bureaucracy. Yet the vision he set forth was clearly a major force in shaping public policy between 1925 and 1928. Activities that could be fitted into it acquired a capacity for survival and growth. Those that could not were vulnerable to cutbacks, abolition, or redirection. And the result, despite Coolidge's emphasis on economy and inactivity, was not really a reduction in governmental expenditures and activities. While pruning took place on one side, the organizers of associational action were creating a kind of "associative state" responsive to their needs but partly financed by public funds. These additions outweighed retrenchment elsewhere, and many Americans accepted them as a superior kind of national progressivism meeting the social needs that could not be satisfied by the bureaucratic and "class legislation" proposals emanating from Congress.

BUILDING THE ASSOCIATIVE STATE

At the center of governmental activism was a dynamic and expanding Commerce Department, reaching out now to draw other areas of the federal bureaucracy within its orbit and halt activities that challenged its own perceptions of the public interest. Initially Hoover had operated alongside and sometimes in conflict with Hughes and Wallace. But after 1924, with Wallace dead and Hughes returning to private life, Commerce burst out of earlier jurisdictional boundaries and sought to function as a "ministry of reconstruction" concerned with all phases of economic organization and decision making. As early as 1922 Hoover had turned what remained of the Labor Department into a cooperative satellite. Subsequently he attached much of the Interior Department, annexing such bureaus as Mines and Patents and shaping policy for most of the others. At the same time he succeeded in making Commerce a dominant force in shaping international economic relations, encroaching in many areas on the traditional jurisdiction of the State Department. And after Wallace's death in October 1924, he was successful in installing William Jardine, a man who agreed with his prescriptions for farm relief, as the new Secretary of Agriculture. Under Jardine the department ceased to be a major center of anti-Hooverism; it purged those who had been guilty of such behavior and became a member of the Hoover team.

In addition, the Hoover organization moved with considerable success to revamp the antitrust and regulatory agencies, not, so it claimed, to permit antisocial behavior but rather to halt destructive organization wrecking and encourage fruitful forms of cooperative action. Under the post-1924 attorney generals, Harlan Stone and John Sargent, the Antitrust Division lent its blessing to a variety of associational activities previously considered illegal. Its job, as interpreted by the new antitrust chief William Donovan, was one of helping constructive cooperationists to avoid legal difficulties. Similarly, the Federal Trade Commission underwent a major transformation. Under the chairmanship of William Humphrey, whom Coolidge appointed in 1925, it drastically reduced its investigatory activities, began negotiating more informal settlements, and started sponsoring trade practice conferences at which private leaders and FTC officials agreed upon codes of ethical behavior for numerous industries. In theory the commission was still carrying out its mandate to eliminate unfair methods of competition. But it was now doing so by devolving its power upon private bureaucracies and allowing them to define what was fair and what was unfair.

Adding such agencies as the Interstate Commerce Commission and the Federal Reserve Board to the Commerce-led team proved more difficult. Plans for a new kind of ICC, which would help the railroads to reorganize themselves into an efficient and responsive national system, failed to materialize. And Federal Reserve policy, as developed by Benjamin Strong of the New York Federal Reserve Bank, was much more concerned with reestablishing an international gold standard than with organizational and managerial reform. It strongly resisted Hoover's repeated efforts to develop new credit controls. Yet both the ICC and the FRB did seek to regulate by devolving power and responsibility upon private groups; and work with these groups, it was assumed, would eventually bring their "regulators" into the larger "cooperative system."

New regulators, in the meantime, were being added not as independent entities or agents of popular action but as parts of the Commerce-led system. New controls over the Alaskan salmon industry, for example, were entrusted to Hoover's Bureau of Fisheries and used to implement conservation measures long urged by the canners' association. A "model" labor mediation system for the railroad industry (set up under the Railway Labor Act of 1926) emerged from Commerce-led efforts to develop control agencies and procedures that both labor and management would support. New safety and operational standards in the aviation field became the responsibility of Hoover's Aeronautics Branch and its outcropping of collaborative associations. And in the radio field, a frequency allocation system developed by the Commerce Department finally received statutory sanction and became the basis for ordering access to a new resource. In each case the aim was to reinforce private ordering mechanisms with governmental power or approval, and in each this was accepted as necessary for further development of progressive organization and practice.

The promise, however, was that this union of public and private power could be held to a manageable minimum or would be needed only for a temporary or emergency period. The real faith of the Hooverites was not in statist coercion but rather in publicly endorsed agreements that had an approved yet extralegal status and would therefore lend quasi-official standing and protection to private compliance efforts. It was through such agreements, they believed, that one could achieve a fruitful balance between order and liberty, and by 1928 they were pointing proudly to three bodies of agreement that had allegedly done so. One consisted of publicly endorsed pledges to refrain from antisocial employment practices, the most cited examples here being the steel industry's agreement on an eight-hour day and joint commitments elsewhere to safety and factory standards. The second consisted of over a hundred federally approved standardization and conservation agreements, each credited with helping to build the new mass-consumption economy or to curb wastage of resources. And the third consisted of more than fifty trade practice codes, certified by the FTC as specifying unfair methods of competition and spelling out the obligations of the ethical and socially responsible competitor. Together, it was said, these represented a new triumph for the American way, and together they constituted both an implementation of wartime lessons and the foundations for a new and superior kind of socioeconomic order.

As of 1928, Hoover seemed convinced that the major threats to this developing associational action were being effectively contained. It was not until later that he became much concerned with the market riggers, corporate plunderers, and protectors of inefficiency who were operating behind the associational façade. And state-approved associational action, he continued to believe, was helping to check big government and class-oriented "syndicalism," not to move the nation toward them. His chief concerns were with agriculture, the sick industries, and electrical power, areas where, as he saw it, failure to develop healthy forms of association and public-private cooperation had allowed state coercionists to gain political followings. Yet even in these areas he could find relatively little to worry about. Congressional attempts to legislate statist solutions had been turned back. Time had been gained for reeducation and for the building of truly progressive forms of collective action and cooperative endeavor.

CONTAINING CONGRESSIONAL INITIATIVES

Of the statist solutions that Hoover worked to block, the most prominent and in his eyes the most threatening was the one embodied in the McNary-Haugen bill and supported by a movement generally designated as McNary-Haugenism. Sponsored by Senator Charles McNary of Oregon and Representative Gilbert Haugen of Iowa, the bill would allegedly make the tariff effective for farmers. Under it a federal agency would support and protect domestic farm prices, seeking to give such goods the "fair exchange" or "parity" value they had sold for in the prewar period. This agency would then dispose of accumulated surpluses abroad, taking losses on such transactions, and would finance its operations by assessing "equalization fees" against farm producers. The scheme had first appeared in 1922, in a pamphlet by former war administrators George Peek and Hugh Johnson. It had subsequently won the support of Secretary of Agriculture Wallace, the American Farm Bureau Federation, and a number of business leaders. And while it had gone down to defeat in 1924, its supporters had not given up. Peek proceeded to build a powerful legislative lobby, and a collapse of cotton prices in 1926 brought growing support in the southern as well as the western states.

In 1927 and again in 1928, McNary-Haugenism developed enough strength to put its program through Congress. But on each occasion President Coolidge imposed a veto that could not be overridden. Relying heavily on memoranda supplied by the Commerce Department, he condemned the scheme as class and bureaucratic legislation that would have disastrous effects on private initiative, constructive cooperation, and the relations of the United States with other nations. The real answer, said Coolidge, was further encouragement to educational services and cooperative marketing. And apparently without much enthusiasm, he lent his support to the Hoover-Jardine plan to assist such organization with federal credits. This was a proposal that Hoover had been refining since the early 1920s. It could, so he argued, fill the organizational gap responsible for farm difficulties and such phenomena as McNary-Haugenism; and while farm leaders were in no mood to listen in 1927 and 1928, he seemed convinced that they soon would be.

Movements analogous to McNary-Haugenism also developed in some of the sick industries. There, as in agriculture, there was agitation for state-supported cartels or for using governmental power to put a floor under prices and wages, and in Congress this was reflected in proposals for antitrust revision, fair trade laws, and special price-and-wage controls for such industries as bituminous coal. Unlike the McNary-Haugen bill, though, such measures never came close to displacing Hoover's operations or to confronting the President with unwelcome legislation that he felt compelled to veto. The only sick industry to be the subject of new legislative action was shipping, and there the enhanced subsidies and new credits followed the administration's prescriptions and remained within its definition of what constituted appropriate and necessary governmental action.

Tax and welfare policy also continued to follow administration prescriptions, although in these areas they came more from Andrew Mellon than from Herbert Hoover. In 1926 congressional defenders of graduated income and estate taxes were unable to prevent further reductions; the maximum surtax dropped from 40 to 20 percent. And having failed to establish the constitutionality of federal laws prohibiting child labor and protecting working women, the advocates of welfare statism largely withdrew from the federal arena and concentrated what energies they could still muster on the state level. In their present weakness they could not even save the limited funding for infant and maternity health that had been established under the Sheppard-Towner Act of 1921. In 1927 the program was extended for another two years but only on condition that it would then be phased out.

In most fields proposals for government-operated enterprise had even less congressional support. Yet in one area this was not the case. By 1926 the abuses of private power and fertilizer companies, coupled with the failure to find acceptable lessees for the wartime developments at Muscle Shoals, on the Tennessee River, had opened the way to limited "experiments in socialism." A growing bloc of congressmen, led by Senator George Norris of Nebraska, came to support federal expansion and operation of the Muscle Shoals facilities. And in May of 1928, despite strong opposition from the power lobby and the Coolidge Administration, Congress passed a measure under which a federal corporation would develop the Tennessee Valley, produce large quantities of cheap power, and work out a "yardstick" for measuring the fairness of private power rates. As with the McNary-Haugen bill, the President's veto became the instrument of containment. With Congress adjourned, he gave the measure a pocket veto and passed the issue on to his successor.

On the river development question as a whole, however, the administration's stand was not entirely negative. The American solution, so Hoover's Commerce secretariat kept insisting, lay neither in Norris's "socialism" nor in an unregulated and haphazard system of private exploitation. It lay rather in a "partnership" or association of federal, local, and private agencies, all working together to curb abuses, bring engineering expertise to bear, and implement cooperatively developed regional and national plans. It was this notion that Hoover articulated in a series of "superpower" conferences, in agitation for a national waterway plan, and in protracted negotiations looking toward the development of the Colorado and Columbia river basins and a St. Lawrence seaway. And Coolidge did eventually accept an enlarged sphere of federal responsibility and sign two major developmental measures into law. One authorized an extensive flood control program for the Mississippi River, the aim being to prevent future floods from having the disastrous effects of the one in 1927. The other implemented an interstate compact dividing the waters of the Colorado River and authorized federal construction of a huge Boulder Canyon dam and an accompanying water-delivery system. Under the compromise finally adopted, the federal government was also to install and operate a hydroelectric power plant but was to sell power only at wholesale to a specified group of private and municipal distributors.

For the most part, then, congressional initiatives that challenged administration prescriptions were effectively contained. In Congress men with different visions of government and different perceptions of progressive organization were able to win substantial followings. But what they could produce in the way of new laws and programs was either negated by presidential veto or reshaped to fit the administration's definitions of what was American and progressive. As of 1928 the Hooverian views on these matters seemed destined to remain at the core of national economic policy. But should the forces keeping them there weaken, challengers would have foundations upon which to build.

ETHNOCULTURAL TENSIONS AND ISSUES

Though ethnocultural tensions remained high, they were now producing remarkably few eruptions in either Congress or the administration. In this area, to be sure, there was little philosophizing about the emergence of a new and superior synthesis. But many Americans preferred the situation that existed to the changes that various groups were advocating, and it was people of this view who were making national policy. Both the "hundred percent Americans" and their opponents tended to withdraw from the national legislative and administrative battlegrounds and channel most of their energies into agitation on the state and local levels or into struggles for control of the Democratic party.

On the matter of immigration, for example, majority sentiment in Congress continued to support the central features of the legislation enacted in 1924. Although a number of ethnic minorities continued to criticize the ethnocentric and racist ideas reflected in the quota system, they were unable to influence many legislators. And while organizations espousing "hundred percent Americanism" continued to urge new Americanization programs and other measures to reduce alien influence, they had no success in bringing about legislative action. The only protesters with much impact were the German and Scandinavian ethnic groups, who wanted to retain the 1924 quotas and prevent those based on "national origins" from being implemented. The changeover, they argued, would necessarily be based on arbitrary determinations and would be hardest on would-be immigrants from Germany and the Scandinavian countries, people who had made and would make good Americans. They strongly supported the one-year postponements passed by Congress in 1927 and 1928; and given Hoover's sympathy with their position, they had hopes of making the postponement permanent in 1929.

Congressional and administrative responses to those dissatisfied with the existing status of minority rights were also minimal. Although battles over feminism, cultural freedom, and the civil liberties of "un-Americans" continued in local governments and the federal courts, there was little support for altering decisions through national action. And to the protests of the black minority against racial discrimination, the responses were limited to those that would not arouse fears of a new "Black Reconstruction" or challenge the legitimacy of the southern establishment and its institutions. They consisted only of a few additional appointments to federal offices, a slight increase in the support for black educational institutions, some improvement in civil service job opportunities, and an occasional rhetorical gesture.

Perhaps the most unstable of the accommodations that had emerged by 1925 was that in regard to prohibition. On this, to be sure, a kind of balance had been struck, one that allowed prohibitionist ideals to be embodied in federal law while tolerating inadequate enforcement, continued drinking, and massive bootlegging. Yet even as Coolidge backed away from actions that could upset this balance, the stage was being set for new and fiercer battles over the issue. Gaining strength from 1925 on was a repeal movement led by a newly formed organization, the Association against the Prohibition Amendment, supported by many urban Democrats and financed by some of the nation's wealthiest men. No longer satisfied with mere toleration of illicit activities, the movement was advancing new counterimages that many Americans of the period found appealing. Increasingly opinion makers were adopting the view that prohibition, far from being a liberating and progressive reform, was a repressive denial of cultural and individual freedom, a breeder of crime and corruption, and a burdensome imposition on the nation's taxpayers. And increasingly social drinking was being associated not with the moral evils and un-American behavior of the old-time saloon but with fashionable living and liberated comportment, the assertion of individual and minority rights, and the romance of adventurous youth, the new woman, and the workingman's club. If such counterimages should prevail, even a prohibition that did little prohibiting would soon be in jeopardy.

The response of the Anti-Saloon League and its allies was one of mounting alarm and heightened fanaticism rather than of concessions designed to deflate the repeal movement. Proposals for partial repeal or for redefining intoxicating beverages so as to exclude beer and wine were denounced as compromises with evil; the new life styles, despite their popular appeal, were condemned as degenerate, immoral, and un-American. In prohibitionist circles the political success of Alfred E. Smith, culminating in his capture of the Democratic party machinery in 1928, became a resurgence of evil forces threatening to undo what had been accomplished through a hundred years of effort. Bent upon defeating Smith, the dry leaders organized Democrats for Hoover. Having become aroused by the repeal threat, they were determined that Smith's defeat must be followed by vigorous action against lawbreakers and those who condoned or excused their behavior.

Indeed, Smith's nomination and Hoover's willingness to become the candidate of the anti-Smith forces had the effect of reopening the congressional and administrative arenas to the kind of ethnocultural warfare that Coolidge had avoided. The years after 1928 would bring not only a severe test for Hoover's associationalism but also for his assumption that he could satisfy the Hoover Democrats without doing severe political damage to himself and his party.

THE INTERNATIONAL SCENE

Also to be tested after 1928 were the Republican formulas for international order and progress as developed by Hughes and Hoover and continued during the Coolidge Administration. To a later generation these would seem to bear part of the responsibility for a world depression and the coming of a second world war. Yet as the Coolidge era drew to a close, these formulas seemed to have the world moving in conjunction with American interests and dreams. Reporting to Congress in December 1928, Coolidge could note the prevalence of peace and good will, coming, he said, from mutual understanding and from "the knowledge that the problems which a short time ago appeared so ominous are yielding to the touch of manifest friendship." And according to Secretary of State Frank B. Kellogg, the irascible but generally competent lawyer-politician who succeeded Hughes in 1925, the actions of the period had laid the foundations for what could be a new era of permanent peace.

To the Hughes system of the early 1920s the post-1924 policy makers sought to make three major additions, two of which failed to win acceptance. One was American membership in the World Court, strongly endorsed by both Coolidge and Kellogg but finally blocked by Senate reservations that the court members found unacceptable. The other countries objected in particular to allowing the United States to block advisory opinions in cases where it had or claimed to have an interest; and as of 1928 the efforts of Elihu Root and a League committee to reach an acceptable compromise on this issue had not yet borne fruit. The other attempted addition was extension of the Washington naval limitations system to include noncapital as well as capital ships. In 1927, responding to a growing concern about international rivalry in cruiser construction, President Coolidge called for a new naval disarmament conference to meet in Geneva and complete the work begun in Washington. His call was accepted by Britain and Japan, but from the beginning the negotiations went badly and were under constant attack from nationalistic and big-navy groups in each country. After six weeks of deliberation, the conferees conceded failure and disbanded without a new limitations agreement.

The addition that did win approval and become part of the American design for permanent peace was the Kellogg-Briand Peace Pact, signed in Paris in August of 1928 and eventually subscribed to by most of the nations of the world. In part this was an outgrowth of pacifist idealism, especially of the post-1921 movement for outlawing war as an instrument of national policy. But also involved was Kellogg's determination to guide the movement into constructive channels and prevent the French from using it to involve the United States in their security system. His response to Aristide Briand's proposal for outlawing warfare between France and the United States was to urge a multilateral pact that committed all signatories to renounce aggressive war as a legitimate tool for advancing national interests. It was this conception that prevailed and won the Nobel Peace Prize for Kellogg. The pact would later be criticized as amounting to little more than an "international kiss," but a good many New Era diplomats were convinced that commitments of this sort would help to deter aggressive militarism and strengthen the other ordering mechanisms that America had helped to establish. A few even argued that the lack of enforcement machinery was a guard against abuse and that this made the peace-keeping properties of such arrangements superior to those of the League covenant.

While lauding the creative balance between nationalism and internationalism, New Era statesmen also assumed that the measures taken to promote European recovery from the war had been effective. In the wake of the Dawes Plan and the refunding of war debts in accordance with "capacity to pay," American capital was flowing into Europe, especially into Germany. In all, Americans bought a total of about $2,500,000,000 in German securities during the years 1924–1928. And with the proceeds from such loans Europeans were not only making reparations and debt payments but modernizing and developing their economies. Growth, so it was thought, would enable them to pay for the use of the borrowed capital and continue to meet their obligations.

Only a few Americans at the time seemed aware that much of this exported capital was being misused or wasted; that the envisioned growth patterns were basically inconsistent with the protectionism still practiced by the leading industrial nations; or that the remaining international debt burdens (around $625,000,000 a year for Germany and a funded total of $11,671,400,000 owed by European nations to the United States) constantly threatened the currency systems of the nations involved. On occasion, Herbert Hoover, Owen D. Young, and Dawes Plan administrator S. Parker Gilbert did issue warnings against one or another of these weaknesses. But neither they nor others in positions of power were willing to support such remedies as state or state-controlled lending, full cancellation of the debts, or an end to protective tariffs. On the contrary, American policy moved in the opposite direction. And the result, by 1928, was an increasingly shaky structure, more and more dependent on a continued outflow of American capital that had little prospect of being sustained indefinitely.

During this same period American efforts to stabilize East Asia were also encountering major difficulties. In Japan anti-Americanism again became a major force, reflecting itself in protest over American immigration policies and a reassertion of Japan's "special interests" in China. That Japanese imperialism could be contained by the Washington treaty system seemed increasingly problematical. China, moreover, was undergoing new upheavals, manifested in civil war, violence against foreigners, and bitter conflict between the left and right wings of a rising nationalist movement. At Nanking in 1927 nationalist soldiers slaughtered a number of foreigners and American gunboats helped to restore order. Yet in spite of these developments, much of the optimism of the earlier period persisted. American goals, it was thought, were still realizable, and in 1928 two forces in the area were believed to be enhancing the chances of realization. One was the continuing influence of Japanese moderates, an influence that the United States might strengthen through constructive diplomacy. The other was the new nationalist government that had finally won recognition in China and with which the United States reached agreements settling the Nanking claims and recognizing China's tariff autonomy. Chiang Kai-shek, so a number of American diplomats had come to believe, was the leader of the moderate and progressive elements in China. Properly encouraged, his government could become the vehicle for containing radicalism and imperialism and achieving the kind of East Asia the United States desired.

Policy makers also seemed convinced that Western imperialism was being liberalized and steered into constructive channels. In the Near East the struggle against "closed doors" had finally brought a multinational consortium allowing American firms a share in oil development and permitting future entry through a subleasing system. And elsewhere the efforts to make colonialism pay through price-raising cartels supported by governmental power seemed to be in retreat. Against these the Commerce Department had waged a series of campaigns, seeking in particular to mobilize and bring pressure through American buyers, lenders, and competitors. And while these had encountered strong resistance from noncooperators and from congressmen unwilling to grant new antitrust exemptions, Hoover believed that they deserved considerable credit for the demise of the British rubber cartel and other foreign combinations. The world, so it was thought, was being nudged away from an exploitive and war-breeding imperialism toward the kind of "cooperative competition" that could bring orderly progress. Still hidden from view were the intensified economic nationalism and the anticolonial upheavals that would really characterize the 1930s.

Beneath the surface, then, developments were under way that would eventually lead to a worldwide depression, another world war, and revolutionary upheaval in the underdeveloped world. But as the architects of America's post-1921 diplomacy surveyed their work in 1928, they did not consider any of these things at all likely. On the contrary, they saw themselves as having found ways to attain the benefits of international order and progress without giving up those that derived from national independence and individual enterprise.

REPUBLICAN DIPLOMACY AND THE PAN-AMERICAN VISION

Meanwhile, efforts were continuing to build a new Pan-Americanism, one that could provide stability, protection, and expanded commerce yet retain the good will and support of the Latin-American republics. Although Hughes was no longer Secretary of State, his designs for improved peace-keeping machinery and the phasing out of gunboat diplomacy were being followed. The new Central American system seemed to vindicate itself when cooperative action restored order in Honduras, and in August of 1925 American marines left Nicaragua. Nor had the Commerce Department abandoned its vision of an ever larger market created through the joint activities of American capitalists, trained economic experts, and cooperative Latins. Under its auspices business contacts continued to be systematically organized, uniform standards and laws promoted, and pressure brought against operations considered economically unsound. Its job, as Hoover and his assistants defined it, was both to create vehicles for constructive forms of economic association and to defend the instruments of progress against the encroachments of statists, imperialists, and cartellizing extortionists.

 In late 1925, however, two developments inaugurated a train of events that would severely test the Hughes and Hoover policies. One was the outbreak of civil war in Nicaragua, touched off by Emiliano Chamorro's seizure of government power and continuing even after the United States had helped to force Chamorro out and install Adolfo Díaz as his successor. By the end of 1926 a rival government under Juan Sacasa held substantial areas of the country, and as fighting intensified pressure for American military intervention was building. The other development was a resurgence of revolutionary nationalism in Mexico. There a new administration under Plutarco Calles proceeded to scrap the agreements reached in 1923, sponsor new legislation requiring foreign oil companies to exchange their holdings for long-term leases, launch a bloody anticlerical campaign, and offer recognition and aid to the Nicaraguan rebels. To a number of Americans the Mexican Revolution seemed to have got out of hand again,

and by early 1927 there was considerable clamor for armed intervention in Mexico as well as Nicaragua.

Coolidge turned a deaf ear to the clamor for war with Mexico, especially after the Senate voted unanimously in favor of peaceful arbitration. But Nicaragua was another matter. There the President yielded
to pressures for intervention, sending in a force of 5000 marines to
support the Diaz government and in the process arousing a storm of
criticism in both the United States and Latin America. The whole
vision of a new Pan-Americanism seemed in jeopardy, revealed, so its
critics declared, as only a façade for an exploitive imperialism backed
when necessary by armed force. If Pan-Americanism was to be saved,
this relapse into gunboat diplomacy had to be liquidated. And the
result, in April 1927, was a special pacification mission, headed by
Henry L. Stimson, once Taft's Secretary of War. In May Stimson was
successful in persuading the warring factions to lay down their arms,
allow Diaz to complete his term, and accept the results of an
American-supervised election in 1928. Only one small rebel band,
under Augusto Sandino, held out against this arrangement; and once
the election was held and José Moncada, military commander of the
rebel forces, installed as president, most of the marines were again
withdrawn.

Meanwhile, the Mexican problem also seemed to be moving toward
resolution. In September 1927 Coolidge replaced Ambassador James
Sheffield with Dwight W. Morrow, a House of Morgan partner with
unusual persuasive and diplomatic skills. Some three months later
Morrow persuaded America's hero aviator, Charles A. Lindbergh, to
make a good-will flight to Mexico City. Taking advantage of the new
cordiality, Morrow was able to arrange face-saving formulas that
allowed foreign companies to retain subsoil rights acquired prior to
1917, mitigated or postponed actions against American landowners,
and brought a truce in the battle between church and state. His diplomacy achieved no permanent resolution of the tensions between the
new Pan-Americanism and Mexico's revolutionary nationalism, but,
as one historian has noted, Morrow did demonstrate that "with tact
and patience the peace could be kept."

Thanks to the work of Stimson and Morrow the way seemed open
to a further development of the envisioned Pan-Americanism, and in

late 1928 three actions seemed to indicate that further progress was being made. In November President-elect Herbert Hoover began a lengthy good-will tour of Latin-American nations, articulating his hopes for greater hemispheric cooperation. In December a Pan-American Conference on Conciliation and Arbitration assembled in Washington, eventually producing new agreements and agencies for handling international disputes. And in the same month Undersecretary of State J. Reuben Clark finished a new policy memorandum repudiating the Roosevelt Corollary to the Monroe Doctrine and declaring that the doctrine did not justify American police actions in Latin America. Although not published until 1930, and although the diplomatic establishment then showed a reluctance to embrace it as "official policy," the memorandum was a milestone in the retreat from interventionism. And to the surprise of many, this retreat would survive the subsequent economic breakdown. Despite renewed pressures for armed intervention and the collection of debts by force, the Hoover Administration would not relapse into a new round of gunboat diplomacy and military occupations.

Continuing commitments to nonintervention, however, would not mean realization of the vision's other aspects. Despite claims to the contrary, the proponents of Pan-Americanism had not developed machinery that could sustain the flow of American capital into the region or insure that it would be used there for reproductive purposes. As subsequent investigations would reveal, the financing operations involved large elements of misrepresentation and economic malpractice. As in Europe, a shaky structure was being built that could not withstand a decline in American capital exports. When this occurred, the result would be not the peaceful and prospering hemispheric community that was envisioned but rather a Latin America forced into wholesale debt repudiation and general economic contraction, torn by political upheaval and instability, and convinced that it had again been victimized by "Yankee imperialists."

In the end, whether in Latin America, Europe, East Asia, or the United States itself, the New Era formulas for orderly progress would fail the tests to which they were eventually subjected and would be labeled either as naïve and unperceptive or as smokescreens for rapacious private interests. Yet failure and the subsequent labeling should not be permitted to obscure the genuine achievements of those seeking to apply such formulas. Nor should they obscure how perceptive the analysis of alternatives often was or how much of a later design for orderly progress was foreshadowed or anticipated. While resisting the initiatives of statists and League advocates, the policy makers of the period were not merely reactive or negative. They were the heirs and transmitters of managerial visions which included embryonic forms of corporative planning, world community building, and "alliances for progress."

CHAPTER 7

Alternatives to the Mainstream

Americans, so a succession of historians have noted, have prided themselves on being a practical people, confident that they can solve problems as they arise and retain solutions found to be workable or functional. Yet, as an equal number have noted, they have also been an intensely ideological people, raising liberal dogmas into a national philosophy and using this to define rival systems as inherently unworkable. Along with tests of workability they have insisted upon tests of "Americanness," ruling out support for those who have challenged the national philosophy itself. And only when existing arrangements have been perceived as meeting both these tests have such arrangements been relatively free from criticism and demands for reform.

Such was the case with the mixture of public and private activities that took shape in the 1920s. Many saw the New Era arrangements both as a flowering of American liberalism and as a huge practical success, and many others believed them sufficiently effective and safe as to be tolerable. Many, however, did not mean all. Outside the mainstream a variety of critics challenged the dominant perceptions, depicting a society mired in error and perversion and offering alternatives both to New Era Americanism and to the American system itself. They too were part of America in the 1920s, and segments of their part were to be of major significance for the decade that followed.

COMPETING VISIONS OF A NEW LIBERALISM

Of greatest significance, perhaps, were critics who envisioned a new liberalism yet denied that the New Era arrangements were bringing or could bring it into being. Modern technology, they believed, was capable of providing an uplifting and liberating abundance, and the realization of this potential was compatible with and perhaps dependent upon the retention of a capitalist economy and a liberal political order. But the notion that it could be done through capitalist syndicates and the machinery of private bureaucracies was to them both fanciful and dangerous. Such institutions were inherently incapable of developing the necessary vision and responsibility; and their inevitable tendency, if unchecked by other forces, was toward exploitation, tyranny, and a waste of natural and human resources. It was only through an enlightened governmental apparatus, using its power to obtain decisions that private organizations could not make, that designs for a new liberalism could actually be realized.

Just what this apparatus should consist of, however, and just what decisions it should make and enforce were questions upon which the liberal critics of New Era arrangements found it difficult to agree. They disagreed, in particular, about the kinds of action that could take place in the private sector, about the capacity of government to plan, and about the potential abuses of power that must be guarded against. Given these disagreements, the result was an array of differing and often competing designs for an expanded public sector.

To some critics, for example, the major deficiency in the New Era arrangements was their inability to produce the spending decisions needed for sustained growth and continued social progress. Fordism and private planning activities were steps in the right direction, but ultimately they were incapable of curbing or correcting the destructive aspects of a maturing capitalism. This would require governmental power, specifically the transfer of a larger portion of the spending decisions to the public sector and the development there of an apparatus to insure that they were made in the interests of the system as a whole. So said such unconventional economists as William T. Foster and Waddill Catchings, especially in such widely read works as

Business Without a Buyer (1927) and *The Road to Plenty* (1928). By 1929 leaders who agreed with this analysis had formed a Planned Prosperity League, presented a plan for prosperity reserves to the state governors, and developed a vision of enlarged federal construction managed in the interests of overall economic stability. In particular, they were urging commitments to a superhighway system and the gearing of its construction to a prosperity index.

A second vision of enlarged government came from those still committed to the "new freedom" ideology of the prewar period. Many of them were still active in the rural wings of both parties and in the service of small-business and consumer groups. And their prescriptions for a new liberalism continued to discount the human capacity for planning and to stress the ability of enforced competition to make private activities serve the public good. The fatal flaw in the New Era arrangements, as they saw it, was the assumption that special interests could be enlightened or professionalized and thus turned into social interests. The release of such interests from market discipline was an invitation to social disaster, and under modern conditions the maintenance of this discipline could not be left to natural law or private action. It required a powerful government engaged in constant action against market riggers and in a constant process of taking over and operating sectors that were inherently monopolistic. Hence the first priority of the true progressive should be the rescue of the antitrust and regulatory agencies from their captors, and the second should be the building of governmental organizations with the ability to sustain market discipline and to conduct efficiently those enterprises in which release from such discipline was a social necessity.

Still another vision of enlarged government came from the heirs of the "new nationalism" and others convinced that a planning and welfare state could serve liberal ends. Like the antitrusters, such critics rejected the assumption that special interests could be enlightened or professionalized. Yet at the same time they regarded the notion of government-enforced market discipline as unworkable and antimodern. The answer lay not in an apparatus that supported entrepreneurship but rather in one that would free scientific professionals from the grip of pecuniary-minded men and allow them to use their talents to serve public interests. The true founts of wisdom were such critics as Thorstein Veblen and Simon Patten, not Louis Brandeis or Woodrow Wilson. And as the decade progressed, such theorists as John Dewey, Charles A. Beard, Stuart Chase, and Rexford G. Tugwell were sketching the outlines of a planning and welfare apparatus believed capable of speeding up and managing national progress. In essence they proposed the transfer of key decisions from the private sector and partisan political arenas to an elite of national planners acting in the interests of the people; and, as a number of social workers had continued to advocate, they would couple this new discipline with tax-supported social action programs designed to break the chains of poverty, ignorance, and disease. This was the vision that continued to appear in the pages of the *New Republic* and the *Survey,* in some of the calls leading up to the Progressive party convention of 1924, and late in the decade in the formation of a League for Independent Political Action.

Also operating in liberal circles were reformists who could accept the central coordinating mechanisms of the New Era political economy but wished to erect alongside of these a new set of governmental welfare structures. Much of what they believed necessary for enlightened national progress had first been enunciated at the National Conference on Social Agencies and Reconstruction in November 1918. It consisted not so much of a planning or antitrust or managed spending apparatus as it did of an enlarged public sector that would enforce fair labor standards, protect the weak from economic exploitation, provide public health and housing services, and operate new systems of health, unemployment, and old-age insurance. Real social welfare, they insisted, the kind essential to the realization of liberal goals in an industrial and urban age, could come only through a national system of public institutions, not through extensions of private philanthropy and local community action. And working through such organizations as the National Child Labor Committee, the American Association for Labor Legislation, the National Federation of Settlements, and the American Association for Old Age Security, these reformists continued to develop designs for the envisioned institutions and to agitate for programs of implementation.

Included in their ranks were such people as Isaac Rubinow, Paul Kellogg, Edward Devine, Abraham Epstein, Julia Lathrop, and Mary Dewson.

Another kind of new liberalism came from those opposed to governmental bureaucracies yet seemingly convinced that their own private bureaucracies and syndicates could employ governmental power as an instrument of national progress. Modern democracy, as these liberals saw it, must function not through an enlarged state but through corporative institutions resembling those of the war period. These, so they maintained, were the tools really capable of defending and advancing liberal values. And unlike the men associated with the Hoover operations, they believed that the building of such institutions would require, for a time anyway, substantial grants of governmental power to those engaged in it. This view appeared in much of the agitation for the McNary-Haugen bills. It was a view espoused by some labor and welfare leaders, and in business circles it continued to generate designs for a planning and welfare system administered through government-supported cartels. By 1929 these designs were coming particularly from the leaders of the National Civic Federation, from writers associated with *Forbes* magazine, and from minority elements in the Chamber of Commerce. In their more extreme form, they were also ₊being set forth in the literature of the Committee on Industrial Coordination and in such books as Benjamin Javits's *Make Everybody Rich* (1929).

Finally, from still other quarters came visions of a new apparatus moving to end racial and ethnic discrimination rather than economic disorders. The crucial defect in the American system, so these critics argued, was not in its treatment of the majority. It was in the unprogressive, unjust, and wasteful basis upon which minorities were allowed to participate. And until this defect was remedied—something that would require extensive state action against discriminatory institutions—the system was in constant danger of degenerating into disorder, irrationalism, and tyrannical capriciousness. So said a variety of minority group spokesmen; and moving beyond the concerns of particular groups, such politicians as David Walsh and Fiorello La Guardia envisioned a new America enriched by cultural diversity and equipped with institutions guaranteeing equitable treatment for its racial, ethnic, and cultural minorities.

Outside the mainstream, then, liberals of various sorts continued to view the New Era arrangements as prescriptions for disaster rather than progress. Pointing to major flaws in the period's underlying assumptions, they set forth competing versions of a new liberalism. And when post-1929 developments seemed to confirm their prognoses, their solutions would acquire greater credibility and growing public support.

ALTERNATIVES ON THE RIGHT

America, so Herbert Hoover liked to say, was "a nation of progressives," a country whose disagreements were over the means to liberal ends rather than the ends themselves. In the 1920s the many though divergent efforts to design a "new liberalism" seemed to bear out such perceptions. Yet there were also critics of another sort, people whose quarrel was not with an "old," "new," or "false" liberalism but with liberal thought and liberal ends themselves. Rejecting the visions born of the Enlightenment and adopted as part of the national philosophy, such critics offered alternatives aimed not at liberating mass man but at protecting society from him or eradicating his desire for individual fulfillment.

For some of them the great shortcoming of American society was its failure to develop the kind of aristocratic institutions capable of nurturing cultural creativity, protecting traditional wisdom, and restraining mass appetites. Promising beginnings along this line had been cut off by concessions to popular agitation and acquisitive materialism. And the result was a society catering to its worst elements and stifling those who possessed the greatest creativity and wisdom. Among some intellectuals this produced a counsel of despair, a conviction that escalating concessions to the masses must eventually destroy everything of real social value. Among other critics there was talk of a "sav-

ing remnant" that would withdraw into isolation and survive the barbarian onslaught. But for still others there was hope that America
might now correct nearly two centuries of error. If the power of
popular demagogues and aggrandizing bureaucracies could be curbed
and held in check, then a genuine aristocracy might emerge, gain
social legitimacy, and establish institutions that would liberate the
creative and the wise.

As to where this aristocracy would come from there was nothing
approaching full agreement. But the most likely spot, so a number of
conservative critics believed, was the business elite that had survived
the competitive tests of the past three decades. This survival, to be
sure, had depended upon the possession of certain undesirable
qualities, among them a "ruthless individualism" and an "eye for the
main chance" that were incompatible with the role envisioned for an
American aristocracy. But the survivors were also men of wisdom and
ability, with demonstrated leadership qualities, a growing appreciation of the finer things of life, and a growing interest in developing the
institutions that could nurture and train a genuine aristocracy. If they
could be protected from populist impulses—and some organizers of
antiradical and antibureaucratic groups hoped to provide such protection—then evolution might well take care of the rest. Permanence and
natural development could transform the inheritors of the great
entrepreneurial fortunes into an American gentry capable of turning
back the barbarian onslaught and correcting the nation's past errors.

This dream was not, however, shared by all those who hoped to see
the development of aristocratic institutions or suitable substitutes for
them. The nation's business elite, as some saw it, had remained far too
individualistic, divided, and mass-oriented to fill the role being outlined for it. It had internalized too much of the libertarian rhetoric
being used to counter populist and working class impulses. And for
these reasons it had little potential for developing into the kind of
aristocracy that conservative critics yearned for. If such an aristocracy
was to emerge, it would have to come from other sectors of the
nation's society; and in the conservative visions of the 1920s several
such potentialities were set forth and debated.

To a few intellectuals, for example, the major hope of redemption
lay in reviving and developing the kind of agrarian "aristocracy" that

had once ruled the South. There, so it was argued, the United States had once had the basis for a truly organic, integrated, and wholesome society, built around an "innate code of obligations" and a "mutuality of interests." If Americans could only see how liberal fallacies and corporate capitalism had destroyed this hope for a wholesome and meaningful way of life, then redemption from the fragmenting cleavages and social disorders of the modern era might begin. Such views were expressed by a number of conservatives, but none did so more eloquently than a group of writers, literary critics, and historians associated with Vanderbilt University. In the work of these "southern agrarians," men like John Crowe Ransom, Allen Tate, and Donald Davidson, the institutions of the New Era were indicted not so much for their economic evils as for their psychological costs to the human organism. To such critics "economic progress" was in reality the generator of moral ruin, atomistic isolation, and debilitating maladjustments; and as the decade ended they gathered their indictments into a symposium under the militant title *I'll Take My Stand* (1930).

Envisioning still another kind of aristocracy were the "new humanists," led by such critics as Irving Babbitt, Paul Elmer More, Stuart P. Sherman, and Norman Foerster. For them the model was neither the antebellum South nor an emerging industrial gentry but rather the learned Puritan divines who had provided moral leadership in colonial New England. In the Puritan leaders, it was maintained, America had once had an elite capable both of disciplining itself and of devising machinery that could protect the wise and cultivated from mass bestiality. It had also had one possessed of the reason and will necessary to discern the ethical absolutes underlying all moral progress. And hence the great task of genuine "humanists" should be one of exposing the heresies of the nineteenth century, upholding such standards and restraints as had survived, and thus paving the way for another aristocracy in the Puritan mold. As the decade ended, moreover, a few such critics seemed convinced that their remedy for the sorry condition of American civilization could actually be implemented. In a manifesto entitled *Humanism and America* (1930), they argued that the nation's intellectual climate was now swinging back to an appreciation of permanent values and of a social order able to protect and sustain them.

Even more designs for a redemptive aristocracy were set forth in the America of the 1920s, designs whose formulators looked back to Hamiltonian federalism and religious authoritarianism or abroad to nations ruled by military, religious, and statist hierarchies. But spokesmen for these had neither the eloquence of the "southern agrarians" and "new humanists" nor a "cult of the commercially successful" upon which to build. They received little attention, even among those who yearned for an aristocratic order, and these yearners never became more than a tiny minority within a larger conservative constellation. Much more attuned to American values were those alternatives that idealized traditional middle-class life and looked to a resurgence of the older middle class for moral regeneration and social redemption. It was this middle-class "right," appealing especially to those with vested interests in traditional norms and relationships, that constituted the largest group of Americans viewing the New Era arrangements as too liberal or too progressive. Although it produced few fascists in the European mold, this group's penchant for doctrines of "social fundamentalism" and "radical restorationism" did bear striking similarities to rightist developments abroad.

BETWEEN FUNDAMENTALISM AND FASCISM

At the core of middle-class rightism, as it appeared in the America of the 1920s, was an idealized community in which sturdy farmers, enterprising but community-spirited businessmen, and industrious and cheerful workmen lived side by side in peaceful and prosperous harmony. The members of this community recognized the mutuality of their interests; and in well-filled churches, character-building homes, and community service organizations, they learned the fundamental truths that allowed them to live rewarding and moral lives. Having discovered a body of higher law, they needed little government. And having developed time-tested and unquestioned methods of allocating wealth and status, they enjoyed a community life free of envy, conflict, and resentment.

That America had ever contained such communities was dubious. But among middle-class rightists their existence in a golden past was an article of faith. America, they insisted, had once been a land in which adherence to social and economic fundamentals resulted in a rewarding and harmonious community life. And America, they also insisted, could become such a land once again. Given proper encouragement and protection and proper antidotes against the poisons that were weakening and corrupting them, the spirit and the community institutions of the golden age could regain their vitality and restore national virtue.

For some, proper protection meant action against the very heart of the "new economy" of mass production and mass marketing. It meant action to protect traditional crafts and occupations and especially to protect the livelihoods of traditional merchants and farmers. But many more seemed to assume that the real corrupter was not economic change, that participants in the "new economy" were still capable of participating in a rebirth of the golden age. The real sources of corruption, as they saw it, were modernist ideas, alien value systems, and imported social misfits, all working to foster an "un-Americanism" incompatible with the attainment of social virtue. And the real remedy lay in moving beyond the kinds of protection and antidotes provided by New Era politicians. It lay, more specifically, in increasingly stringent and selective immigration measures; stronger curbs on subversive forms of association and expression; fuller protection for the traditional family, school, and church; and firmer defenses of the ethnic and racist distinctions embedded in traditional society.

Among those who expressed such ideas there was never full agreement. Some concentrated on one foe to the exclusion of others; some were more inclined toward statist measures than others; some were willing to sanction violent and illegal methods while others were not; and some saw the need for action as pressing and imminent while others favored a gradualist approach. There were also partisan differences and disagreements about the boundary between the American and the un-American. Yet rightist coalitions were able to bridge these divisions, win control of a variety of business, patriotic, and religious societies, and put together such new vehicles as the Sentinels of the Republic, the Crusaders, and the American Vigilant Intelligence

Federation. Through such educational and social action groups they were able to exert political influence and keep their vision of an alternative America before the country.

For a time it even seemed that America was about to produce its own variant of the fascist and "radical right" movements that had appeared on the European continent. Marrying the doctrines of middle-class rightism to traditional bigotry and war-fostered vigilanteism, a rapidly expanding Ku Klux Klan emerged as the most prominent manifestation of the traditionalist counterattack against modern ways. Between 1920 and 1925 the "invisible kingdom" grew from two thousand members to two million, attracting not only rural defenders of traditionalism but substantial elements from the "older settlers" in the expanding cities. And although most of its leaders condemned European fascism as an alien ideology, commentators then and later were quick to note some striking similarities. As the historian George Mowry has pointed out, both movements were ideologically grounded in village or preindustrial ideals; both called in almost mystical terms for a return to the virtuous life of the past; both were intensely nationalistic, with a stress on folkish and racial purity; both attacked minorities as being of inferior or defective stock; and both condemned most aspects of the new urban culture, especially its polyglot racial mixtures, its intellectuality and leftist politics, and its new standards of moral behavior. Both, moreover, considered themselves the organized good of the community, and both saw the return to virtue as being achieved through an arduous struggle with pernicious and subversive influences.

At the peak of its strength, the Klan offered a chilling glimpse into New Era America's potential for fascism. It found and recruited a deeply troubled group of middle- and lower-middle-class Americans. It showed how appealing a distinctive garb, supersecret rituals, and guarded open-air meetings could be to those yearning for a touch of the mysterious. It tapped the darker sides of nationalism and folkishness, and in the name of popular virtue it challenged the basic concepts of human dignity and individual rights. For a time, moreover, it seemed to thrive on exposés of its extralegal and terroristic activities— on a kind of vicarious participation in its direct methods of dealing with sinners, corrupters, and social enemies. Yet America, as developments in the later 1920s demonstrated, was neither Italy nor Germany. It lacked the surviving elements of an "old regime" who saw fascism as the road to another kind of restoration. It lacked the linkages between managerial bureaucracies and middle-class rightism that developed abroad. It lacked an intelligentsia willing to develop a respectable ideological cover. And it possessed what Germany and Italy did not: a set of deeply rooted commitments to a liberal polity and a politics of accommodation. It gradually became apparent that much of the Klan's growth was due less to underlying fascist proclivities than to a temporary emotionalism incapable of sustaining itself; from 1925 on the movement rapidly lost its appeal and most of its membership and power.

What also hastened the organization's decline was its susceptibility to capture by politicians interested in using its ready-made "political machine" for their own purposes. In such states as Texas, Louisiana, Oklahoma, Kansas, and Indiana, the Klan served as a vehicle through which political spoilsmen of less than savory character elevated themselves into positions of power. In office they became involved in political and personal scandals, the most notorious of these revolving around sexual misbehavior, election frauds, and political graft in the state of Indiana. And as such behavior was disclosed, it accelerated the organization's mounting membership losses, its loss of standing with the general public, and its growing tendency to disintegrate into warring factions. By 1930, despite desperate efforts to find fresh issues and new menaces, membership had dwindled again, to an estimated 100,000. As the decade ended, America had lost most of its potential nucleus for a "radical right."

Even as the Klan faded, however, a considerable group of Americans continued to see their homeland as a nation fallen from grace and corrupted by false ideals, alien influences, and inferior human stock. In an array of rightist organizations the vision of restoring a golden age through a return to social fundamentals persisted. And in the 1930s it would gain new adherents, both from the victims of economic catastrophe and from those who saw redemption being blocked by another injection of poisonous un-Americanism.

THE ANTICAPITALIST LEFT

Curiously, many of the rightist images of New Era America could also be found at the other end of the political spectrum. In leftist perceptions, too, the institutions being built by New Era capitalists and administrators were dehumanizing and incapable of meeting man's need for a wholesome community life. Where the perceptions differed was in their view of what was at the root of the difficulty and what must be done to overcome it. For the left the basic source of corruption was neither a departure from tested fundamentals nor failure to fill institutional vacuums. It was rather the disintegrating and corrosive impact of capitalist acquisitiveness and institutionalized greed. The good society could not be a capitalist society, and it could not be attained without abolishing private ownership of capital and putting an end to production for profit. On this central point the great bulk of the anticapitalist left accepted the teachings of Karl Marx and equated true progress with the coming of communal property and socialist institutions.

One variant of the Marxist solution had long stressed a gradualist strategy. It envisioned capitalist corruption gradually yielding to an expanding welfare state responsive to an ever widening popular participation, the end result being the attainment of a socialist commonwealth. In Europe this had become the ideology of Social Democratic parties, and in America such a party had seemed to be taking shape during the quarter-century prior to 1917. The war, however, had brought divisions and repression. And while party membership had climbed again in early 1919 (reaching a peak of about 109,000), the subsequent impact of antiradicalism from without and antigradualism from within had left the Socialist Party of America in a shambles. Having failed to capture the organization, the advocates of "revolutionary socialism" broke away to form the Communist and Communist Labor parties. Apostates of other kinds also left, either withdrawing into political inactivity or seeking other channels for realizing their social visions. By 1921 Socialist party membership had dwindled to barely 13,000, and in popular imagery "socialism" had become solidly linked with "un-Americanism." Few doubted that most of the 915,000 votes cast for Eugene Debs in 1920 had been expressions of personal empathy or of concern for civil liberties rather than votes for a socialist America.

In the mid-1920s the remnants of the Socialist party, with such leaders as Victor Berger, Morris Hillquit, and Otto Branstetter, continued to champion a gradualist strategy for attaining the socialist commonwealth. In 1922 the party accepted an invitation to the Conference for Progressive Political Action, and in 1924 it supported Robert La Follette in the hope that his organization might develop into something comparable to the British Labour party. It also worked for the formation of state labor parties to which socialist units might attach themselves. But all initiatives seemed only to bring further decline. By 1928, when Norman Thomas became the party's presidential candidate, its membership had dwindled to less than 8000 and it had become increasingly an organization of ministers and intellectuals rather than industrial workers. Outside a few urban strongholds (places like Lower Manhattan, Milwaukee, and Reading, Pennsylvania), organized American socialism was hard put to bring a few civil liberties cases into court and keep the idea of social democracy alive among a few intellectuals and youth groups.

The other major variant of Marxism was that envisoning the attainment of the socialist commonwealth only through violent revolution and a "dictatorship of the proletariat." Gradualism, so Marxists of this sort argued, could never achieve the necessary transfers of power. These could come only by following the Russian example; and for a time, especially in early 1919, their hopes were high that America was about to do so. Stimulated by news from abroad, they organized themselves as the Left Wing Section of the Socialist party, and by late 1919 the section had spawned separate Communist, Communist Labor, and Proletarian parties. And even as the authorities responded with mass raids and deportations, these groups stuck with the Russian analogy. Their strategy was to "go underground" and develop disciplined revolutionary conspiracies, as radicals had done in Czarist Russia. By 1922 the Communist and Communist Labor parties both had underground organizations, each with an attached "open" party serving as its legal periscope.

From the beginning, too, organized American communism had been quick to send emissaries to the Soviet Union and surrender most of its autonomy to the Moscow-controlled Third International. It was under the tutelage of Third International representatives that the separate organizations were finally joined in a single party and the "underground" policy abandoned. And it was from Moscow that the orders came for expelling such heretics as the Trotskyists and Bukharinists, for shifting from "dual unionism" to "boring from within" and then back again, and for subordinating American considerations to the building of socialism in Russia. In theory such subservience was supposed to hasten the day when capitalism could be overthrown everywhere. But in operation it became another element that discredited the critiques and prescriptions emanating from the Communist apparatus. As of 1929 Communist efforts to develop a base in the labor unions had turned into a dismal fiasco; similar efforts to capture reform-minded political groups had either failed or left the would-be captors holding empty shells; and party membership had dwindled to less than 10,000, about one-fifth of what it had once been. Circumstances, it seemed, would have to change drastically before many Americans turned to revolutionary Marxism.

Also populating the anticapitalist left at the time were a variety of syndicalist groups, mostly tiny remnants of the Industrial Workers of the World, the Syndicalist League of North America, and earlier flirtations with guild socialism and functionalist democracy. They had in common a vision of the syndicalist commonwealth, purged both of market capitalism and the political state and reorganized around the factories, mines, and other places of production. But there were drastic differences on the methods through which the vision could be realized. At one extreme were those who saw it coming through sabotage and mass protest, culminating in a general strike. At the other were those who saw the modern corporation or worker-management councils as the instruments of transition. And in the center were theorists who looked to a new kind of unionism that would gradually take over managerial prerogatives and reorganize society along syndicalist lines.

In some quarters the syndicalist vision had become fused with notions of a technocratic order run by production engineers and soviets of technicians. Technological advances and engineering methods, so theorists of this sort argued, had put a liberating abundance within the reach of the American people. But this could not be attained in a system that remained subject to capitalist "sabotage," worker romanticism, and political adventurism. Its realization required that the system of production and distribution be taken over by an engineering directorate and that this directorate be given full power to allocate resources, assure full utilization of manpower and equipment, and gear production to scientifically determined social needs. In time, moreover, these technocratic radicals expected such a directorate to be installed. It would come, as some saw it, through a gradual expansion of the technostructure within the capitalist order. It would come, as others saw it, through a general strike of the technicians supported by workers' organizations. Or it would come, as still others saw it, through a breakdown of the existing system and an abdication of its ruling elites.

One center of such thinking was an organization known as the New Machine, founded by the management engineer H. L. Gantt. In the years from 1916 to 1919 it brought together a number of radical engineers, efficiency experts, and other technocratic theorists. Another center, appearing in the mid-1920s, was Charles Ferguson's Technarchy. But the group associated with the economist Thorstein Veblen attracted the most attention during the period. At the New School for Social Research, in New York City, Veblen had continued his analysis of business waste and "sabotage" and had begun exploring the possibilities of organizing engineers for the revolution, a project eventually leading to his *Engineers and the Price System* (1921). Among his associates were Howard Scott, Guido Marx, and Otto Beyer; and for a time they organized and operated a Technical Alliance that urged surveys of waste and conducted conferences on the engineer's social function. The Veblen group won few followers at the time and subsequently disappeared from public view. But a number of them would reemerge as leaders or supporters of the Technocracy movement that gained attention in 1932 and 1933.

Finally, still another kind of anticapitalist radicalism envisioned a collectivist commonwealth to be attained through cooperative economic organization, farmer-labor parties, and radicalized pressure groups. Here radical consumerists and laborites had some effect, especially in trying to envision an American kind of collectivism purged of

European ideologies and appealing to collectivist impulses of indigenous origins. But most of the ideas and most of the support came from remnants of an earlier agrarian radicalism. It was to such groups that the Farmer-Labor parties of 1920 and 1922 sought to appeal. And it was as a champion of public enterprise in farm-related industries that the National Non Partisan League emerged as a political force in the upper Midwest. Founded in 1916 by Arthur Townley, the league enrolled thousands of members in some fourteen states; and in North Dakota league-backed politicians did gain control and put through a program of state-operated banks, packing houses, elevators, flour mills, and insurance services. These enterprises, however, fared badly in the recession of 1920–1922. League-backed officials were ousted in a recall election in 1921, and thereafter, although it continued to exist, the league's influence rapidly dwindled.

New Era America, then, was not without its anticapitalist left. Visions of a socialist or collectivist commonwealth continued to be offered as alternatives to the existing system, and theoreticians continued to debate the strategies best suited to realizing these visions. But in a nation enjoying rapid material gains and disposed to see departures from the national philosophy as subversive or pathological, such visions had minimal appeal, especially after efforts to escalate wartime expectations into support for radical change ended in failure. Neither the working class nor depressed farmers nor middle-class engineers and technicians could be turned into instruments for attacking capitalism itself. Nor did the disillusioned intellectuals of the period, disdainful though they were of the "new capitalism" and America's "business civilization," see much merit in socialist critiques and prescriptions. It was not until the early 1930s, when economic catastrophe seemed to lend credence to Marxian and Veblenian analysis, that a number of them found the answers and formulas of the anticapitalist left both perceptive and persuasive.

What was true of the anticapitalist left was also true of the antidemocratic right, the quasi-fascist elements of the middle-class right, and the "new liberalisms" that tried to challenge antistatist and antibureaucratic traditions. Although part of the 1920s, their formulas for a different America failed to mobilize the social groupings and strata to which they were addressed, and powerful challenges to the claims and credibility of New Era spokesmen failed to emerge. So long as growth continued to ease social conflict and the dislocations of growth remained containable through New Era prescriptions, it seemed doubtful that such challenges could emerge. The chance for those with visions of an alternative America would come when growth turned into contraction and New Era formulas appeared increasingly inadequate to deal with the new situation.

CHAPTER 8

Social Rebels and Social Orderers

If American society in the 1920s resisted political radicalization, it was not a society without dislocations and concerns about social order. Throughout the period the growth of the "new economy" continued to disrupt existing institutions and patterns of life. It brought with it another wave of migration to the cities, this time mostly from the rural South and West rather than from Europe. It withdrew economic support from older forms of family, community, and religious life. It posed new problems that existing educational and welfare institutions found difficult to deal with. And it created a social context in which rebellions against established ways could sustain themselves and force accommodations in the mechanisms being used to maintain order and stability. In the social sphere the decade was an "unsettling" one, productive both of social rebels and of new kinds of social orderers. Or, as various historians have argued, it was a period during which social progressivism meant both a liberation from traditional constraints and the constitution of new social authorities steeped in a new wisdom drawn from a new priesthood of social scientists.

This is not to say, of course, that all Americans in the 1920s were affected by all these social changes. Nor is it to deny that the changes were part of a larger story reaching back into the 1890s and forward into the 1960s. But a history of the decade without them would be hopelessly incomplete. Accompanying the postwar quest for an ordered and professionalized capitalism was a simultaneous and highly significant search for new forms of the family, the school, the press, the church, the community, and the delivery system for social services.

THE OLD FAMILY AND THE NEW

In the society of nineteenth-century America the family had served as a major agency of socialization. Indeed, it had borne much of the responsibility for shaping and buffering the individuals who competed for economic rewards. And while the discharge of these obligations had come through an institution with diverse and variant forms, the dominant structure, especially among the nation's broad middle classes, had been one emphasizing parental control, sexual discipline, and deference to the husband-father as family head and provider. Such a structure, so the dominant culture held, was essential to social health and well-being; and outside the family, society had been arranged to uphold it. Those rebelling against approved roles had found few alternatives available, and efforts to create such alternatives had met with stiff resistance.

By the 1920s, however, the supportive context in which the traditional family functioned had weakened considerably. The new forms of economic growth had provided alternatives for those rebelling against established roles. Mass communication and widespread mobility had heightened the awareness of such alternatives. And from society's standpoint the family had become less important, It provided less of the training needed for effective economic performance and less of the socialization upon which stability and order depended. In the newer context, moreover, family heads frequently appeared as something other than wise and benevolent wielders of institutional power. Their kind of wisdom had depreciated in value, and their authority was more frequently seen as working against the interests of society as a whole. In too many instances, so a growing array of critics charged, it was being used to block needed social adjustments, warp and repress individual personalities, or sustain exploitive, despotic, and morally repugnant relationships.

As societal supports weakened, rebellion had got under way. The prewar years had had their "liberation" movements, extolling the virtues of sexual freedom, sensual gratification, and parental permissiveness. And despite efforts to check the process, the years from 1919 to 1929 witnessed the growth of a youthful subculture embracing these counterestablishment ideals and equating them with modernity and sophistication. The colleges had their "flaming youth," kicking over parental traces and tasting hitherto forbidden pleasures; middle-class homes, especially in the cities, had their "problem children" and adolescents out of control. Under the impact of the new subculture the rules and conventions that had once governed courting behavior and family formation were disintegrating. The chaperone all but disappeared from the scene, parental control over marriage decisions underwent a drastic decline, and respectable families condoned "necking" parties in the privacy of apartments and automobiles.

Also joining the rebellion against traditional patterns was the "new woman," no longer willing to play the roles of homemaker, subservient mate, and moral exemplar. The prewar years had also witnessed the birth of counterestablishment feminine ideals, especially among the wing of the feminist movement concerned more with oppressive social institutions than with achieving political citizenship or economic protection. By 1915 enough "new women" had appeared for Henry L. Mencken to announce the arrival of the "American Flapper." And in the 1920s, as the drive for suffrage succeeded and that for better economic protection faded, changes in feminine demeanor and social behavior continued. More women and especially more wives sought and found careers or avocations outside the home. More women rebelled against masculine possessiveness and double moral standards. More were willing to sever the bonds of unhappy marriages, more practiced birth control and planned parenthood, and more engaged in the period's symbolic acts of liberation. They smoked cigarettes, went to speakeasies, talked openly and frankly about sexual subjects, and dressed in a style that combined short skirts and make-up with bobbed hair and the boyish figure. Although full equality with men was not achieved, society was now tolerating behavior once regarded as insufferable.

One factor that helped such rebellions to sustain themselves was the support they received from taste makers and the mass media. Through such support they acquired an identification with sophistication, modernity, and personal liberty, all things that their opponents found difficult to attack. And reinforcing this kind of support was that derived from the new social sciences. If the traditionalists still invoked biblical authority and the "wisdom of the ages," the rebels had found Sigmund Freud, John B. Watson, and Havelock Ellis. Sexual and family relationships, they could argue, were man-made and culturally determined, not ordained by God or by an unchangeable human nature. They could be altered and molded to enhance human happiness, and those inherited from America's past were badly in need of alteration. They were survivals from an unenlightened age and generators of social dysfunctions, mental illness, and crabbed, unhappy, and maladjusted human beings.

Rebel success, however, did not mean the dissolution and disappearance of the family itself. Although liberationist logic might call for a postfamilial society of autonomous, freely associating, and "freely loving" individuals, there were clear limits as to how many such individuals the existing power structure would tolerate. Social well-being, so most Americans still believed, required familial functions that such individuals could not effectively perform. Nor were most of the rebels themselves willing to pursue "liberation" to its logical ends. Having tasted a liberty that left them without dependable human ties or authoritative standards of conduct, they drew back, reconsidered, and began a search for "modern" forms of bonding and authority. The need, as they perceived it, was not to abolish the family but to find ways of humanizing and rationalizing it. And by 1930 their search for a new and better family had branched out along three general paths, each stretching into the future yet each beset with numerous difficulties and pitfalls.

One path was that of the "loving family," supplanting hierarchical relationships with stronger bonds of romance and affection and thereby finding the means to reconcile a new individualism with orderly and proper behavior. In the new ideal, as reflected in numerous vehicles of popular culture, love became less a means of tempering established authority and more a force for guiding autonomous equals into fruitful, lasting, and socially beneficial partnerships. Love, so it was held, not only "conquered all" but could serve as the "guiding light" in a truly humane and modern society. Yet in practice families attempting to realize this ideal seemed both unstable and productive of new psychological disorders. In numerous cases young people entered marriage with unreasonable expectations and had difficulty in handling failures that allegedly stemmed from their inability to be sufficiently "loved" and "loving."

The second path was that of the "practical family," leaving the roles of its members to be determined by bargaining, compromise, and accommodation. In essence, the market mechanism was to be injected into family life, the assumption being that this was both democratic and modern. And what emerged as bargains and agreements, it was also assumed, would constitute a workable balance serving both individual and social needs. Not much thought was given to the psychological costs of fluctuating roles and bargaining mentalities. Nor was the need seen for social machinery that could provide a stable framework for bargaining and insure that it remained free and fair. Although a few reformers envisioned a supporting system of domestic codes and conciliators, institutions of this sort were slow to develop.

The third path was what might be called, for want of a better term, the "managerial family." In its ideal form the family would function as a domestic team, tied together not so much by affection or practical bargains as by a new wisdom emanating from trained experts in such areas as child care, domestic relations, character building, and household management. It would operate, in essence, as part of an administrative network through which a "domestic science" might be applied to family life. And in the 1920s the creators and would-be appliers of this scientific knowledge were rapidly expanding their domains. Specialists in child nurture, juvenile delinquency, and exceptional children were all developing arrangements through which their expertise could be institutionalized and brought to bear. So were home economists, family rehabilitators, youth leaders, and professional character builders; and claiming to reflect the latest in scientific

wisdom were a variety of manuals on sexual techniques, marital relations, and child psychology. In theory this institutional growth provided "helping hands," allowing the family team to draw upon outside
resources to create a better product. But in practice the tendency was
for the "helping hands" to become new centers of authority without
much in the way of accountability. The change was directed toward a
new effort to harmonize family loyalties with those needed in an
expanding industrial society—toward a family system that could reinforce and complement the other institutions characteristic of an emerging managerial order.

Against each of these solutions the traditionalists continued to
argue. The only real remedy for social ills, they insisted, was a return
to the traditional family structure with its supporting moral code and
societal arrangements. But that such a restoration could actually be
brought about became an increasingly dubious proposition. Despite
the problems inherent in the new ordering mechanisms, they did work
to mitigate the dislocations generated by economic change and mass
mobility. And more and more Americans sought to order their family
life through these new mechanisms.

More, however, did not mean all or in all probability even a
majority. Such changes and conflicts, it should again be emphasized,
were much more characteristic of the middle class than they were of
Americans occupying the lower rungs of the social ladder or the poorly
rewarded sectors of economic life. For these groups the story of changing family structures revolved less around individualistic rebellion or
bureaucratic impulses than around the impact of agricultural
depression, uprooting migrations, and ghetto life on traditions already
at variance with the dominant one. In some cases the change was
toward structureless demoralization and disorganization resulting in a
"free-floating" individualism that was regarded as pathological yet in
some respects was strikingly similar to the "free-loving" association-
ism idealized by middle- and upper-class rebels. In other cases the
change was toward a matrifocal structure in which a strong female
figure with a dependable source of income became the stabilizing core
and new source of authority. And in still others, indeed in the great
majority that have been studied by historians, the change was toward
a household structure with elastic boundaries, taking in relatives, out-

siders, and subfamilies as the need arose and proving amazingly adaptive to coping with the burdens of lower-class life and defending the subcultural traditions that were at variance with New Era ideals. Significantly, the penetration of managerial ordering mechanisms into family life made less headway and met with far greater resistance at lower-income levels than it did in the middle ranges of the social structure.

REFORM AND THE EDUCATIONAL SYSTEM

If family life in the 1920s was an "unsettled" area of social behavior, the same was also true of school life and educational relationships. Traditional educational patterns, like the traditional family structures, were losing societal support and being challenged by educational rebels and modernizers. They were unsuited, so it was claimed, to modern citizenship, modern economic life, modern pursuits of happiness. And despite stiff resistance from educational essentialists and fundamentalists, the American school system was being reshaped along lines that were expected to meet modern needs.

For one thing, the system was being rapidly expanded, the reigning assumptions being that modern society needed more education and that more of it should come through the schools rather than other institutions. Enrollment in the public schools grew from 23,278,000 in 1920 to 28,329,000 a decade later; most of the expansion was at the secondary level but some of it was via the addition of kindergartens and the extension of elementary education to previously neglected groups. During the same period enrollment in institutions of higher learning nearly doubled, from 598,000 in 1920 to 1,101,000 in 1930. And expanding also was that portion of the educational system devoted to the search for and production of new knowledge. Business, governmental, and foundation researchers were increasing, and so were scholar-teachers with combined instructional and research missions.

As the system grew, it was also changing in other ways. Country schools were giving way to consolidated operations. Educational

governance, despite resistance from school boards and trustees, was
moving into the hands of technical specialists and professional
administrators. Teachers were being required to meet higher
professional standards and learn new and allegedly more scientific
teaching methods. And reflected now in numerous curricular reforms
was the view that modern education should move beyond traditional
goals and equip students with the social, political, and vocational skills
needed for modern life. At all levels offerings were being broadened,
vocational and citizenship training expanded, and traditional subjects
remolded to meet mass needs.

In part the changes were responses to altered patterns of educational demand and continuing concern about social disorder and
instability. But also involved was the ideology of "progressive education" associated with the philosopher John Dewey and others who
followed his lead. The function of education in a progressive society,
so Dewey had argued, was to create an enlightened and adaptable citizenry capable of making rational choices and adjusting to the social
roles that continued progress required. It would make modern
democracy possible, both by unmasking the irrationalism in traditional arrangements and loyalties and by equipping individuals to participate in modern forms of cooperative action. And it was to these
dual missions of "liberation" and "resocialization" that the educational modernizers of the period claimed to be dedicated.

Keeping the two in tandem and balance, however, was no easy task.
And unbalanced, "progressive education" could veer in directions that
Dewey had never intended. It could, on the one hand, become an
instrument of managerial manipulation used for antidemocratic and
antiprogressive purposes. This possibility loomed especially large in
the drive to supplant liberal with technical education and in such
phenomena as the Americanization programs, the scientifically
managed school, and the institutionalized partnership between corporate and academic researchers. On the other hand, there was the
danger that "unmasking" would destroy older loyalties and identities
without creating new ones to take their place and would thus produce
disintegration and anarchy rather than progress. This possibility
loomed large in the notions of an education built around myth destruction, responses to felt needs, and the satisfaction of natural curiosities.

To educational traditionalists such dangers seemed to outweigh any possible benefits. Modernism, as they saw it, was pushing the school into areas where it did not belong, destroying its capacity for moral training and social integration, and undercutting popular authority as institutionalized in elected school boards. It was, they believed, a recipe for social disaster rather than social progress. And throughout the period they organized countermovements calling for a return to essentials, the maintenance of traditional core curricula, and less autonomy for teachers and administrators. As the decade ended, however, the modernizers seemed to be winning most of the battles. It was their ideas that were being implemented. But whether this would continue to be the case when economic depression generated charges of economic failure remained to be seen.

THE PROVISION OF PUBLIC INFORMATION

The institutions through which public information was gathered and disseminated were also undergoing change and engendering debate in the 1920s. These, like traditional education, had once been used to reinforce village ideals or to service small educated elites. But from the 1880s on, this older system had gradually yielded to a "mass journalism" involving large corporate organizations, an emerging journalistic profession, and information tailored to meet growing mass demands. Such publishers as Joseph Pulitzer, William Randolph Hearst, and S. S. McClure had developed mass circulation papers and magazines filled with popularized reportage and special features. And despite their dependence on advertising revenue, these publications had succeeded in establishing themselves as gatherers and dispensers of factual information. The potential for abuse, it was argued, was held in check by rising professional standards, acknowledged lines of demarcation between reportage and special pleading, and competing sources of information.

In the 1920s this system of "mass journalism" continued to expand and develop new offerings. The decade witnessed such "successes" as the tabloid, the news digest, and the syndicated feature. It witnessed the further growth of newspaper chains and cooperative services, and it became, to the dismay of some traditionalists, the age of the media figure and the "big story," with journalists linking millions in shared vicarious experiences.

This pattern was one that the new medium of radio followed rather than broke. There too the gathering and dissemination of public information was entrusted to organizations whose principal revenues came from advertisers. And there, as in newspaper journalism, the emphasis was upon building and holding mass audiences, rationalizing operations through consolidation and cooperative activities, and arguing for a nongovernmental discipline grounded in professional obligations and competing information sources. Although federal licensing became necessary to achieve orderly use of the air waves, radio journalism was neither nationalized nor subjected to any very stringent set of quality controls.

As mass journalism grew, two other developments were taking place. One was the rapid proliferation of specialized informational agencies, serving, for the most part, the nation's newly forming trade, professional, and special-interest communities. America in the 1920s was not only a nation informed through mass circulation media but one that supported an expanding array of trade and professional journals, specialized informational exchanges, and organs addressed to limited and special publics. The other development was a rapid expansion of the public relations apparatus that had first appeared in the prewar period and burst into full bloom under the war system. Staffed by press secretaries and publicity experts, this new institutional structure depicted itself as a bridge between wielders of power and a democratic citizenry. It existed, so it was argued by such publicists as Edward Bernays and Ivy Lee, to enlighten public opinion and help secure constructive social action. But its real purpose, so critics insisted, was to manage informational flows in the interests of those who hired its services. It was a medium in which information was processed into political or commercial weapons, and the people staffing it were best seen as hucksters or propagandists rather than true journalists.

As with "progressive education," the champions of the new media envisioned a continued development that would have both liberating and ordering effects. On the one hand, it would work to overthrow traditional authority and unfetter those kept in ignorance of the outer world. On the other, it would facilitate a "new citizenship" and the formation of new kinds of community ties and cooperative endeavors. Yet, as with education, the task of holding these two things in tandem was not an easy one. Liberation, it seemed to some, was opening the way not for a new citizenship or new communitarianism but for a mindless and socially destructive consumption of journalistic sensationalism. And the search for a new order, so others felt, could lead not to informed community action but to misinformed puppets manipulated by information managers or the interests that such managers had agreed to serve.

As in the educational field, moreover, traditionalists doubted that the benefits of change outweighed the costs and the dangers. As the older standards and behavioral patterns crumbled, some traditionalists sought to reimpose them through a network of community censors. As small-town and local journals folded, a number of Americans urged that they be given special protection and encouragement. And as modernizers and reformers reached for public support of their informational services, they encountered traditionalist charges that they were subverting free institutions and wasting the nation's resources. If modernizers continued to win most of the battles, it was by no means clear that the institutions they were creating could withstand the pressures of a society undergoing economic depression and depression-induced social trauma.

RELIGIOUS MODERNISM AND THE FUNDAMENTALIST CRUSADE

If the schools and the press were "unsettled" areas in the 1920s, the most heated controversies seemed to revolve around religious modernism and its challenges to established teachings and values. As in other areas, the roots of this modernization reached well back into the nineteenth century, and by the second decade of the twentieth it had already altered much of the nation's religious life. New doctrines reconciling religious teaching with scientific evidence had gained widespread acceptance in mainstream Protestant denominations. Ministers had lost much of their traditional status and authority. And "creeping secularism" had found expression in a new gospel of social and environmental reform, a conversion of churches to what critics considered mere recreational societies, and a tendency to downgrade the importance of religious experience. Being weakened, too, was the nation's informal Protestant establishment. Catholics, Jews, and skeptics were no longer staying in the roles they had been assigned, and efforts to keep them there were losing societal support.

In the 1920s these alterations of American religious life continued to gain momentum. The teachings of such modernist theologians as Harry Emerson Fosdick, A. C. McGiffert, and Henry Preserved Smith gained further acceptance, especially among urban congregations and seminary students. The churches, like the schools and the press, underwent consolidation and the introduction of managerial and technical expertise. Worldly pursuits of happiness and conversions to scientific materialism continued to encroach upon religion's place in American life. And many religious leaders, having frankly embraced evolution and the higher criticism, proceeded to abandon theological exegesis for some version of the "social gospel" or some vision of an ethical world built around a "new humanism." In many quarters support for the older kind of Protestant domination continued to weaken. Catholics, Jews, and unbelievers, it was argued, were entitled to their own beliefs and at the same time to full citizenship in the American republic. It was only by recognizing these rights and working toward a pluralistic order based on mutual toleration and cooperation that one could adapt the nation's religious system to modern needs and sensibilities and yet preserve it as a source of moral guidance and spiritual inspiration.

Religious modernizers, then, like their counterparts in the educational and informational fields, saw themselves as both liberators and orderers. Yet to their enemies they were subversives and heretics, denying God's dominion over human affairs, rejecting revealed truths, and undermining the foundations upon which moral behavior rested. In the religious field, moreover, this antimodernism seemed stronger and more active than elsewhere, enhanced perhaps by a history of rigidity and defensive militance as acceptable responses to pressures for change. In any event, antimodernists were able to mount major counteroffensives that made the decade of the 1920s one of heightened religious tensions and conflicts.

One such counteroffensive was directed against the notion of a new pluralistic order recognizing equality of status for non-Protestants. To substantial numbers of Americans, especially in the South and Midwest, this kind of liberalism amounted to dangerous nonsense and fundamental error. They reacted by espousing militant forms of anti-Catholicism, anti-Semitism, and anti-intellectualism, joined, in many instances, with the political doctrines of hundred-percent Americanism or the Ku Klux Klan. And from the early 1920s on, these reactions manifested themselves in a literature of intolerance, a variety of political activities, and other attacks on religious minorities or those who would tolerate them. Anti-Catholics worked to close the parochial schools, uncover "papal plots" against American liberties, and bar Catholics from positions of political or social influence. Anti-Semites resurrected and spread charges of an international Jewish conspiracy to control the world. And urged on by such newspapers as J. Frank Norris's *Searchlight*, religious militants set out to expose the atheists and unbelievers who had allegedly infiltrated into the nation's educational and intellectual institutions. Nor was this intolerance to be found only in lower- or middle-class groups. As non-Protestants sought access to the nation's elite colleges, clubs, services, and board rooms, they were met with new and more formalized barriers, often in the disguise of merit systems or tests of character.

A second counteroffensive, building in the prewar years but now greatly intensified, was directed against modern science and modernist heresies within the Protestant camp. The biblical scriptures, so religious fundamentalists continued to insist, were to be interpreted literally. Any deviation from this was an attack on fundamental truth; and especially pernicious, as they saw it, was the Darwinian notion that man had evolved from lower forms of animal life. In the early 1920s the fundamentalists campaigned to purge "atheistic evolutionists" from the churches and schools. And once William Jennings Bryan, the old spokesman for rural and evangelical America, had joined the crusade, it was carried to state legislatures and church governing bodies all across the country. Only in the South, however, primarily in what detractors called the "Bible Belt," did the cause develop strong popular support and have a measure of success. In North Carolina and Texas educational authorities forebade evolutionary teachings. And in Tennessee a purge of university professors was followed by an antievolution law; in 1925 it became illegal for instructors in the state's schools or colleges to teach any theory denying the biblical account of creation.

In the wake of this legislative action the American Civil Liberties Union offered to finance a constitutional test of the statute. And when John T. Scopes, a young high school teacher in Dayton, Tennessee, purposefully violated the law, the stage was set for the "monkey trial," one of the decade's great journalistic sensations. William Jennings Bryan was engaged for the prosecution. Clarence Darrow, the famed criminal trial lawyer and an avowed agnostic, joined the defense; and the resulting clash became front-page news all over the world. In the end Scopes was found guilty (the sentence, however, was later reversed on a technicality), and subsequently the antievolution law was upheld by the state supreme court. But the real climax came shortly after the verdict. On July 26, 1925, while still in Dayton, Bryan became ill and died—a victim, so his followers said, of his strenuous efforts to defend the true Christian faith.

In the months that followed Bryan's death, the antievolutionists formed new organizations and intensified their activities. Through such groups as the Bryan Bible League, the Bible Crusaders, and the Supreme Kingdom they brought pressure to bear on other legislatures and worked for an antievolution amendment to the federal Constitution. But substantial success eluded them. By 1928 they had secured antievolution measures only in Mississippi and Arkansas, the latter acting through a popular initiative that bypassed the legislature. And by 1929 the crusade was ebbing. Modernists and liberals were successfully holding the line, at least to the extent of blocking antimodernist efforts to dictate what should be taught in the nation's public schools.

As the decade ended, it seemed clear that America's religious traditionalists lacked the power to halt or reverse the developments associated with modernization. The real potential for greater order, so it appeared, lay not in their efforts but in those of modernist theologians, religious pluralists, and formulators of a religious relativity attuned to constant change. Yet the power that they retained in American society was far from insignificant. If they could not restore the "old-time religion" of an earlier America, they still provided alternatives for those disillusioned with modern life, liberal formulations, and frightening uncertainties.

COMMUNITY LIFE AND WELFARE SERVICES

Bemoaned as well in the 1920s, particularly by those with roots in a rural or small-town past, was the loss of traditional community structures and established patterns of community life. In the past these had defined the status, obligations, and identity of many Americans. And as economic change weakened their capacity to do so, one response had been a variety of movements urging some form of "community restoration." These had constituted one aspect of prewar reform; and in the 1920s the idea continued to serve as the rallying cry of local merchants fighting the chain stores, farmers battling urban sin and monopolistic industries, and local establishments resisting further progress of the organizational revolution. America, so these groups argued, must not become a land of communityless human atoms manipulated by communityless holders of power. Yet if the "pillars of the community" were to be destroyed, such a land would be the eventual result.

Similar warnings came from some academic sociologists. The disintegration of the older community life, they feared, could mean a permanent state of social "disorganization" and individual "anomie." Yet more than countering this view were perceptions of a community-minded people substituting modern forms of community life for those now on the decline. Occupational and interest groups, so it was argued, were developing into functional communities committed to the proper organization and conduct of modern social functions. An expanding social science was equipping these functional communities with a new and more scientific social consciousness. And even as the pillars of the older edifice gave way, mutually interdependent functional groups were fusing into new social units and erecting the framework for modern forms of community endeavor and collective solidarity.

The decade, moreover, despite its reputation for individualism and self-centeredness, was one in which a variety of activities were carried on in the name of community service or community building. It was a period of expanding service clubs engaged not only in after-dinner oratory but also in local and national projects, of an organized philanthropy consciously seeking modern substitutes for the vanishing processes of village life, and of corporate managers seeking recognition as community trustees and restorers of social harmony. It was a period as well of "community development" operations, mostly under private auspices but with some encouragement from the Department of Commerce and other public agencies. And in the name of community welfare or civic betterment, it became an era of urban zoning laws, scattered experiments in community planning, and numerous exercises in bringing functional representatives together in community federations and councils.

Upon examination, too, social researchers usually found not a growing mass of human atoms but an ongoing and adaptive group life developing its own group pressures and sanctions. The organization building of the period reflected not only managerial promotion but new patterns of group loyalty, especially to the profession, the company, the trade, and the club. Factory labor, so researchers at Western Electric found, did not consist of undifferentiated human atoms responding uniformly to changes in their environment. It consisted rather of informal worker groups of varying degrees of cohesion and autonomy. And despite the attack on ethnic loyalties, an attack carried on by modernizers and hypernationalists alike, ethnic-based communitarianism showed an amazing resiliency. Instead of dissolving, it became the basis for an expanding civic and political activism and for an ideology that equated the liberal dream with enhanced status and greater freedom for ethnic subcultures. Ethnicity, it seemed, might be a much more adaptive loyalty than once thought; it might find ways to survive and grow in a society that was replacing traditional arrangements with modern ones.

Among black Americans there were also indications of a new community spirit and cohesion. On the one hand, the continued migration to the North brought disorganization, explosive racial tensions, and all the miseries of life in the black ghettos of the big northern cities. Yet at the same time it formed the basis for a heightened racial solidarity that brought blacks together in an expanding network of community programs. Mutual-aid societies and neighborhood improvement associations offered themselves as instruments of racial affirmation and progress. Programs for studying black history and culture aimed both at changing white attitudes and at fostering a more intense feeling of racial worth and pride. And two phenomena of the 1920s indicated the developing potential for a racial nationalism that went beyond efforts to attain full citizenship in an American republic.

① One of these was the search among black intellectuals for African roots and distinctive forms of black art and literature, a search most apparent in the cultural movement known as the Harlem Renaissance. ② The other was the mass appeal of Marcus Garvey's Universal Negro Improvement Association, a quasi-militaristic organization that preached a form of black Zionism and sought to organize a return to an African homeland. Founded in 1914 by a Jamaican immigrant who saw himself as the "Black Moses," the organization expanded rapidly in the wake of the race rioting of 1919, and in the early 1920s it had hundreds of thousands of adherents and sympathizers, most of them drawn from the urban ghettos and most rejecting, at least temporarily, the integrationist goals of the older black leadership. What outsiders had perceived as a demoralized and structureless mass had become the base for a reforming and allegedly redemptive and purifying nationalism. And while the late 1920s saw the group fade into obscurity, a victim of frustrated expectations and fraudulent promotions, its achievements between 1920 and 1925 revealed a potential for racial nationalism that could bring new vehicles of community action and community discipline into being.

Americans in the 1920s, then, were not only severing old community ties but forming new ones. And for a good many this meant that the "community," defined as a changing mixture of the old and the new ties, could retain its role as the chief developer and dispenser of social welfare services. If the older structures were no longer adequate, new structures were rising; and around them, provided destructive kinds of community conflict could be avoided or contained, Americans could build a modern welfare system without giving up the benefits of community feeling and initiative. They were not faced with a choice between impersonal commercial services and the kind of impersonal and unfeeling statist bureaucracies that had been set up in Britain and Germany.

Occupying a central place in the envisioned welfare system was the rationalized community unit bringing the leaders of specialized public and private agencies into a joint welfare council and entrusting the execution of council policy to a professional welfare expert. Such arrangements represented the welfare sector's counterparts to trade and industrial associations; and through them, it was argued, one could combine the benefits of professional expertise and consolidated budgeting with those of agency autonomy and voluntary action. As the decade progressed, a number of such units did come into being. In some areas they developed as extensions of the earlier Charity Organization Societies or the war-born Community Chests. In others they grew out of community responses to emergency situations. And in still others they were promoted by schools of social work or professional organizations of social workers. Under the Iowa Plan, for example, a projected scheme of organization initially adopted in 1913, the State University Extension's Bureau of Social Welfare organized such community units in twenty-two counties in Iowa.

Three other sets of institutions occupied important positions in the envisioned system. One was another structure of community welfare units, based not on the county or city or neighborhood but on the newly forming corporate, occupational, and ethnic communities. This structure was taking shape in corporate welfare programs, group insurance plans, and other expressions of this new community spirit; as envisioned, it would supplement and intermesh with the geographically based units. The second was a set of coordinating and promotional organizations, working to foster more efficient intermeshing and action and helping communities to mobilize and expand their resources when confronted with emergency situations or new needs. In part, these were to operate as permanent agencies, set up on a continuing basis in both private and public sectors. In part, they were to be reserve bodies, capable of springing into action to cope with emergency or special situations and of being retired when these passed. And finally, filling out the picture, was an emerging set of special funding agencies, increasingly professionalized and allegedly capable of raising and managing funds upon which straitened community units and other parts of the welfare apparatus could draw. Operating through a network of foundations, specialized philanthropies, and organized appeals, this component of the system was supposed to minimize public funding and thus avoid the evils of "politicization."

As the decade ended, some critics had already labeled this "American solution" a pipe dream and a failure. Most of it, they claimed, was unrealizable, and the part that was realized had already demonstrated its inability to deal with wasted human potential, mass insecurity, and the persisting misery of those at the bottom of America's social scale. As yet, however, such views were relatively rare and without much influence. Defenders of the solution could point to the active formation of new welfare units, to encouraging developments in individual and corporate giving, and to what were cited as highly successful responses to the mass unemployment of 1921 and the catastrophic Mississippi flood of 1927. Most Americans seemed to believe that they had found a superior approach and that this approach was being implemented and was proving itself in practice. As of 1929 they had little doubt that the emerging welfare institutions of the New Era could deal effectively with whatever the future held in store.

In other respects, too, most Americans seemed confident that their society was closing the "institutional gap" opened by economic and technological change. If there were dislocations and rebellions, there was also movement toward a new order to be achieved through new and allegedly modern forms of the family, the school, the press, the church, the community, and the social service system. The New Era dream was of an intelligent and humane society rationally adapting to economic and technical progress while avoiding the twin perils of anarchy on the one side and statist "politicization" on the other. And while some viewed this as an impossible and dangerous dream, doomed to collapse of its own contradictions, the American people as a whole were still caught up in it. It was not yet the "shattered dream" that it would soon become.

CHAPTER 9

Intellectual and Cultural Pursuits in a Modernizing Era

For students of American culture the decade of the 1920s has had a powerful fascination. It was a time, so it was once thought, when an established cultural and epistemological consensus broke asunder and gave way to clashing conceptions advanced by rival cultural and intellectual elites. And although recent research has tended to push the occurrence of this phenomenon back into the prewar period, the decade was certainly one during which those cleavages deepened and intensified. The sciences became battlegrounds between an older scientific absolutism and the champions of relativity and also of narrowly conceived problem solving. High culture, as expressed in literature and art, tended not only to attack scientific and popular values but to develop deep schisms over what constituted literary and artistic excellence. And popular culture, as reflected in mass tastes and mass consumption of cultural products, not only followed paths that alienated the nation's cultural elites but came to embrace differing and competing responses to mass anxieties and aspirations. If there was a unifying pattern to the period's cultural pursuits, it lay in the common stimulus provided by economic and institutional change. The responses to this stimulus were divergent and dissonant.

For better or worse, the cleavages and disjunctures of this period have remained enduring features of twentieth-century American culture. They were not, so it seems, merely manifestations of a chaotic and irresponsible interlude sandwiched between the decline of one cultural consensus and the rise of another. They indicated instead a passage into the modern cultural condition. And for those who would understand that condition, the intellectual and cultural history of the 1920s can be highly instructive.

SCIENTISTS AND SCIENTIFIC ENDEAVOR

For American scientists the years from 1917 to 1929 were years of expanding opportunity and numerous achievements. The war period had brought increased support for nationally approved research. And while efforts to institutionalize continuing support of this sort eventually failed, the postwar decade did bring a new willingness to channel corporate, public, and endowment funds into a support system for scientific endeavor. Science, so the New Era leaders kept saying, was the "new frontier," capable of generating innovations that would keep America open, growing, and progressive. And as support grew, the "new pioneers" were making discoveries that New Era society was putting to practical use. Their achievements could be seen in such science-based industries as chemicals and electronics, in the new feats of production and marketing engineering, and in the new tools and insights available to doctors, lawyers, teachers, managers, and social workers.

Such achievements in applied science were also accompanied by impressive advances in basic scientific knowledge. In physics a variety of experiments and observations lent confirmation to the new theoretical constructs of Albert Einstein, Louis de Broglie, and Werner Heisenberg. Much of the physical world, it was shown, followed the principles of relativity and quantum mechanics rather than those associated with Isaac Newton. In chemistry similar advances took place, especially in the understanding of chemical processes and their manipulation to create new materials. In biology the decade witnessed not only new insights into the needs of healthy organisms but a fuller understanding of how new species evolved and how hereditary traits were transmitted. Especially important here was the work of such men as Edmund B. Wilson and Thomas Hunt Morgan. And in psychology, where the study was now giving way to the laboratory or controlled observation, a growing body of data became unexplainable through the older theories of innate drives and human rationality. It seemed on the contrary to support some combination of the theories advanced by John B. Watson and Sigmund Freud, theories that stressed the causal role of environmental conditioning or of an irrational subconsciousness rather than the older determinants.

In the social sciences, too, the period was one of intellectual excitement, rapid methodological innovation, and renewed convictions that a true "science of society" was possible. It could not be built, so the innovators argued, through deductive reasoning from self-evident truths. There were no such "truths" that could be accepted as first premises. But trained investigators could assemble aggregations of empirical data, subject these to rigorous analysis, and arrive at an ever fuller understanding of how operating societies worked and why they worked as they did. Such were the beliefs underlying a new wave of research activities. And as the decade progressed, all the social sciences were affected. A "new sociology," centered especially at the University of Chicago, specialized in factual surveys, team observations of community life, and ecological investigations of the city. A new "institutional economics," developed by such economists as Wesley Mitchell, John R. Commons, and John M. Clark, turned from classical theory to historical reconstruction and detailed institutional analyses, seeking a science based on verified institutional experience rather than a priori assumptions about "economic man." A "new realism" in political and legal studies focused on such phenomena as judicial and voting behavior, interest group interaction, popular stereotypes, and political propaganda. A new anthropology jettisoned unilinear theories of cultural development and began reconstructing cultures as independent, self-fulfilling, and equally valuable wholes. And a "new history," pioneered by such historians as James Harvey Robinson and Carleton J. Hayes, stressed social and scientific developments as the keys to understanding modern processes of historical change.

Like the businessmen, engineers, and social workers, New Era scientists and social scientists also sought to rationalize their activities and make them more efficient and productive. They established the wartime National Research Council on a permanent basis and in 1923 added a new Social Science Research Council; both were conceived of as rationalizing bodies. The scientists preached a "cooperative individualism" in which research teams and professional orders would play key roles, and a number of them worked to build institutions that could reach the general public and the holders of power and turn them into supportive components of the envisioned system. From their efforts, for example, came a Science Service designed to popularize scientific developments and foster scientific-mindedness, an array of advisory committees for public and private agencies, and a national committee devoted to fostering scientific-mindedness among corporate givers and foundation executives. The assumption, especially among such enthusiasts as Robert A. Millikan and George Ellery Hale, was that an efficient and productive science, rationally organized and properly justified, could serve not only as the new agent of national progress but as the instrument through which cultural fragmentation could be halted, reversed, and eventually ended.

This dream, however, remained a largely unrealized one. Despite the work of the rationalizers, American science retained much of its prewar pluralism and segmentation. If anything, the walls between disciplines tended to harden, while methodological and epistemological battles grew more intense. And despite the efforts at cultural reintegration, the sense of estrangement between scientific endeavor and the values held in other sectors of American society seemed to deepen and intensify. In popular culture the scientist was seen not only as the "new pioneer" but also as an ivory tower innocent, a keeper of strange mysteries, a potential danger to human welfare, democratic institutions, and public morals. In business circles he was seen more as a resource to be used and controlled rather than as a model of social virtue. In literary and artistic circles he was frequently depicted as cold and alienating, more machine than human. And within the scientific community such misunderstanding and lack of appreciation reinforced perceptions of an outer world that was basically hostile or at best indifferent to the values and qualities of mind that could save it from catastrophe. From such a world, insulation was to be sought and preserved.

The sense of estrangement was also intensified by the continuing battle over evolutionary theory and by new scientific discoveries that seemed to undermine the very foundations of the American national philosophy. From the new physics, especially that built around Einstein's theories of relativity, came the startling proposition that the layman could never hope to understand the physical world in which he lived. It was comprehensible only to the few minds capable of mastering a rarefied mathematics, and their conclusions would have to be accepted on their authority. From the new psychology and social sciences came a similar proposition, that only a few were truly capable of understanding human and social problems. Most people could never do so and were therefore incapable of making sound decisions and wise policy choices. And from articulate minorities in a variety of disciplines came challenges to the whole conception of natural and human progress. The growth of science, so it now appeared, might mean not only the decline of religion but a crisis for the liberal postulates that constituted the American national faith; and the result in some quarters was strong resistance to inquiries that did not recognize other sources of truth and confine themselves to socially approved areas.

Even as this resistance developed, moreover, other discoveries were undermining the claim that scientists were themselves capable of discerning and understanding one objective reality. Ironically, the new physics was now disclosing a universe that was indeterminate, at least at the atomic level. It was suggesting that nature itself was irrational and could never be entirely known, even by trained scientific minds. And in the social sciences, the weapons previously used to attack traditional wisdom were now being turned against that claiming a scientific basis. Perceptions of social reality, it was argued, were inevitably conditioned by the experience and perspective of the perceiver. Scientists, like other people, perceived different realities and built consensuses through social pressures against the heretical; and like others they still lacked the key that could eventually unlock all the mysteries of human behavior.

As the 1920s drew to a close, then, scientific endeavor still occupied an uneasy place in American society. On the one hand it was hailed as the new fount of progress, given more support than during any previous peacetime period, and lauded for its advances along a new frontier. Yet to the dismay of early enthusiasts, its findings frequently ran counter to established cultural axioms; its practitioners often behaved in ways that confused and alienated nonscientists; and its claims to possess a true power of revelation were undercut by exposures of its methodological and epistemological limitations. Its prestige and achievements were such that it could resist efforts to make it wholly subservient to commercial, political, or religious endeavors. But they were not such that it could become the core of a new cultural consensus or the apex of a new social order.

THE LITERARY AND ARTISTIC ELITE

The position of science in New Era America had its counterparts in the isolation and fragmentation of other forms of intellectual endeavor. Increasingly the literature and art of the nation's cultural elite was not the literature and art appreciated by the masses or by other elites. And increasingly this was seen less as a gap between vanguard and followers and more as a condition imposed by the very nature of literary and artistic endeavor. Once writers and artists had believed themselves capable of changing or reinforcing national values, and for a time the modernist rebellion against genteel standards had been waged in the name of mass liberation and social uplift. But as the decade progressed, "modernism" in high culture frequently ran directly counter to "modernization" in the economic, social, and political sectors. It not only attacked traditional values but also expressed a marked revulsion against mass aspirations, organizational elites, and scientific rationality. And it became associated not with democratic reform or technocratic rationalization but rather with sensitive individuals repelled by traditional society yet unable to find satisfying and respected places in a world of mass production, impersonal relationships, and bureaucratic orders.

In traditionalist circles this kind of "modernism" was still denounced as immoral and socially subversive. But by the mid-1920s efforts to ban or repress it were losing strength. If New Era leaders questioned its value, they seemed willing to tolerate it as relatively harmless; and if appreciation of its output was limited, there was enough to allow a tolerated activity to grow and prosper. Recognition abroad raised its status at home, especially among those anxious to overcome America's reputation for cultural backwardness. And one result of the enhanced appreciation and status was a new complex of supporting institutions. By the end of the decade the modernists had their own art galleries, museums, and publishers, their own outlets for experimental theater and music, their own array of judges and interpreters, and their own forms of association and community support. Their institutional base was small when compared with what it would become in the 1950s and 1960s, but it was of sufficient strength to survive the assaults of a new wave of antimodernists and social redeemers in the 1930s and 1940s.

During the 1920s, moreover, such support did seem to release wellsprings of insight, energy, and creativity. It brought substantial freedom not only from the esthetic canons of the past but from mass tastes, political movements, and idiosyncratic patrons. And taking advantage of the opportunities that this provided, American writers and artists embraced an exciting experimentalism and left behind them a body of work that was remarkable in both quantity and quality. Incorporated in it were breakthroughs to new forms and subjects, new perceptions of the human and artistic predicament, and a multifaceted search for new standards, purposes, and identities.

For the American novel the decade was one of exceptional richness. For an older literary naturalism it was a time of fruition, a period when Darwinian determinism was reinforced by the findings of the new psychology. The result was such novels as Theodore Dreiser's *An American Tragedy* (1925). And for an emerging group of younger writers, a group that Gertrude Stein characterized as the "lost generation," the 1920s were years of successful experimentation with new forms and new material. Such writers as Ernest Hemingway, Sinclair Lewis, F. Scott Fitzgerald, and James Branch Cabell developed new and highly influential styles, modes in which stripped and taut sentences, skillfully crafted dialogue, and satirical symbolism became central features. They and others also cracked most of the remaining taboos on subject matter, and in the world of the 1920s novelists discovered new social types and new kinds of human experience worthy of extended scrutiny. They wrote of individuals scarred or destroyed by the war experience, of the hypocrisy and smugness of small-town life and business boosterism, of degenerate elites and doomed pleasure seekers, and above all, it seemed, of those who realized the hollowness of human dreams and strove restlessly to make their peace with this disturbing insight.

One side of such writing set forth a searing critique of New Era America and its dominant value systems. Another exposed and ridiculed those who believed that redemption could come through political reform, material gains, or shifts in social leadership. Yet taken as a whole, the novels of the 1920s were neither completely negative nor entirely devoid of values. They can also be studied, as the intellectual historian Roderick Nash has pointed out, as manifestations of a pervasive search for alternative values. Some novelists tried to find these in an idyllic primitivism, but the majority offered such "modern" solutions as a naturalistic morality, a retreat into bohemian countercultures or knowing laughter, and an existential affirmation of unbending struggle in the face of inevitable failure. Beneath the bitter satire and iconoclasm of H. L. Mencken, editor of the *American Mercury* and high priest of literary innovation, lay a quest for new standards of excellence and civilization. And beneath the nihilistic despair expressed in the works of Hemingway and Fitzgerald lay the outlines of an existential heroism, achieved not by attaining glory or suffering martyrdom but by grace and courage in the face of impending doom.

Despite modernist victories, traditionalism remained alive and productive in the 1920s, stimulated, so it seemed, to new levels of achievement. It was represented now by the New Humanists and Southern Agrarians and by such established novelists as Edith Wharton, Willa Cather, and Ellen Glasgow. And from it came another stream of literature that combined criticism of New Era values with assertions of alternatives. For the most part, however, the alternatives offered in such writing were drawn from the American past rather than the liberated imagination. They came embodied not in existential rebels or creators of a new morality but in portraits of those who had remained anchored to moral absolutes, had recognized and lived by traditional wisdom, and had built the agrarian-oriented and allegedly more wholesome societies of the Middle Border and the South.

American literature in the 1920s, then, was not without positive values. Nor was it characterized by complete rejection of national history and traditions. Yet its value systems and symbols were incapable of becoming the nuclei of a new cultural consensus. And its creators and defenders, whether of the modernist or the traditionalist variety, had little but disdain for efforts to fashion high art from the technical achievements, social visions, and popular triumphs of the New Era. In the mass media a new set of heroes appeared, a breed of men who were taming the techno-organizational revolution and turning it toward beneficent ends. But such themes did not attract talent of the first order, and the decade ended without a major novel built around these feats and their performers.

What was true of prose writing was also largely true of other areas of artistic endeavor. In poetry and drama, for example, the decade witnessed similar modernist breakthroughs, characterized by an exciting experimentalism, an exploitation of new themes and subjects, and numerous innovations in form and structure. Among its artististic triumphs were the grim tragedies of Eugene O'Neill, the theatrical realism of such playwrights as Maxwell Anderson and Laurence Stallings, the new intellectual poetry of T. S. Eliot and Ezra Pound, and the unconventional verse of such rebels as Robinson Jeffers, E. E. Cummings, and Edna St. Vincent Millay. Yet it was a decade as well of a more traditional kind of creativity, a decade when Stephen Vincent Benét tried to capture the national heritage in epic poetry, when the southern "Fugitives" offered romanticized images of their region's past, and when Robert Frost lit "poetic bonfires" illuminating mysteries in New England settings. By 1930 modernists and their opponents could both look back upon an era of remarkable creativity. But again both groups seemed repelled by New Era goals and visions. Only in Carl Sandburg's affirmations of national vitality or in Hart Crane's *The Bridge* (1930), written as a refutation of Eliot's *The Waste Land*, was there anything approaching a celebration of the courage, faith, and skill that had wrought technological and industrial marvels.

In painting the pattern was much the same. Coming to fruition now were two aspects of the prewar revolt against academic painting, one being the seamy realism of the "Ash Can" school of painters and those associated with them, the other an abstract modernism embracing and building upon a variety of European movements. In the first category such painters as John Sloan, George Bellows, and Edward Hopper left a vivid pictorial record of the darker and drabber side of American life. In the second were the cubist works of Charles Sheeler and Joseph Stella, the expressionism of Georgia O'Keeffe and Stuart Davis, and the efforts of such artists as John Marin and Max Weber to capture moods and emotions on canvas. Yet modernist triumphs did not prevent good traditional work from being done. Nor did they prevent the beginnings of a folkish regionalism portraying the dignity and strength of rural traditions. It was during the late 1920s that such regionalists as John Stuart Curry, Thomas Hart Benton, and Grant Wood began the kind of work usually associated with the 1930s.

As in the literary arts, painters in the 1920s explored man's animalistic urges and subterranean psyche, his existence in an unfeeling and decaying social order, and his possession in the past of more wholesome ways of life. But like the writers, only a few sought to maintain the earlier linkages between art and reformist or radical politics; and still fewer sought to capture on canvas the vitality, achievements, and visions of New Era industrialism. The European movements proclaiming an esthetic of the factory, a technocratic redemption of the future, or an erotic vitalism of the machine—movements that were in part inspired by European perceptions of Taylorism and Fordism—failed to attract American talent of the first order. And while cubists like Joseph Stella and Niles Spencer did seek esthetic inspiration in the dynamism and engineering feats of modern America, they tended to be exceptions with few imitators or followers.

Nor was the pattern substantially different in the musical arts. There, as in literature and painting, the period became one of exciting experimentation with new forms and themes, some of which was hailed as providing a foundation for an independent American music. Such modernist composers as Aaron Copland, Henry Cowell, and Roy Harris became musical pioneers, both in developing freer forms and in using native themes; and with assistance from friendly publishers and conductors, they succeeded in breaking into the repertoires of established performing groups. During the same period Charles Ives composed works for which he would later be recognized as America's most accomplished and original composer. And while composers like Deems Taylor, Howard Hanson, and Ernest Bloch stuck closer to the classical approach, they too began to utilize and exploit themes drawn from American history and experience. Yet declaring independence from European tutelage and Victorian constraints did not, as some enthusiasts had hoped, bring a music that all Americans would find meaningful, enjoyable, and expressive of their collective life. On the contrary, the gap between "serious" music and the popular variety seemed to widen. And such bridges as were attempted, as in the efforts to join the polyrhythms of jazz to symphonic forms, were spans not to the dominant forms and central images of popular music but to the innovative and primitivistic portions that liberated intellectuals found appealing.

Seen in perspective, then, the period was one during which cultural modernizers and liberators won a substantial measure of the freedom for which they had been agitating. Old constraints weakened, impulses toward political control faded, and institutions that valued innovation and continuous experimentation developed. Greater freedom brought a remarkable burst of creativity. It seemed to stimulate both modernists and traditionalists to their best efforts, and along with the negativism it allowed came an active search for new esthetics and moral values. It did not, however, lead to new ideals upon which writers and artists could agree, let alone to a synthesis that could unite art with national life. Nor did it lead to a society in which artistic talent and creativity served to enrich the lives of the expanding middle classes. Most of those liberated by the new affluence and leisure became consumers not of high culture but of the burgeoning mass variety. And high art, even more than high science, became the province of an elitist subculture existing in a state of tension with American society at large, and engaged in work that most of that society found baffling and misdirected if not socially harmful.

CULTURE AND THE MASSES

If high culture in the 1920s can be seen as the creative outpouring of an estranged and increasingly autonomous subculture, the period's popular literature and art are best viewed as an array of commercialized responses to mass leisure and affluence. Coming together at the time were a growing mass demand for cultural products, a widening gap between high art and mass tastes, and an expanding structure of cultural industries attuned to mass markets. Their convergence produced the rapid growth of a sphere in which cultural experiences were manufactured for mass sale. And in this sphere—the sphere of popular writing, commercial showmanship, and pleasers of the popular ear and eye—the kind of experiences provided depended less upon their artistic merits and demerits than upon their mass marketability or their capacity to meet tests imposed by community censors or by those in control of the production and distribution machinery.

One set of such cultural products became the means through which the newly prosperous sought a sense of upward movement into more refined social circles. For substantial numbers of Americans, upward movement had long been associated with the ability to afford cultural refinements. And now, as demand for these increased and older prescriptions for attaining them became suspect, cultural "developers" built ever larger markets for mass-produced replicas of certified art and culture, for commercialized adaptations of the new artistic styles, and for refined versions of the popular. If the 1920s had their "lost generation" and their breakthroughs in form and subject matter, they also witnessed the successful launching of the Book-of-the-Month Club, the rapid growth of pretentious theater and packaged cultural experiences, and an amazing proliferation of what arts critic Gilbert Seldes called "arty conglomerations of middle-class seriousness and bourgeois beauty." For some observers, this constituted evidence of rising tastes and the spread of cultural riches to a broader proportion of the population. But whether those who made such enterprises prosperous were really enriched by the products consumed is highly dubious. As Seldes put it, the principal ecstasy provided seemed to be an unfulfilling snobbism.

Livelier and less pretentious were those products purchased for entertainment, distraction, or escape rather than as symbols of social refinement. For these, too, the period brought larger mass markets, and as markets grew the tendency was toward heavy reliance upon set formulas, stereotyped characters, and habit-forming experiences. Much of the output was closer to the realm of narcotics than to that of art, and much of it was produced under stipulations that virtually forebade the expression of profound feelings or insights. Yet there was creativity of a sort, especially in building new media audiences, adapting to market changes, and frustrating the designs of cultural uplifters. If the movie, radio, and musical industries showed little concern for creative art, they did attract organizers, technicians, and craftsmen of the first rank; the result was often well-crafted and superbly executed productions of mass melodrama and fantasy. From these standpoints there was much to admire in the screen spectaculars of Cecil B. De Mille, the musical revues of Florenz Ziegfeld, and the production teams that adapted older entertainment forms to radio audiences. And genuine art was easier to find in the mass output of the 1920s than it would be in that of later decades. What uplifters called vulgarity or "philistinism" contained at times a refreshing capacity to unmask pretentiousness; in the comedy of Charlie Chaplin and Harold Lloyd, the films of D. W. Griffith, and the comic strips of George Herriman (creator of "Krazy Kat"), the period yielded works that had both mass appeal and the qualities appreciated by the nation's intellectual and artistic elites.

The 1920s were also notable for the emergence of new themes in popular culture. Its creators now found growing audiences for the glamour of youthful rebellion and urban sophistication, the rhythms and romances of city life, and the triumphs and trials of a machine age. Yet even as these audiences grew, works that reasserted earlier values and ideals enjoyed immense popularity. Perhaps partly as compensation for bureaucratic and urban reality, large numbers of Americans immersed themselves in romanticized celebrations of heroic frontiersmen, noble primitives, and self-sufficient individualists. And partly because ethical certainty was under attack, millions found comfort and reassurance in works celebrating the triumph of traditional standards and virtues. Measured solely in terms of mass sales, the great popular works of the decade were the fictionalized sermons of Harold Bell Wright, the western morality tales of Zane Grey, the "Tarzan" adventures of Edgar Rice Burroughs, and the sugary myths of Gene Stratton Porter.

For still other Americans in the 1920s, however, the popular culture most in demand was that in which the new appeared as terrain still inhabited and rendered worthwhile by the old. Eager for the benefits of progress yet deeply troubled by the transforming effects of economic and social change, they hungered for heroic figures who performed great feats in the modern world yet remained embodiments of traditional virtue. Such, for example, were the media images of big sport's Babe Ruth, big entertainment's Will Rogers, big industry's Henry Ford, and big administration's Herbert Hoover. Such was also the image of the decade's greatest media hero, Charles Augustus Lindbergh, conqueror of the Atlantic through his solo, nonstop flight to Paris in May of 1927. And with slight variations and adaptations, figures of the same sort peopled the pages of inspirational works, juvenile literature, and contemporary versions of the personal success story. Vicariously at least, one could function and rise in the modern world without losing one's soul; and in one stream of related literature, that seeking to sanctify the "new capitalism," this message was made particularly explicit. The most prominent examples were the best-selling works of advertising executive Bruce Barton, especially his *The Man Nobody Knows* (1924) and *The Book Nobody Knows* (1926). In these he offered comforting parallels between the activities of early Christianity and those of modern American business.

Much of popular culture in the 1920s clearly supported the existing order, either by embracing its ideals and prescriptions for progress or by providing safety valves through which cultural strains and tensions could be eased. Yet New Era leaders were not entirely happy with what the cultural "developers" of the period were doing. They saw connections between certain themes and appeals in popular culture and the aggravation of such problems as urban corruption and lawlessness, anti-institutional and anarchistic attitudes, and popular resistance to modern technology and its organizational imperatives. They worried also about the impact that the marketers of popular pleasures and cultural experiences were having on the work ethic, the drive to get ahead, and the pool of talent from which institutional leadership had to be drawn. And a portion of the associational code system through which they were seeking to regulate economic and social behavior was pushed into the sphere of popular culture, producing there a network of rules and ethical standards governing the output of motion picture producers, radio broadcasters, organized baseball, and mass-oriented publishers. In the New Era establishment there seemed to be much more concern with keeping popular culture in line than with the negativism and alternative values of high culture.

This concern, moreover, was a persisting one, reflecting to some extent the weaknesses of the control system but indicating as well that popular culture could develop a life of its own and follow paths incongruent with those in the economic sector. If it remained estranged from high culture and the core of scientific thought, portions of it also remained in conflict with the New Era economic and organizational visions. And while these segments seemed unlikely to coalesce around a coherent countervision, they did seem capable of sustaining themselves as still another manifestation of cultural fragmentation.

IMPULSES TOWARD DIFFERENTIATION AND SEPARATISM

There was another form of cultural fragmentation in the 1920s, one that stemmed not from divergent and conflicting responses to economic and social modernization but rather from the determination of particular groups to have their own cultures and maintain them as separate entities with unique perspectives on the human condition. One manifestation of this phenomenon was the effort to throw off European domination and establish "American" styles in serious art and music. Another was the continuing effort of a few radicals to create a "proletarian" art and literature expressive of working-class perspectives. And a third was the reassertion and defense in the cultural sphere of particular regional experiences. Each of these, however, would become much more pronounced after 1930 than before. The more prominent manifestations in the 1920s were those associated with ethnic and racial minorities, a separate youth culture, and the much publicized rebellions against middle-class respectability and life styles.

Ethnic-oriented cultural activities were in part a reaction to the expanded Americanization programs of the period. They were the work in particular of culturally aware individuals, often the children or grandchildren of immigrants, who were torn between pride in an ethnic heritage and pressures to renounce it. Such individuals were determined to awake fellow members of their ethnic groups to an appreciation of their cultural heritages. They were also convinced that new creativity could flow from the unique perspectives provided by their backgrounds and experiences. And while they produced little that approached the status of great art, they were successful in establishing new cultural programs and in sustaining alternatives to the cultural experiences being manufactured for mass sale. Their critique of assimilation also helped to raise doubts about its application elsewhere. Another development during the decade was the appearance of a movement recognizing the value of native Indian cultures and seeking ways to recover, preserve, and build upon them.

Developing along similar lines but having wider ramifications and generating greater creativity was the movement through which black artists and intellectuals proceeded to identify their racial heritage and exploit it for cultural purposes. Joining in what became known as the "Negro Renaissance," they were responsible not only for new cultural recovery and appreciation programs but also for an outpouring of ethnic-oriented novels, poems, plays, drawings, and music. Especially prominent were such writers as Langston Hughes, Claude McKay, Jean Toomer, and Countee Cullen, all of whom focused on the black man's unhappy situation in American society and in doing so produced prose and poetry that ranked with the best literary production of the decade. Of lesser stature was the work in music, painting, and drama. But it too had a range of appreciation extending far beyond the black community.

Also developing as a separate entity during the period was a set of youth-oriented cultural activities glorifying the special perspectives and capabilities of the young and depicting the attitudes and teachings of elders as being outmoded, harmful, or absurd. What made this possible was the prolongation of adolescence resulting from higher living standards, fewer child laborers, and extended education. But involved as well was an institutional gap opened by the weakening of traditional authority and left open when modern substitutes proved unable to channel all youthful endeavor into preparation for adult roles in the new organizational society. Youth, so those who resisted such socialization were told, was a time for experimentation, daring adventure, and rejection of the hypocrisies and false ideals that had poisoned human relationships. Those who possessed it had the potential either to redeem society or to create within it a sector of experiences that made life worth living. And in the name of building this redeeming sector, rebellious youths and their allies and exploiters in the intellectual community and the popular arts began to identify appropriate forms of cultural activity and defend them against those who regarded such forms as immature, mindless, or pathological. As the decade progressed, the new subculture acquired its own distinctive literature and art, its own forms of expressive behavior and social intercourse, and above all its own forms of music and dance. Jazz, once the music of New Orleans brothels and the black ghettos, owed much of its rise and development to its association with the new youth culture and its activities.

Finally, as still another manifestation of cultural separatism in the 1920s, one can note the much publicized growth of a bohemian counterculture centering in the cafés and gathering places of Greenwich Village, in New York City, and in similar communities, quarters, or "institutions" elsewhere. An object of fascination to journalists then and since, this growth has been much exaggerated. But clearly the number embracing bohemian life styles did increase, the circles in which they were admired widened, and visits to the Left Bank in Paris were followed by efforts to create its spirit and values in the United States. A significant subculture emerged, loosely joined in various ways to the youth, ethnic, and intellectual rebellions yet also embracing a substantial number of people who were neither adolescents nor members of minority groups nor genuine connoisseurs of artistic genius and intellectual achievement. Their central bond was a shared aversion for ordinary pursuits and bureaucratic organizations, and it was around activities through which they could assert, justify, and act out this aversion that the new subculture was built.

As America entered the 1930s, then, a new cultural consensus seemed further away than ever. The advance of science and the weakening of traditional authority and standards had not, as some had hoped, brought a new unity between intellectual and popular life. Major portions of the cultural sector had not followed the central thrusts of economic development. Nor had discordant subcultures disappeared from the national scene. On the contrary, new impulses toward fragmentation and separatism had shown a surprising strength; and by invoking the values of tolerance, diversity, and freedom of expression, these had been able to sustain themselves against mass standardization and against pressures for imposing and enforcing a cultural orthodoxy. In modern America, it appeared, the search for a new cultural coherence and stability might be a long, frustrating, and eventually unsuccessful one, a search that would only generate new versions of the cleavages and estranged enclaves that were characteristic of cultural development in the 1920s.

Yet it was by no means clear that the failure to achieve cultural coherence and stability acted as a bar to creativity or subtracted from the quality of American life. If cultural conflict and disorder allowed vulgarity, pretense, and irresponsibility to flourish, they also helped to stimulate the burst of intellectual and artistic creativity for which the 1920s are now remembered. And if they made the tasks of economic and political leadership more difficult, they also served as checks against those who would organize an end to individual liberties. The totalitarian-minded of the period also had their visions of a new order, with controlled scientific and cultural activities used to build and sustain it. And whether there could have been· greater cultural "rationalization" without opening the way to such designs or to something resembling the wartime abuses in the cultural sphere is difficult to tell.

CHAPTER 10

The New Day and the Great Crash, 1928–1930

For some Americans the year 1927 revealed a flawed underside to the New Era's dreams and assumptions. In Chicago dozens died in gangland warfare, a manifestation, so it was said, of the lawlessness that prohibition had bred. In western Pennsylvania coal operators evicted striking miners from their company homes, organized private armies, and imported strikebreakers by the thousands. In the lower Mississippi Valley a disastrous flood exposed both the emptiness of engineering claims and the appalling conditions of those at the bottom of the South's rural social structure. In Michigan Henry Ford closed down his plants for retooling, laying off thousands and aggravating a slump in business activity and employment totals. And in Massachusetts Nicola Sacco and Bartolomeo Vanzetti, convicted of murder in the nation's most celebrated case of "red scare" justice, were denied pardons and died in the electric chair. The "American system" had its victims as well as its beneficiaries; and, as some saw it, any system that allowed these kinds of victimization was in need of drastic changes.

For the great majority, however, these were minor flaws in a system that was still moving toward ever higher levels of technical achievement, material benefits, and spiritual enrichment. During the same year Lindbergh had crossed the Atlantic; Babe Ruth had hit sixty home runs; Warner Brothers had brought the marvel of sound to the silver screen; and Owen D. Young, dedicating the new Baker Foundation at the Harvard Business School, had proclaimed the arrival of professionalized business orders intent upon ending the "economic blot" of unemployment, creating modern substitutes for local community opinion, and establishing an economy in which all were free to develop culturally and all worked with "zest and spirit and pride of accomplishment." The slump, moreover, had seemed to respond well to the monetary and educational correctives applied by public and private authorities. And the flood area had become one more arena in which Herbert Hoover had demonstrated his organizational and administrative prowess. As head of the President's Flood Relief Committee, he had mobilized and coordinated a remarkably effective set of cooperative endeavors, thus validating, so it seemed to many, his organizational and social ideals.

As the year 1928 dawned, then, most Americans seemed more inclined than ever to credit New Era claims and formulas. If they saw defects in the existing order, their solution was to broaden the area in which managers like Hoover could exercise their organizational talent. And to a remarkable extent, the story of American history from 1928 to 1930 revolved around the figure of Herbert Hoover and the functioning of the institutions he had identified as the agents of national and international progress. It was the story, first of all, of increasing acclaim for the Great Engineer and his prophecies of a "New Day," of political currents and developments that installed him in the White House, and of his efforts to create a presidency suited to the realization of his designs. It was the story, secondly, of the failure of the New Era's planning and coordinating apparatus, especially of its failure to check the kind of economic imbalances and irrational behavior that it was supposed to prevent. And it was the story, thirdly, of a stabilization and countercyclical program based on Hooverian prescriptions yet unable to halt the forces that would soon make a mockery of his campaign promises. In sum, it was a period that witnessed both the apogee of a dream and the first stages of an economic nightmare.

A NEW KIND OF PRESIDENT

In the presidential nominating conventions of 1928 both major parties chose men who differed markedly from those chosen in the past. The Democratic nominee, Alfred E. Smith of New York, came neither from the rural hinterland nor from the older middle and upper classes. He was a representative instead of the urban metropolis and of that immigrantized, polyethnic, and boss-ordered America for which nativists and hypernationalists had such an aversion. And while the Republicans nominated a man of sterling respectability and village origins, they also broke with their pattern of rewarding electoral success, party work, and standing in the older professions. Herbert Hoover was the first presidential candidate to emerge from the managerial and technical elites spawned by the organizational revolution, and at the time his choice seemed to signify a closing of the gap between the new economic and technical order and the older American polity.

The Republicans were the first to meet in 1928. They convened in Kansas City on June 12, and by this time it was clear that Hoover would be their nominee. Coolidge had taken himself out of the contest. He had declared in the summer of 1927 that he did not choose to run again and subsequently had given no encouragement to a "draft Coolidge" movement. Such contenders as Vice-President Charles G. Dawes and former governor of Illinois Frank O. Lowden had also failed to develop substantial followings; and neither the skeptical party regulars, the antibusiness progressives, the disgruntled McNary-Haugenites, nor the anti-Hoover elements of the financial community had been able to find a candidate strong enough to check the Hooverites and their energetic gathering of convention delegates. On the first ballot, taken on June 14, Hoover received 837 of the 1084 votes cast. The convention then chose Senator Charles Curtis as his running mate. In his subsequent acceptance speech, the Great Engineer praised the blend of individual and cooperative endeavor that had been developed over the last eight years and promised that its continued development would eventually banish poverty from the land.

The Democratic convention, meeting in Houston on June 26, was more colorful but equally devoid of surprises. By the time the convention met the Smith forces had won control of most of the nonsouthern states. They had no difficulty this time in mustering the two-thirds majority needed to nominate their candidate. And once this became clear, the Southern Democrats concentrated on winning concessions that might make Smith's candidacy more palatable to their region. They were successful in getting Senator Joseph T. Robinson of Arkansas as Smith's running mate and in persuading Northern Democrats not to insist on a platform plank favoring repeal of the Eighteenth Amendment. But Smith was not inclined to placate the southerners any further. Although he promised to enforce the prohibition laws if elected, he also reserved the right to work for repeal.

In the campaign that followed Smith won strong support among urban ethnic groups, antiprohibitionists, Roman Catholics, and anti-Hoover elements in the farm, business, and welfare communities. Indeed, his carrying of the nation's twelve largest cities has been seen as a major milestone in the evolution of a new urban-oriented Democratic party. But his following was no match for Hoover's. Although the latter had no great appeal for ethnic minorities, he was able in 1928 to bridge the gap between modernists and traditionalists, hold the Republicans together, and win the votes of anti-Smith Democrats in the South and West. Many of them, responding to the anti-Smith campaigns carried on by such Protestant leaders as Bishop James Cannon of Virginia, decided that they simply could not vote for a man who was Catholic in religion, wet on the prohibition issue, and associated with a culture alien to the American heartland. In the voting booths the hinterland's aversion to Smith far outweighed the rural disenchantment with Hoover's solutions for the farm problem. When the votes were counted, Hoover had won by a landslide, one that for the first time since Reconstruction had even cracked the solid South and carried seven of the southern states. In the popular column he had polled 21,392,190 votes to Smith's 15,016,443 and in the electoral college had won by a vote of 444 to 87.

In the wake of the election the new President-elect toured Latin America, considered possible cabinet appointees, and laid plans for implementing his campaign pledges. His vision of the future, what he had called during the campaign a "New Day," had apparently been overwhelmingly endorsed by the American people; and presumably his prescriptions for attaining further installments of this uplifting abundance, especially his formulas for fusing a cooperative individualism with scientific management, could now become operative over ever widening areas of national life. Yet he was now entering an arena in which technocratic skills would have to be supplemented with the political arts of compromise, bargaining, and popular arousal. This was particularly true since the congressional majority elected with him consisted chiefly of Old Guard politicos and anti-Hoover progressives and agrarians. And to complicate matters further, the campaign had involved him in ethnocultural issues in which lack of consummate political skills could leave him isolated between polarized extremes. In his quest for votes he had welcomed the support of the anti-Smith Democrats; as a result he was now committed to stronger enforcement of the prohibition laws, new efforts to reduce urban disorder and lawlessness, and party reforms that could give the Hoover Democrats a permanent home in the Republican party. The nation was about to inaugurate a new kind of President. But how he would fare in a polity that had not yet "rationalized" its lawmaking bodies, its party structures, and its ethnocultural divisions remained to be seen.

BEFORE THE CRASH

In staffing the new administration Hoover weighed and acted upon two major kinds of considerations. First of all, there were political powers to be recognized and political debts to be paid. Consequently Andrew Mellon remained at the Treasury. The War, Agriculture, and Post Office departments went respectively to James W. Good, Arthur M. Hyde, and Walter F. Brown, all of whom had played major roles during the campaign. State, which Kellogg was anxious to vacate, finally went to the architect of the Nicaraguan settlement, Henry L. Stimson; and Justice, after an outcry from the "drys," finally went to William D. Mitchell rather than William J. Donovan. Second, there was the need for men who shared Hoover's vision of the future, had helped to build the organizations that were supposed to be realizing it, and could function as his lieutenants in further organizational efforts. Two prominent appointments of this sort were Ray Lyman Wilbur as Secretary of the Interior and Robert P. Lamont as Secretary of Commerce. And below the cabinet level there were numerous others. There the roster of "Hoover men" anxious to participate in new "Hooverization" projects included F. Trubee Davison in the War Department, Julius Klein in Commerce, Ernest Lee Jahncke in Navy, and Charles J. Rhoads as Commissioner of Indian Affairs.

The early days of the administration brought a variety of efforts to establish new and more enlightened mechanisms for coordinating public and private action. Plans were quickly made for a massive study of social trends and for an accompanying series of conferences on such problems as child welfare, housing, recreation, education, and public health. Out of these, it was hoped, would come the machinery for looking ahead and reducing irrational and uncoordinated action in the social welfare field. Plans were also made for a new series of economic studies and conferences, designed to follow up the work of the Commerce secretariat. More immediately, efforts were made to rationalize oil production and to set up a national economic council in which both public and private organizations would be represented. In June of 1929, in Colorado Springs, the administration convened a national oil conference and sought support for cooperative drilling programs and an interstate conservation compact; and in May and June it gave serious consideration to a proposal for formal linkages between federal administrators and representatives of organized business, labor, and agriculture. In neither of these cases, however, was the President willing to push matters, especially if it meant revising the laws governing private combinations and public-private relations. And in neither case did the envisioned agencies and programs materialize.

The major area in which the administration did seek congressional action was that of agricultural organization and relief. Redeeming a campaign pledge, the President called a special session of Congress to deal with the farm problem. And although his proposals for agricultural tariff revision bogged down and were carried over to the regular session, Congress did reject new proposals for export subsidies and pass a measure embodying the Hoover farm relief plan. Under the Agricultural Marketing Act of June 1929 a new Federal Farm Board, organized to represent the various interests in agriculture, was to become the agency for building and financing a new set of marketing associations. Given an initial sum of $500,000,000, it could provide technical and promotional assistance, make loans to facilitate orderly marketing, and form emergency stabilization corporations to deal with demoralized markets. To head the agency, Hoover turned to Alexander Legge, a former member of the War Industries Board. And by late 1929 Legge had most of the major commodities organized and had extended a number of commodity stabilization loans.

By October these actions in agriculture were accompanied by other reform initiatives, some unsuccessful but some laying the basis for more substantial changes at a later date. In the first category, the administration tried but failed to secure repeal of the national origins provision in the immigration law, and it was eventually unsuccessful in efforts to transfer western grazing lands to state control. In the more successful category, it moved quickly to rationalize the system of veterans' benefits, reform and improve the educational and health services of the Indian Bureau, and establish new procedures for making judicial appointments. It also strengthened its relations with labor when a special railroad board endorsed a broad view of employer responsibilities. And following a prison riot at Leavenworth, it opened a campaign of prison reform that eventually produced eight pieces of remedial legislation. The central figure in this was Sanford Bates, a nationally recognized penologist who left his position as head of the Massachusetts state system to take charge of the Federal Prisons Bureau.

The new administration refused to back away from the troubled areas of liquor control and party reform. Spurred on by pressures from the "drys" and by reactions to new outbursts of gangland warfare, it proceeded to reorganize and "depoliticize" the prohibition enforcement agencies, thus setting the stage for a mounting clash with urban politicians and advocates of repeal. At the same time it organized still another major exercise in fact finding, a national study commission composed of eminent lawyers and chaired by George W. Wickersham. And seeking to bring the Hoover Democrats into the Republican party, it lent its support to the "purging" of corruptionists from the southern party organizations, often, so it turned out, corruptionists who happened to have black skins. Ironically, the major result of this policy was to alienate much of the northern black community. In the South the Democrats quickly reestablished themselves as the party of respectable whites, in part by pointing to Hoover's previous ties to black leaders, his continuing concern with improving economic opportunities for blacks, and his wife's decision to entertain Mrs. Oscar DePriest (the wife of Chicago's new black congressman) at a White House tea.

Both the southern policy and that in regard to prohibition seemed likely to involve more political costs than gains. Nor had the administration's handling of the tariff question, the oil problem, and public land reform done much to enhance its political reputation. Yet in mid-October, when the President journeyed to Michigan for the dedication of the new Edison Institute of Technology, he could still be hailed as the architect of a new political economy. His actions still seemed to be moving the nation toward a "New Day," and few suspected that his ideas and policy prescriptions were about to face their most severe test.

PANIC AND CONTRACTION

The panic selling that gripped the American stock market in late October of 1929 marked the culmination of a series of speculative excesses that New Era institutions had been unable to prevent. In 1923 and again in 1926 these had seemed to work. In any event speculation had not become excessive and had been followed by mild setbacks that the economy had quickly absorbed. But the new bull market that began developing in 1928 was accompanied by a get-rich-quick psychology that proved readily exploitable by high-pressure securities merchants and promoters with exaggerated and irrational visions of the future. Intoxicated, so it seemed, by the performance and potentialities of the "new economy," Americans were eager to bid against each other for chances to participate in what was being touted as another and even more astounding phase of development. They also had mounting savings with which to conduct the bidding contest, and, partly because the international situation seemed to demand a low-interest policy that would discourage the flow of gold to the United States, they were able to borrow on easy terms. Once the bidding started, it fed upon itself. The upward spiral in stock prices drew in more bidders and increased willingness to keep borrowing even after interest rates began moving rapidly upward. Under the circumstances the Federal Reserve Board's belated efforts to curb credit and reduce its use for speculative purposes became exercises in futility.

By March of 1929, then, speculative activity had developed a momentum that was difficult to check. It was not about to yield to the new President's efforts to generate warnings from key public and private figures or to his pleas for greater responsibility on the part of investment bankers and securities merchants. Throughout the spring and summer the upward spiral in stock prices accelerated. Over the past year many leading stocks had doubled and tripled in price, this despite the fact that corporate earnings statements told a story of mounting business difficulties. And still the demand seemed insatiable. Promoters were now busy organizing new holding companies and investment trusts for the express purpose of manufacturing more stock. Unscrupulous salesmen had little difficulty in finding gullible customers, and public deference to the new set of "financial wizards" had opened the way to a variety of market-rigging abuses.

Eventually, though, such a bubble would have to burst. It could not sustain itself once the supply of new bidders began to falter, and by September of 1929 this point was being reached. Buy orders were no longer sufficient to fuel the price spiral. And as this became apparent, a number of those who had bought for speculative purposes began looking for the right moment to take their profits. Under the circumstances any downward movement in stock prices could trigger a selling panic, and should the movement become substantial it could force a wave of involuntary selling. Stocks that had been bought with borrowed money and pledged as collateral would have to be sold to cover the loans.

As it happened, the first break in stock prices came as a result of developments abroad. In late September there was a large withdrawal of funds to London, a withdrawal initially triggered by a scandal on the London Exchange and then deliberately encouraged through actions taken by the Bank of England. Prices on the New York Exchange fell, and big speculators started liquidating their holdings. For a time others seemed reluctant to follow suit. But on October 15 a new wave of selling got under way; and by October 24, as brokers began unloading the stock that had been pledged as collateral, this wave was approaching panic proportions. A bankers' pool then stepped in. Under the leadership of the House of Morgan, it began buying stock and succeeded in holding the line for a few days. Its efforts, however, could not reverse the panic psychology that was now developing, and on October 29, Black Tuesday, the bottom again fell out. Over 16,000,000 shares exchanged hands that day, and many leading industrials dropped as much as forty points in this single day's trading. By the end of October stocks that had been worth $87,000,000,000 at the peak of the boom were now worth only $55,000,000,000, and by 1933 they would be worth only $18,000,000,000.

The impact of the stock market debacle was twofold. In the first place, it created an atmosphere of gloom that dampened both investment and consumer spending. Where Americans had once credited roseate visions of their future, they were now inclined to credit cynics and pessimists. Second, it ended the speculative boom that had hidden and temporarily offset serious weaknesses in the New Era system. Had this been working as its theorists claimed, the new setback might have been relatively short lived. But it was not working that way. Structurally the reality differed from the theory in ways that now became increasingly apparent.

For one thing, the system was not as balanced and expansive as New Era theorists argued. It did, to be sure, recognize the importance of mass purchasing power. But it had not yet found ways of expanding this fast enough to absorb the kinds of goods being produced. This was a gap reflected both in the massive growth of consumer debt and in the increasing resort to "hard sell" techniques. Investment opportunities had also become a growing problem. Despite the faith in a new scientific and technical frontier, the late 1920s had not brought forth new industries and technologies comparable to those responsible for earlier investment outlays. Nor were these weaknesses the only ones. To make matters worse, the "balance wheels" that were supposed to come into play when demand faltered were in 1929 largely nonexistent. Construction demand had been largely exhausted by 1927, not built up as a countercyclical reserve. Production for inventory, even if credit could be arranged, seemed highly irrational at a time when consumers and investors were retrenching. And foreign demand had already reached its practical limits, at least without major changes in tariff, debt collection, and foreign loans policy.

Indeed, the system was not only lacking in balance wheels or stabilizers. It was now mined with "booby traps" whose triggering could transform an initial downturn into the greatest economic contraction in the nation's history. A relatively small number of layoffs or wage cuts could have strongly negative effects on the market for consumer durables and thus trigger more layoffs or wage cuts. A relatively small dose of retrenchment could force overcapitalized holding company pyramids into bankruptcy and liquidation, thus triggering stronger pressures for retrenchment. Any new shrinkage in agricultural markets could push the commodity holding operations of the United States and other nations beyond their available resources, thus triggering "dumping" measures that would cause even greater distress in rural areas. Any new decline in the export of American capital could bring down an international trade and monetary system predicated on its continued outflow, thus triggering stronger pressures for withdrawal and contraction. And any one of these developments could trigger what was perhaps the greatest "booby trap," a banking system rigged to collapse when subjected to pressures for monetary liquidity, the desire to hold money. Each of these could reinforce the downward impetus, and organizational development had now greatly reduced the ability of the market place to force the readjustments needed for new expansion. In a contracting economy the institutions that were supposed to organize continuous and orderly growth could become instruments for protecting those whose actions were helping to produce the contraction.

In the wake of the stock market crash, then, the tendency of the New Era economic system was toward continuing contraction. And while there would be brief halts and temporary reversals in this process, contraction would be the dominant feature of the economy's behavior for the next four years. During the year that followed October of 1929 new investment declined some 35 percent, the gross national product fell about 8 percent, and unemployment climbed from an estimated 3 percent of the work force to an estimated 9 percent. And this was only the beginning. By 1933 new investment would dwindle to virtually nothing, the gross national product (adjusted for deflation) would stand at only 67 percent of the 1929 level, and unemployment would reach 25 percent.

HOOVERISM ON TRIAL

For Hooverism the beginnings of economic contraction provided a major test. Since 1920 the Great Engineer had been associated with business cycle control, and in 1929 he was quick to accept the new challenge and apply the formulas that he had worked out over the past nine years. As he saw it, the potential for continued economic growth was still there, especially since the bursting of the speculative bubble had now released capital for more productive endeavors. It was a potential that could be realized not through liquidation or statist measures but through cooperative programs to counteract the psychological effects of the panic and induce compensatory spending. Turning to an elite that was presumably system conscious and willing to absorb temporary losses for the sake of future growth, the President made a strenuous effort to organize such programs. In November 1929 he called the leaders of the economic establishment into a series of conferences at the White House, and by early 1930 three new programs were in operation. The National Business Survey Conference, set up as an adjunct of the Chamber of Commerce and functioning through a committee representing some 170 trade associations, was seeking to dispel gloom and obtain compliance with pledges of wage maintenance and new investment. The National Building Survey Conference, also operating through trade organizations, was seeking to implement pledges of new-or expanded construction, and the new Division of Public Construction in the Commerce Department was working to speed up federal building projects and obtain compliance with state and municipal pledges to increase expenditures on public works.

Along with these programs Hoover also sought and was able to get a number of supplementary measures. He obtained a temporary tax cut, a $400,000,000 increase in public works appropriations, a "labor peace" pledge from union leaders, and monetary expansion measures from the Federal Reserve Board. In addition, the new Farm Board swung into action. Invoking its emergency powers, it formed government corporations to purchase surplus wheat and cotton. And yielding to arguments that domestic stabilization required temporary sheltering from foreign competition, the President worked to secure an appropriate tariff law. He did not, however, show much sympathy for those who wanted to tie macroeconomic stabilization to the legalization of protective cartels. On the contrary, he seemed strongly supportive when his new antitrust officials and a new majority on the Federal Trade Commission proceeded to scrap the policies of the late 1920s, refuse further advisory opinions on projected business agreements, and attack the more restrictive features of the industrial codes and trade association operations. These, so Hoover explained, protected the wrong kind of concerted action.

That the Hoover program had much chance of working is doubtful. But in the spring of 1930 the indexes measuring production and employment did turn up, and even stock prices seemed to be recovering. Addressing the annual convention of the Chamber of Commerce on May 1, the President expressed the conviction that the worst was now over and that rapid recovery was in the offing. A "great economic experiment," he declared, had "succeeded to a remarkable degree," and once recovery was complete he hoped to organize another great national investigation in which economists would join with business, labor, and farm representatives to discover ways of achieving greater future stability. He was also enthusiastic about the prospects of growth in new industries, especially in aviation, where a new Air Mail Act had provided the tools for building a national passenger service.

The latter half of 1930, however, brought new downturns rather than recovery, downturns that Hoover blamed on congressional obstructionism and foreign dumping but which most economists have attributed to a growing business conviction that new investment outlays were unwarranted. In essence, informed business expectations began diverging from those projected by the Hoover agencies, and strengthening this divergence was the inability of the Hoover programs to counter the effects of new depressants. As summer gave way to fall, the economy reeled under the impact of a severe drought in the South and West, a collapse of commodity holding operations abroad, and an intensifying international trade war aggravated by the new Smoot-Hawley Tariff Act that Hoover (ignoring a petition signed by 1038 members of the American Economic Association) had signed into law on June 17. It also suffered from a rising rate of bank failures, especially late in the year as farm and drought distress intensified the strain on rural banks. Between November 1 and December 31 a total of 609 banks with combined deposits of $550,000,000 went under. And since the Federal Reserve Board failed to take compensatory action, the result was a continuing scramble for liquidity that kept shrinking the monetary base.

Confronted with this worsening situation, the Hoover Administration was not inactive. In August it organized a National Drought Committee, an agency designed to mobilize drought relief in much the same way that flood relief had been mobilized in 1927. In October it added a similar agency for unemployment relief, setting up for this purpose the President's Emergency Committee for Employment under the direction of Arthur Woods. During the same month the President deemphasized the developments abroad, arguing that recovery could come along national lines. When Congress met in December, he recommended new expenditures for public works, further support of his cooperative programs, and limited antitrust relief for the natural resource industries. But as the year drew to a close, contraction was still accelerating; and the number of those who believed that Hooverism had failed and should be abandoned was now increasing. In 1931 the President would face growing challenges from old-line liquidationists on one side and from welfare statists, national economic planners, and business cartelizers on the other.

WELFARE, PROHIBITION, AND
THE SOUTHERN STRATEGY

By late 1930 Hoover's difficulties were compounded by growing dissatisfaction with his social welfare, law enforcement, and southern policies. In each of these areas he was alienating important groups and losing political support. And in the press his "political ineptitude" was now being played up. His once cordial relations with the press had soured, especially among those who felt that he was trying to manage the news through canned releases and press favorites. Alienated reporters seemed bent on creating a counterimage of the man they had admired in 1928 and were therefore receptive to Democratic publicity portraying the President as an insensitive political bungler of the first order.

In social welfare the administration's plans for new rationalizing and coordinating mechanisms continued to unfold. A prestigious Research Committee on Social Trends began its studies; a National Advisory Committee on Education produced a design for improved educational organization; a national conference on child welfare led to a new body of recommendations and a new network of committees in that field; and by the end of 1930 the planning for a similar conference on housing was well advanced. But the number of social workers and welfare organizations who believed that federal action should be limited to such informational and stimulative endeavors was now rapidly dwindling. As unemployment put new pressure on welfare budgets and traditional sources of funding, there was a growing demand for federal aid. And as shrinking profits put pressure on corporate welfare programs, the advocates of a tax-supported social security system were gaining new adherents. Throughout 1930 Hoover resisted such proposals, arguing vehemently that federal action of this sort would undermine the private and local institutions essential to American freedom and further progress. But his stand was interpreted as a hardhearted rejection of humanitarian considerations, an unmasking, as it were, of his pretentious claims to the label of the "great humanitarian"; and even within his administration he was now having difficulty in holding certain agencies in line.

The prohibition issue was also continuing to fester. Economic stringency added new arguments to the case for repeal, arguments that were particularly persuasive to business groups. It could now be offered as a way to stimulate recovery and reduce the burden of existing taxes. And as the repeal movement gathered strength, generating new organizations and waves of propaganda, alarmed "drys" talked about a "whiskey rebellion" and intensified their pressures for stronger enforcement. Hoover's policies were now being criticized from both sides, and it seemed unlikely that either better administration or more scientific study could prevent further polarization. In any event a law transferring the Prohibition Bureau from Treasury to Justice had not deflated the issue. Nor had the Wickersham Commission been able to produce a scientific solution.

At the same time, the efforts to reform the Republican party in the South were now having political repercussions that Hoover had never intended. They had brought not a new and more respectable Southern Republicanism but an alienation of black pressure groups, an intensified factionalism in the southern party organizations, and an acerbation of the President's relations with Southern Democratic congressmen. They were also at least partly responsible for the curious coalition of blacks, laborites, and Southern Democrats that was fighting Hoover's nomination of Judge John J. Parker to fill a vacancy on the Supreme Court. An able jurist from North Carolina, Parker had in his earlier career upheld "yellow-dog" contracts—in which employees promised, as a condition of employment, not to join a labor union—and had advocated that blacks be completely excluded from the political process. But the crucial factor that produced the 41-to-39 vote against confirmation was the identification of Parker's appointment with Hoover's "southern strategy." The contest marked the emergence of the National Association for the Advancement of Colored People as an important political pressure group, and it was a significant milestone along the route that would eventually take most blacks out of the Republican party.

One indicator of the changed political climate was the strong Democratic showing in the midterm elections of 1930. In the South the gains that the Republicans had made in the 1920s were virtually wiped out. In northern state contests candidates associated with Hoover fared badly. And in Congress the massive Republican majorities disappeared. In the Senate the new division was 48 Republicans, 47 Democrats, and 1 Farmer-Laborite; and in the House of Representatives, which the Democrats would eventually organize, it was initially 217 affiliated with each of the major parties and one Farmer-Laborite holding the balance of power. If Congress had been uncooperative in 1930, it was likely to be more so in the future.

SETBACKS IN THE QUEST FOR WORLD ORDER

The year 1930 also brought setbacks in the New Era quest for an Americanized world order stabilized through moral commitments, scientific expertise, and cooperative economic development. In this sphere, as in domestic policy, the Hoover Administration had hoped to build upon and improve the system developed in the 1920s. But here too some impressive early achievements failed to correct fatal flaws in the economic structure, and the result by late 1930 was the beginning of an economic breakdown that would usher in a decade of destructive economic nationalism and growing political disorder.

The most impressive of the initial achievements was the Hoover Administration's success in extending and expanding the naval limitations system. Its key contribution to doing so was the new "yardstick principle," which took into account a navy's age, armaments, and other fighting capabilities as well as its tonnage. This allowed the British to accept parity with the United States without giving up the larger cruiser tonnage they insisted upon. At the London Naval Conference, meeting from January to April of 1930, the new formula produced a treaty under which Britain, the United States, and Japan agreed to fixed limitations on the construction of cruisers, destroyers, and submarines. France and Italy did not sign, primarily because the United States still refused to give guarantees of French security and Italy would accept no limitations unless the French did so. But all five powers did agree to extend the Washington Treaty limitations on capital ships for another five years.

Three other developments at the time were also hailed as proof that the New Era approach could achieve its diplomatic goals. One was a new formula under which the United States again committed itself to membership in the World Court. Worked out by an international committee under the chairmanship of Elihu Root, it became the basis for a new treaty submitted to the Senate in 1930. The second development was the passing of a Far Eastern crisis that dominated the international scene in late 1929. In this case American efforts to invoke the Kellogg-Briand Pact and arrange for mediation were rebuffed by the Soviet Union. But fears of a general war subsided when the Russians and Chinese made peace on the basis of the previous status quo. And finally there was the renewed movement toward the Pan-American ideal. Fresh from his good-will tour, Hoover moved to upgrade the diplomatic service in Latin America, encourage new forms of economic cooperation and cultural exchange, and solidify the Nicaraguan and Mexican settlements. He also endorsed the revised view of the Monroe Doctrine set forth in the Clark Memorandum, and despite pressure from American investors he made it clear that there would be no collection of debts by force. The one sore spot during his first year was the situation in Haiti. There a new wave of rioting erupted in late 1929, some of it directed against the American military government. But even here Hoover responded rationally and sympathetically. More marines were rushed in, but this action was quickly followed by the creation of a special commission to devise a plan for American withdrawal.

The Hoover Administration, however, was not successful in protecting the Latin American economy from the effects of the American financial panic and the Smoot-Hawley Tariff Act. For this purpose the cooperative system of the 1920s seemed inadequate, especially since it was now under investigation by critics in Congress. Yet suggested alternatives—such things as government investment guarantees, government loans and grants, or special trading arrangements—were still regarded by the Hooverites as certain to cause more difficulties than they resolved. They believed that the recovery being organized in the United States would soon generate new capital and markets for Latin America. But as it turned out their programs did not bring recovery in the United States, and the new capital and markets were not forthcoming. By late 1930 those Latin American economies that had been linked to the United States were entering a vicious cycle of debt repudiations, capital withdrawal, and shrinking markets, a cycle that would soon make a mockery of the hopeful visions of New Era diplomats, stabilizers, and developers.

In Europe, too, the Hoover Administration failed to find ways of enabling the rickety economic structure of the 1920s to withstand the loss of American capital and markets. There 1929 had brought another committee of experts, chaired this time by Owen D. Young; and from its recommendations had come the Young Plan, which readjusted German reparations downward, linked a portion of them to the Allied war debt obligations, and set up an international bank to facilitate collection. To Young's dismay, however, the Hoover Administration had strongly criticized the linkages between reparations and Allied war debts and had rejected all suggestions of official participation in the new bank. Nor was it amenable to the new crop of economic relief proposals put forth by European statesmen in 1930. Throughout the year it rejected suggestions for trade concessions, monetary support, and debt readjustment; and from mid-1930 on the international debt structure created in the 1920s became increasingly difficult to sustain. Those committed to the task were putting increasing strain on their monetary systems, trade programs, and laboring populations and by doing so were setting the stage for the collapse and disorders of 1931.

For the heralders of a "New Day," then, 1930 was not a propitious year. In 1928 and 1929 the Hooverian vision of national and international progress had reached the apogee of its acceptance and influence, and for a time in early 1930 it had seemed to be proving itself in another major trial. But as 1930 gave way to 1931, its architects were on the defensive and would soon be fighting desperately for their political lives and for the institutions they believed essential to ordered liberty and future progress.

CHAPTER 11

The Hoover Vision at Bay,
1931–1932

For the American people the twenty months from January 1931 to August 1932 constituted one of the bleakest and most unsettling periods since the 1890s. As during that decade, frontiers seemed to be closing, institutions seemed out of control, and a long search for liberal ordering mechanisms seemed to be ending in failure. The Hoover prescriptions, although they continued to bring forth new programs and organizations, seemed incapable of putting idle resources to work or meeting basic social needs. Yet to many Americans the alternatives being proposed seemed to involve forms of coordination that would require the sacrifice of fundamental freedoms and renunciation of the nation's most cherished dreams.

If bleak and unsettling, however, the period was also one of major significance for the future course of American development. Economically it was a period during which the depression became worldwide and reached depths beyond what the most pessimistic had been predicting in 1930. In America manufacturing output declined some 35 percent, farm prices fell to record lows, another three thousand banks went under, and another five million workers joined the ranks of the unemployed. The land of promise became one of increasing distress, not only for those at the bottom of the social structure but for large segments of the middle class as well. And it was under pressure from these worsening economic conditions that two interrelated stories continued to unfold and to dominate national life. One was the story of the Hoover vision at bay, of an administration still committed to the formulas of 1929, fighting desperately now to restore faith in them and to block what it considered prescriptions for bureaucratic despotism and social degeneration. The other was the story of growing support for those who had once been outside the mainstream, especially those who envisioned other kinds of institutions as the tools through which the New Era goals could actually be realized. Much of what would eventually be incorporated in or attempted by the New Deal was now emerging, and once the Hooverian barriers crumbled the American search for a "new liberalism" would veer into these new paths.

PRELUDE TO THE EUROPEAN CRASH

Of major importance in the continuing economic contraction was the European financial panic of May 1931. Indeed, during the four months preceding the panic the American economy seemed to be stabilizing and showing signs of recovery. And consequently much of the political debate in early 1931 revolved not around alternative recovery programs but around such issues as liquor control, drought relief, veterans' benefits, power development, employment service reform, and oil imports. Congress was in a rebellious mood, and it was more responsive to the changing political climate than the administration was. But this was reflected less in an alternative economic or social program than in particular congressional blocs seeking to pass specific pieces of legislation that the administration opposed.

Two of the most heated debates were over the prohibition law and the drought relief program. The first reached a new intensity in January 1931, when the Wickersham Commission finally confessed its inability to agree on a solution and filed a badly divided report that each side tried to use for its own purposes. Journalists had a field day satirizing the report, and congressmen offered numerous analyses of it. But the major effect of the whole experience was further embarrassment for a President who had made expert commissions an integral part of his leadership strategy. Nor did the workings of drought relief, presumably an area in which the President was himself an expert, do much to reestablish his personal and political standing. There his commitments to working through the Red Cross, the business establishment, and local community institutions collided with mounting evidence of severe distress and resources inadequate to deal with it. And although he succeeded in limiting federal feed and seed loans to $45,000,000, blocking federal appropriations for the Red Cross, and restricting the use of a special $20,000,000 loan fund to prescribed rehabilitation activities, these victories cost him dearly in political credits. Many agreed with Will Rogers when he remarked that the more generous congressional proposals were unlikely to give drought-stricken farmers "the gout," and for years Hoover would be subject to the taunt that he was willing to feed the area's livestock but not its starving human beings.

Two other congressional initiatives that the administration strongly opposed were those calling for federal loans to veterans and federal development and operation of the Muscle Shoals facilities. To each of these the President reacted with a veto, but only on Muscle Shoals was he able to make this stick. There his blockage of the latest version of the Norris bill seemed to open the way to his own proposals for cooperative regulation and for a development commission made up of regional and organizational representatives. But in the area of veterans' benefits an overridden veto left the initiative in the hands of the servicemen's lobbies. In 1931 the holders of the World War bonus certificates gained the right to borrow up to 50 percent of their certificates' maturity value, an operation that eventually involved about $1,400,000,000 in federal loans; and this same group would soon be pushing for full maturity value redemption in 1932 rather than 1945.

Also vetoed in early 1931 was a bill to establish federally financed state employment services. Introduced by Senator Robert F. Wagner, a liberal Democrat from New York, it had won the support of numerous labor and welfare groups. But in the eyes of the Hoover Administration it would destroy a developing system of federal, local, and private cooperation, coordinated by the existing Employment Service. And the result, after Congress turned down an administration substitute, was a pocket veto of the Wagner bill. What the President did agree to was a special $500,000 appropriation for expanding and overhauling the Employment Service's existing work. In addition, he signed into law a measure authorizing a new public works planning agency, an agency first known as the Federal Employment Stabilization Board but one that would eventually develop into the New Deal's National Resources Planning Board. This was also sponsored by Senator Wagner, but in signing it the President took pains to link the measure to the public works planning movement of the 1920s and give credit to such men as Edward Eyre Hunt and Otto Mallery.

Finally, another set of political debates swirled around proposals for antitrust or other forms of relief to especially demoralized industries. Oil, coal, lumber, sugar, and textiles were all pushing their cases. But the President, despite his recommendations of late 1930, was not inclined to support either the legalization of cartels or the import restrictions advocated by representatives from the oil states. His answer again was cooperative private and local programs, mobilized around quasi-official informational services yet steering clear of the kinds of collusion forbidden by antitrust law. It was, in short, the creation of new units of "associational action." And efforts to bring these into being did continue. During the early months of 1931 the administration helped to launch new programs of this sort for the oil, lumber, and cotton textile industries.

When Congress adjourned in March of 1931, both the business and the political communities were sounding cautious notes of optimism. Some industries and groups, to be sure, were suffering severely. But in February the indexes of employment, payrolls, and production had steadied; they were now rallying slightly; and, as some analysts saw it, a period of relief from congressional activities and the accompanying political quarrels might induce them to move up more rapidly. This was an analysis, moreover, in which the President seemed to join. In late April, speaking to the Gridiron Club in Washington, he refused to make prophecies; but he expressed the view that "mobilized voluntary action" had "proved its strength," and he noted that recovery from every major depression in the past had "begun in the summer." At the time he was largely unaware of just how threatening the situation in central Europe had become. Nor would he begin to realize the full implications of this until some nine days later, when Ambassador Frederic M. Sackett arrived from his post in Germany for a series of conferences. Unhappily, the second and deeper phase of America's Great Depression was about to begin.

A NEW KIND OF DEPRESSION

Seen in long-range perspective, the European crash of spring and summer of 1931 was a product of wartime dislocations which the peacemakers and New Era diplomats had never dealt with adequately. It was, as the Hooverites would say again and again, the price to be paid for such follies as the reparations assessment, the breaking up of the Austro-Hungarian Empire as an economic entity, and French intransigence toward German reconstruction and world disarmament. Yet one could hardly claim, as the Hooverites frequently did, that American actions and decisions had played no part in this story of folly and breakdown. American policies, after all, had been largely responsible for the emergence of an international exchange system financially dependent upon a continued outflow of capital from the United States. It was the loss of American capital and markets that subjected this system to the severe strains of 1930 and early 1931. And it was American rejection of the relief proposals of 1930 that rendered the development of compensatory programs exceedingly difficult. Although the United States had now replaced Britain as the center of world finance, it refused, in the words of economist Charles Kindleberger, to accept the "role of underwriter" that Britain could no longer play.

The immediate triggering of the crash, however, was largely the result of German, Austrian, and French actions rather than decisions made in the United States. One factor was a March 1931 proposal for an Austro-German customs union, offered as a way of reviving trade but regarded by the French as a projected breach in the Versailles Treaty system. The French reaction made it increasingly difficult for Austria's overextended banking system to obtain needed funds. And in early May, when it was learned that the Credit-Anstalt in Vienna had become the beneficiary of special governmental support operations, the result was a run on the institution that finally forced it to close its doors. Panic liquidation then followed quickly. The next two months brought exchange crises and bank runs throughout central and western Europe. Gold flowed out of Germany and Austria in massive amounts, its owners apparently convinced that the financial system was doomed and that revolution from either the left or the right was imminent. And as capital fled or went into hiding, a hard-pressed German government was forced into austerity measures and crisis taxes that put more pressure on a labor force that was now more than 20 percent unemployed.

In the United States the European crisis brought new downturns in the economic indexes. But throughout June and July the Hoover Administration had hopes of containing and reversing these through a new set of international initiatives. As early as June 5 the President had decided to propose a one-year moratorium on intergovernmental debts; and once he had overcome the resistance of his Treasury Department and gotten pledges of cooperation from congressional and financial leaders, he arranged for an appropriate request from Germany and proceeded to announce his plan. This came on June 20, but it was not until July 6 that the moratorium finally took effect. The French, irritated at not being consulted beforehand, were not in a cooperative mood. It was only after the New York Federal Reserve Bank joined in new credits to Germany and after Hoover threatened to leave the French outside any international agreement that their endorsement was finally obtained. To deal with a continuing banking crisis the Germans then requested fresh loans; but this proposal won little support in either Britain or the United States. The only further relief was a standstill agreement on withdrawals of foreign credits, an agreement that was finally hammered out at a conference in London in late July.

Through such measures Hoover had hoped to restore confidence in the European financial system, gain a year during which armament burdens could be further reduced, and allow the American economy to escape further deflationary pressures. His hopes, however, were not realized. In Europe the months of August and September brought further liquidation, manifested now in a flight from the pound that finally led the British to abandon the gold standard. That action marked the beginning of a more intense trade war, fought with retaliatory currency devaluations, higher tariff walls, and a variety of exchange controls. And as European difficulties intensified, the American depression entered a new and deeper phase. The late summer and fall brought sharp breaks in commodity and security prices, new declines in foreign trade, and further drops in industrial production. Late September and early October also brought major losses of gold; and when Federal Reserve authorities responded with deflationary credit policies, the result was a new wave of bank failures and bank runs. Between September 30 and November 1 private cash hoards increased by an estimated half-billion dollars and another 522 banks, with $471,000,000 in deposits, closed their doors.

Subjected to this new pressure, a number of the earlier Hoover programs broke down and were abandoned. This was true, for example, of the National Business Survey Conference's wage maintenance program, of the stabilization activities in oil, and of most of the Farm Board's operations. Having already invested most of its funds in surplus wheat and cotton and having failed in efforts to bring about voluntary acreage reductions, that agency abandoned its emergency support programs and began liquidating its holdings. Yet even as the earlier programs collapsed, the President's response to the new economic setbacks was further attempts to mobilize cooperative action. In August Walter S. Gifford of American Telephone and Telegraph agreed to head a new President's Organization on Unemployment Relief. It would again attempt to mobilize local and private resources, obtain further state action, and establish spread-the-work and reemployment programs. In October a conference in New Orleans produced an agreement under which organized southern bankers would help to finance cotton holding operations. And in early December the long-planned national housing conference became the vehicle for organizing new efforts to promote construction and make new mortgage money available.

In addition, the President moved to establish a cooperative credit pool that could be used to aid banks in temporary distress. Meeting with key financial leaders on October 4, he persuaded them to organize a new National Credit Association and through it to set up a reserve fund of $500,000,000 from which loans could be made on collateral not eligible at the Federal Reserve Banks. The financiers, however, were decidedly skeptical about the new program. Their action was conditioned on the President's pledge that should the measure prove inadequate he would ask Congress to establish a governmental lending agency similar to the old War Finance Corporation. And if the bankers were now skeptical about Hooverian diagnoses and formulas, this was even more the case with many other Americans. The new phase of the depression was now bringing forth not only new applications of the Hoover approach but also a burgeoning anti-Hooverism that was beginning to move beyond its purely negative stage and generate rival diagnoses and rival prescriptions.

THE ANTI-HOOVERIAN ALTERNATIVES

For a relatively few Americans the events of 1931 were proof not merely of Hooverism's loss of contact with reality but of the need to replace liberal capitalist institutions with another kind of social order. In intellectual circles there were new admirers of Stalin's Russia, Mussolini's Italy, and America's preindustrial aristocracies. And in farm and labor circles anticapitalist radicals enjoyed more receptive hearings than at any time since 1922. They developed followings among coal miners, textile workers, sharecroppers, agrarian protesters, and ethnic minorities; and they were active in organizing hunger marches, strike activities, agrarian resistance to foreclosure proceedings, and defenses of civil rights. Yet even among those who were most receptive to such radicalism, its appeal tended to be limited and tenuous, and among other groups it was rejected as being both impractical and incompatible with American ideals and values. For the overwhelming majority of Hoover's critics, the alternative was not a rejection of the capitalist system but institutional reforms that would make it function properly.

For a relatively large group of such critics, moreover, the reforms needed were not in the core of the Hooverian apparatus but rather in support mechanisms that Hoover had failed to develop properly. In particular they saw such things as the new tariff structure, monetary mismanagement, and defective publicity as being responsible for the larger economic failure. And while they believed that Hoover had committed grievous errors, they tended to see these as being confined to one particular policy area. Such was the case with "old Wilsonians" like Cordell Hull, who were now prescribing tariff reductions and reciprocal trade treaties; with a wide spectrum of monetary reformers prescribing new monetary bases or new kinds of banking systems; and with critics envisioning different tools of informational and public opinion management.

For a second and expanding group, however, the fault did lie with the central core of ordering and coordinating mechanisms. The failure of Hoover's economic programs, so these critics argued, stemmed from the fact that they lodged or left economic power in the wrong hands and thus allowed it to be used in ways that left imbalances uncorrected and resources idled. The organizations that were expected to implement the programs were either too weak or too lacking in system consciousness to do so. To remedy this the critics proposed either to lodge more power in the hands of the truly enlightened, democratize industrial government so as to lay the basis for true cooperation, or restore an order in which natural forces would act to compel proper economic behavior.

One set of prescriptions was concerned primarily with new ways to obtain the spending decisions that were necessary for renewed growth and fuller utilization of economic resources. Here the main line of development came directly from the economics of William T. Foster and Waddill Catchings as publicized by such groups as the Planned Prosperity League. When the depression deepened, Foster and Catchings began to sound like major prophets, with a growing body of converts in business, labor, welfare, and congressional circles; and by late 1931 their notion of a new sector of public spending used to offset destabilizing private decisions had become embodied in a wide variety of compensatory spending proposals. Public spending, geared to different needs from those recognized by the Hooverites and in theory financed so as to enhance price stability, was now emerging as a major alternative to Hooverian recovery policies. And not surprisingly, the theory that made it a means of recovery rather than an economic burden was seized upon by groups who saw needs to be met but were unable to secure funding from traditional sources. Welfare and relief workers, highway and other public works constructers, would-be subsidizers of industrial and railroad modernization, advocates of a larger and better equipped military, and spokesmen for commodity price supports were all developing arguments to show that the funding of their programs would foster general recovery.

As the "spending" challenge developed, a second major challenge was also taking shape, this one manifested in new "planning" proposals that rejected Hooverian formulations and called for stronger planning agencies, stronger sanctions against noncompliers, and stronger instruments for mobilizing participatory solidarity. Of these proposals the largest number still envisioned such planning as taking place only in particular industries or sectors. In essence they would utilize such new agencies and powers to deal with "sick" or "chaotic" areas, the argument being that restoring economic health and order to these areas would allow the economy as a whole to recover. But there were also proposals now for new planning systems that would embrace the whole national economy. Former war administrators, especially Bernard Baruch and William Gibbs McAdoo, were suggesting that recovery could be organized through a Peace Industries Board. Such liberal intellectuals as Stuart Chase, Charles A. Beard, and George Soule were publishing "national plans," schemes that, in general, would use a national planning board and cooperating functional syndicates to correct economic imbalances and put idle resources to work. And of greatest importance for the immediate future, the business movement for antitrust relaxation was now generating proposals for lending governmental power to a planning and welfare system administered through industrial cartels. By late 1931 the leaders of the Chamber of Commerce were pushing one plan of this sort; Gerard Swope and Owen D. Young of General Electric were pushing another; and those associated with the National Civic Federation had developed still others.

Paradoxically, though, while the events of 1931 propelled these "planning" and "spending" challenges to the fore, they also sparked a return to classical economic fundamentalism. For a number of economic and political leaders, the New Era and New Day deviations from this established wisdom became the explanation of why the depression had persisted and recovery had failed to come. And from those accepting this diagnosis came a third major challenge to Hooverian policy, one that manifested itself in proposals for unleashing or revitalizing natural market forces and allowing them to compel the kinds of behavior that would restore the economy to working order. In most of these the central prescription was for recovery through government shrinking, the argument being that cutbacks in the Hooverian state itself would broaden the area subject to market imperatives and thus enable these to do their restorative work. But there were also those who wished to use government to shrink the domains in which private institutional power served as a shield against market imperatives. A new group of antitrusters saw strengthened antitrust laws and expanded antitrust agencies as the answer, and a new group of antiunionists saw recovery coming through government-supported wage cuts and union busting.

In late 1931 the great majority of Americans remained committed to liberal and capitalist institutions. There was no political polarization of the kind occurring in Germany during this same period. Yet the number committed to the Hooverian version of a "new liberalism" was rapidly dwindling. In this sense what had once been the "center" was eroding. And as it did so, more and more of Hoover's energies were going into defensive or "containment" struggles similar to those he had once waged against the McNary-Haugenites, the Muscle Shoals "socialists," the Dawes budget cutters, and Daugherty's anti-trust division. Increasingly unable to make his system work, he still saw it as the fount of future progress and social well-being. And perhaps partly because the crisis of the system had now become a personal crisis, a problem whose resolution was necessary to continuing self-esteem, he remained determined to save his approach from the latest breeds of spenders, planners, and liquidationists.

A NEW SET OF PROGRAMS

Throughout the summer and fall of 1931 Hoover seemed to dread the coming of the new Congress. It was, he realized, likely to reflect the new challenges to his programs and philosophy. And as part of an effort to forestall or contain congressional initiatives, the Hoover

Administration opened campaigns to expose the "fallacies" in the new proposals and rechannel the demands for action into beneficial forms of planning, economizing, and reflating. The Commerce Department began a drive to expand orthodox associational activity and persuade business groups to steer clear of the "grandiose schemes" now being proposed. The President held a series of "economy conferences," intended to draw distinctions between desirable cutbacks and undesirable ones; and once it became clear that the National Credit Association could not restore confidence in the banking system and bring reflation through private credit expansion, the administration swung its support behind a new program of public-private cooperation in the credit field. As outlined in the President's message to the incoming Congress, this would involve a new federal lending institution similar to the War Finance Corporation, a new system of home loan discount banks, new lending powers for the Federal Reserve and Federal Land banks, and new measures to hold down the federal deficit and safeguard the gold standard.

As Hoover had expected, the challenges to his version of a "new liberalism" quickly made themselves felt in the new Congress. The Senate Committee on Manufactures, under the chairmanship of Robert M. La Follette, Jr., promptly opened hearings on the new planning proposals. The farm, labor, veterans, and "government economy" blocs quickly pushed forward measures incompatible with the administration's recovery design. Bills calling for large-scale federal employment and relief programs were introduced and pushed forward by such legislators as Robert Wagner, Edward Costigan, and David Lewis; and a presidential veto finally became necessary to block a measure altering the powers of the Tariff Commission. Yet despite these displays of independence, Congress also proved willing to enact the legislation needed for the President's new credit program. In January 1932 it authorized the creation of the Reconstruction Finance Corporation (RFC), empowered to lend up to $2,000,000,000 to credit institutions and needy railroads. By February measures expanding the lending powers of the Farm Loan and Federal Reserve systems had also been passed. And in July, after several frustrating delays, a new system of discount banks for home mortgages came into existence.

Discarded along the way were several lending powers and banking reforms that the President had desired. But the final result was remarkably close to what he had recommended in late 1931.

Hoover also moved to obtain new forms of private cooperation and new legislation to offset gold drainages and quiet concerns about fiscal irresponsibility. Three supplements to the new credit measures were the Citizens' Reconstruction Organization, set up to conduct a campaign against hoarding; a Reconstruction Conference organizing a public-private division of railroad credits; and a new network of Banking and Industrial Committees, set up in each Federal Reserve district to promote credit expansion. Another was the Glass-Steagall Act of February 1932, authorizing the use of government securities as backing for Federal Reserve notes and thereby countering the credit contraction caused by gold withdrawals. Others, all enacted by June 1932, were a surplus disposal law, authorizing Farm Board surpluses to be turned over to the Red Cross for distribution to the needy; a Revenue Act intended to increase federal revenues and thus quiet fears about the soundness of government credit; and an Economy Act cutting federal salaries and services and authorizing administrative reorganization.

Still, as enacted and implemented, the new Hoover program seemed to have no greater success in bringing recovery than similar programs had achieved in 1930 and 1931. New government loans and purchases were made, but these were used primarily to enhance the liquidity of the borrowers and to build up excess banking reserves, not to release new flows of private credit and put them to work. Private lenders were reluctant to lend and borrowers to borrow. And while Hoover blamed most of this on congressional perversity and rebelliousness, this was not the view of his critics. As they saw it, the fault lay with his continued reliance upon private groups to implement public policy, his acceptance of a diagnosis that missed the system's crucial structural defects, and his perverse belief that raising taxes would somehow stimulate more private spending.

Any real answer, the critics insisted, must involve a rejection of the Hooverian formulas themselves; and for some of them, the only new measures of any real value were those that Congress had pushed upon a reluctant president. They thought it fortunate, for example, that a congressional rebellion led by Congressman Fiorella La Guardia had been able to block the passage of a federal sales tax and thus prevent the Revenue Act from doing even more damage. They were pleased when Congress insisted upon retaining a veto over administrative reorganization. And they looked upon the Norris–La Guardia Labor Relations Act of March 1932, a measure that Hoover signed with some reluctance, as being one of the few truly "progressive" measures since Woodrow Wilson's administration. Under it labor unions gained further immunity from the antitrust laws, and court injunctions could no longer be used to enforce antiunion employment contracts or to prevent strikes, boycotts, and peaceful picketing.

Despite the new programs, then, Hoover's support continued to erode. In business, labor, and farm circles the idea of compulsory "planning" through corporative institutions kept gaining new adherents. By June of 1932 there were vigorous movements for state-supported industrial proration, state-imposed agricultural allotments, state-enforced wage and hour fixing, and state-developed agencies of coordination. Especially prominent was a movement through which former war administrators, supported by industrial groups and the American Legion, were urging a new "economic government" to be formed through a revitalized Council of National Defense. And while these movements attacked Hooverism from one quarter, those for market restoration and compensatory spending were also becoming stronger. The former was unsatisfied with the Economy Act, and the latter had now brought forth two major challenges to the President's definitions of sound and desirable federal expenditures.

One of these, on the verge of passage by late June, was the Garner-Wagner relief bill, a measure calling not only for emergency RFC credits to state and local governments (as Hoover was now advocating) but also for a new $2,000,000,000 federal works and loans program. The other was Wright Patman's bonus bill, calling for maturity-value redemption of the World War bonus certificates with the money to be raised through the issuance of $2,400,000,000 in greenbacks. After gaining House approval on June 15, this had stalled in the Senate. But gathered in Washington now was a "bonus army" of nearly 20,000 veterans, disappointed by the Senate's action but determined, so its leaders said, to force reconsideration. Unless something intervened, the steamy Washington summer promised to be hot in more ways than one.

RESPONSES TO INTERNATIONAL DISORDER

By mid-1932 it had also become increasingly clear that Hoover's hopes for the international arena were unlikely to be realized. In February, to be sure, a world disarmament conference had finally convened in Geneva, and in its proposals of April 11 and June 22 the United States had urged the outlawing of certain offensive weapons and a flat one-third reduction in all military forces. But the Hoover Administration was not receptive to French proposals for substituting an international police force and collective security guarantees, and the Allied powers were loath to concede the arms equality now demanded by the Germans. Given these differences, no agreement seemed possible, and a subsequent German decision to withdraw from participation, announced on August 31, would make the outlook even bleaker.

Disarmament seemed inappropriate, moreover, at a time when Japanese imperialism was reasserting itself in the Far East. There, in September 1931, the Japanese army in Manchuria had manufactured a suitable incident along the Japanese-owned South Manchurian Railway, blamed this on the Chinese, and proceeded to seize Mukden and several other Manchurian cities. For a time the moderate elements in Japan had resisted further military commitments. But in December a reorganized government under Premier Inukai had decided to occupy all of Manchuria, and by early 1932 this had been completed and a new puppet government had been installed there. The Japanese militarists, moreover, were in no mood to brook retaliations against their actions. Their response to Chinese economic warfare was to occupy the city of Shanghai and hold it until the boycott had been lifted. And while they were unable to prevent a League of Nations investigation, their eventual reaction to a report branding them as "aggressors" was to withdraw from the League. Their conquest of Manchuria stood as a major and, as it turned out, irreparable breach in the Versailles system.

The conquest also constituted a major breach in the Washington Conference system and in the moral commitments created by the Kellogg-Briand Pact. This the Hoover Administration realized, and in early 1932, through an enunciation of what became known as the Stimson Doctrine, it tried to invoke the moral sanctions that were supposed to repair such a breach. On January 7 the Secretary of State informed Japan and China that the United States would never recognize any changes in the area that were brought about in violation of the principles set forth in the Nine Power Treaty and the Kellogg-Briand Pact. Subsequently the United States also cooperated with the League investigators and threatened to reconsider its pledges not to fortify its outlying island possessions in the Western Pacific. But none of this seemed to have much effect on Japanese behavior, and the President was opposed to and quickly repudiated the idea of threatening economic sanctions. Such an action, he feared, would only strengthen the Japanese militarists and bring the kind of confrontation from which the United States stood to lose much more than it could gain. It was not the way to bring the Japanese moderates back to power, the goal for which the United States should be working. And to the dismay of Secretary Stimson, Hoover required a public announcement that no such sanctions would be used.

Even if the President had favored stronger actions, moreover, it seems doubtful that he could have mobilized the political and public support needed to undertake them. Public opinion at the time attached little value to the maintenance of the "open door" or the preservation of China's territorial integrity, and many Americans now were in favor of liquidating American holdings and commitments in the Far East rather than expanding them. As economic conditions had worsened, the movement for giving the Philippine Islands their independence had picked up strong support from those who wanted to exclude Filipino products and immigrants. Such support had pushed a Filipino independence bill, complete with severe trade and immigration restrictions, through the House of Representatives; and as of mid-1932 it was becoming increasingly doubtful that administration opposition, even if it came to a presidential veto, could keep such a measure from becoming law.

In Latin America the Hoover Administration faced no crisis comparable to that in the Far East. And despite further debt repudiations and political upheavals in the region, it stuck by its pledges of nonintervention, its refusal to serve as debt collector for private creditors, and its program for gradually liquidating the Haitian occupation. The only displays of military force were limited to upholding the settlement in Nicaragua and providing coastal protection for Americans in Honduras, and the nonrecognition weapon was used only in Central America and against a semisocialist regime in Chile. Yet this kind of "good neighborism" did nothing to halt the further collapse of the economic structure that had been erected during the 1920s. The Hoover Administration gave no support to those urging a debt moratorium or standstill agreement for Latin America; and it remained firmly opposed to the kinds of trade concessions, investment guarantees, and special aid programs that would-be revivers of a Pan-American economic community now believed necessary to halt the contraction.

Similar efforts to refloat the European economic structure of the 1920s also seemed doomed now. The agreements of 1931 had not brought German recovery. On the contrary, German efforts to stay on the gold standard after Britain left it had produced more deflation and higher unemployment rates, accompanied by increasing disorder and violent clashes between political extremists. Meeting with German representatives at Lausanne, Switzerland, in June of 1932, the Allied powers finally agreed to cancel most of the reparations provided a satisfactory agreement could be reached on the war debts owed to the United States. But the Hoover Administration was having none of this. While Stimson was sympathetic, the President was unwilling to go beyond a possible reapplication of the "capacity to pay" formula to each individual country. And even if authorizing legislation for such negotiations could be secured, they seemed unlikely to provide any substitute for the outflow of American capital that had sustained the system of the 1920s.

The chief ray of hope in the international economic picture of mid-1932 was the plans being made for a world monetary and economic conference. The British had agreed to be the hosts, and the President and his advisers hoped that the conference would find some way to reestablish a prosperous, peaceful, and progressive world order. But this was in the future. The more immediate concerns in the summer of 1932 were with the impact of continuing distress on the domestic situation.

THE SUMMER OF 1932

Economically the summer of 1932 brought slight upturns. But politically it was a time of continuing failure for the Hoover Administration. In its battles against federal relief, its handling of the "bonus army," and its efforts to deflate the pressures for compulsory planning and cartelization, it took actions and positions that further eroded its political base and strengthened its opponents.

The relief issue came to a head on July 9, when Congress ignored administration warnings and proceeded to pass a modified version of the Garner-Wagner relief bill. Two days later the President responded with a stinging veto message. Such a measure, he declared, would put the government into business in such a way as to violate the very principles upon which the nation had been founded. And when it became clear that the veto could not be overridden, the sponsors of the measure agreed to settle for what the President would allow. As finally approved on July 21, the Emergency Relief and Construction Act authorized the RFC to lend up to $300,000,000 to needy states, the money to be repaid by reducing appropriations for federal-aid highways. In addition, the agency could lend up to $1,500,000,000 for self-liquidating public works, and it was now required to report all its loans to Congress. The latter was a provision strongly opposed by the administration, but the President finally accepted it when congressional leaders promised to keep the information confidential.

In one sense Hoover had been victorious. The new legislation was essentially of the kind that he had proposed in May, and RFC control meant that "need" and "self-liquidating" would not be loosely defined. But in terms of his political future the struggle had been costly. During it his opponents had depicted him as hardhearted and callous, talking about "moral fiber" and "social principles" at a time when millions were without basic necessities, and therefore thoroughly fraudulent in his pose as a "great humanitarian." Even more damaging politically, they established him in the public mind as a social reactionary defending a "trickle-down approach" that allowed government aid only for bankers, railroad owners, and other millionaires. For many Americans he had now become a tool of entrenched wealth and privilege rather than a builder and manager of socially progressive institutions.

What was true of the relief debate, moreover, was even more true of administration policy during the "bonus riot" of July 28, 1932. Anxious to get the "bonuseers" out of Washington, the administration had secured legislation under which they could borrow money to pay for their transportation back home. But when approximately 8000 of them still refused to leave, it also decided to press matters by evicting them from federal properties along Pennsylvania Avenue. The result, on the afternoon of July 28, was violence in which two of the veterans were killed; and, acceding to a request from the District of Columbia Commissioners, the President decided to use the troops being held in readiness. Under the command of General Douglas MacArthur, a specially trained riot force of about 550 men entered the area, used tear gas, bayonets, and cavalry charges to clear it, and as of 9:00 P.M. appeared to be carrying out its orders to force all rioters into the camp at Anacostia Flats and take such actions as were necessary to identify and arrest those responsible for the rioting. At this stage, however, General MacArthur decided to take matters into his own hands. Convinced that the "bonus army" had now become a radicalized insurrectionary force, he authorized operations that routed the veterans out of Anacostia and finished burning those hovels that they had left standing. By morning the "bonus army" had been reduced to a jumble of ragged and confused groups wandering through the streets of the District and seeking any means of leaving.

The President was not pleased with MacArthur's actions. But after meeting with the general and with Secretary of War Patrick Hurley, he too became convinced that the "bonus army" had been a dangerous group increasingly controlled by Communists and criminals. His decision was to defend MacArthur's actions rather than repudiate them, and not surprisingly a subsequent investigation did its best to document the allegedly subversive character of the "bonuseers." The public, however, was not much impressed with the flimsy and contrived evidence that was offered, and the outcome of the investigation was a strengthening of the belief that Hoover was insensitive, vindictive, and paranoiac. To the image of harshness and reaction was now added that of a man who had turned the nation's arms against the very people who had saved it twelve years earlier.

Meanwhile, during the same period that the relief and bonus issues were coming to a head, the President was also planning an operation that might simultaneously promote recovery and deflate the pressures for compulsory planning and cartelization. It was to take the form of another great voluntary effort, built primarily around the new Banking and Industrial Committees in the Federal Reserve districts but calling as well for new agencies to spread work, stimulate capital expenditures, and cope with disorderly markets. In addition, the relief and welfare agencies were to be mobilized again; and farm distress, which was now generating threats of "farm strikes" and mob action against foreclosing judges, was to be relieved through new agricultural credit associations and mortgage relief conferences. In August and September much of this new plan was put into effect, at least on paper. At conferences in Washington and Chicago the new agencies were created and a new framework provided for what Hoover called "coordinated effort on the economic front." The nation, so he told the conferees, had now won its economic "battle of Château-Thierry." It had brought its financial structure "safely through the world-wide collapse." But it must now re-form for its economic "battle of Soissons."

War metaphors or not, recovery still did not come. On the contrary, late September brought another economic downturn, one that Hoover attributed to fears of what might happen in the coming elections, but one that his critics quickly associated with his new recovery framework and the evidence thus provided that he was still clinging to a discredited and unworkable approach. Nor was he able to deflate the movements for compulsory planning and cartelization, whose advocates could now point to the new failures as further evidence that obstructive and shortsighted elements must be forced into line. Ironically, some segments of this latest administrative framework would become vehicles for promoting the kind of politically enforced coordination that the administration had hoped to block.

As the summer of 1932 ended, the Hooverites still had hopes of carrying their designs for a "new liberalism" safely through the economic storm and making them the basis of a new era of economic growth and social progress. But that they could do so had now become increasingly dubious. The world-wide collapse of 1931, the failure of the new programs of late 1931 and early 1932 to work as expected, and the seeming impotence of the latest set of recovery agencies had continued to undermine the credibility of Hooverian formulas and lend credence to charges that they were formulas for permanent depression rather than perpetual prosperity. In the political arena anti-Hooverism had now become a potent force, fed by frustrated expectations, the need for a national scapegoat, and the negative images emerging from the relief debates, the "bonus riot" episode, and the controversies over prohibition and southern party reform. Along the economic policy front, the lines that the Hoover Administration was still holding against the new spending, planning, and market restoration movements had become perilously thin. The era of "Hooverism at bay" seemed about to give way to an era in which alternative formulations of a "new liberalism" could no longer be contained and would become the paths along which the continued search for a new institutional order and effective mechanisms of organizational coordination would proceed.

CHAPTER 12

From Hooverism to the New Deal, 1932–1933

Viewing each other across the transfer of power in 1933, the Hooverites and the New Dealers tended to see much greater differences than recent historical scholarship has been able to discern. The Hooverites, it now seems clear, were not the laissez-faire fundamentalists excoriated in New Deal rhetoric. Nor were the New Dealers the collectivizing anticapitalists depicted in Hooverian oratory. On the contrary, both are best seen as seekers of a managed capitalist order committed to the realization of traditional liberal ideals. Both drew much of their inspiration from the organizational experience of the war period. And the early New Dealers, at least, were remarkably similar to the Hooverites in their willingness to work through private orders and established organizational elites, their efforts to achieve coordination through concerts of organized interests, and their belief that unbalanced budgets were impediments to recovery rather than ways of promoting it. Far from being an application of socialist theory or radical redistributionism, much of the early New Deal might more aptly be labeled "Hooverism in high gear."

Nevertheless, within the broader story of America's continuing search for liberal ordering mechanisms, the transfer of power in 1933 stands as a major watershed. It marked the end of efforts to implement a "new liberalism" that in theory could allow Americans to meet modern needs without developing a welfare and regulatory state. It removed the barriers against the kind of government-backed cartelization, public works spending, and dismantling of the Hooverian state that the outgoing administration had strongly resisted. And it brought to power a group of leaders who were less committed to a particular set of ordering mechanisms, were inclined to believe that statist bureaucracies could be effective tools for meeting certain social needs, and were more open than the Hooverites to pressures from insurgent groups and antiestablishment critics. In the realm of public psychology, moreover, as distinct from public policy, the watershed was even greater—a fact that may explain the persisting myths that quickly grew up around it. On one side of the dividing line, as much of the American public perceived it, stood a demoralized society rejecting a discredited leader, a man who had been exposed now as cold, uncaring, doctrinaire, and incapable of acting against those responsible for popular distress. On the other side, again as widely perceived, stood a reinvigorated society infused with optimistic activism and responding to a new and dynamic leader, a man of warmth, vitality, immense political skill, and an almost magical capacity to ferret out and foil the enemies of the people.

In part, then, the history of the American nation from September 1932 to March 1933 is a story of heritages bequeathed across a political and rhetorical divide. In part it is a story of public policy breaking into new paths and embracing new instruments. And in part it is a story of a society under stress looking for scapegoats and saviors and inclined to accept perceptions of the period that provided them. Each of these deserves careful scrutiny, and it is to this story of a troubled, myth-shrouded, and multidimensional transition that we now turn.

ELECTION AND INTERREGNUM

For Herbert Hoover and his supporters the month of September 1932 was one of shattered hopes and mounting frustrations. At the Republican convention, meeting in Chicago on June 14, they had encountered no serious challenges. The President and Vice-President were easily renominated; and through August there were still hopes that the new recovery organizations, coupled with concessions to the antiprohibitionists, could somehow turn their political fortunes around. But September brought new economic downturns and the full backlash of the relief debate and the "bonus army" episode. It also brought Democratic victories in traditionally Republican Maine, an indication of how low Republican fortunes had now fallen. From September on, Republican oratory was largely reduced to claims that the Hoover Administration had done all that was humanly possible to fight the depression and warnings that a Democratic victory would delay sound recovery and imperil future progress. His actions, the President claimed, had saved the country "from a quarter of a century of chaos and degeneration." But those who believed this to be the case were now a dwindling and dispirited band. Many more saw him as the apostle of what his political opponents were calling the four Ds, "Destruction, Delay, Deceit, and Despair."

It was clear, moreover, that the Democrats had now found a leader who could unite their party and allow it to take full advantage of the anti-Hooverism that pervaded the political scene. Triumphant in the gubernatorial contests of 1928 and 1930, Franklin D. Roosevelt of New York had emerged as the man capable of fusing Smith's new urban Democracy with the old Wilsonian coalition. He had gathered about him a group of astute political managers and articulate intellectuals; and at Chicago, where the Democrats met on June 27, a "stop Roosevelt" movement had been of no avail. On the contrary, House Speaker John N. Garner had quickly swung his delegates over to Roosevelt's support, thus giving the latter the nomination on the fourth ballot. And following Garner's nomination for Vice-President, Roosevelt had decided to break with tradition and deliver his acceptance speech at the convention. Speaking there on July 2, in an atmosphere of buoyancy and excitement that contrasted sharply with the mood at the earlier Republican proceedings, he had pledged himself and his party to "a new deal for the American people."

To the political columnist Walter Lippmann, the Democratic candidate was essentially a "nice young man who would like very much to be President." But as the campaign unfolded in 1932, it offered an early illustration of the appeals and strategies that would enable Roosevelt to remain in the White House until his death in 1945. One element was the forging of bonds and rapport with the masses, a mixture here of antiestablishment appeals to the "forgotten man" with a charismatic radiation of warmth, confidence, compassion, and energy, the latter despite the crippled legs that were a product of his 1921 bout with polio. A second was the invocation of a political demonology, in this case the Hooverites and the other architects of disaster and injustice that they were allegedly protecting. And a third was the accommodation or balancing of conflicting prescriptions and pressures for change. In speeches addressed to each of the anti-Hoover groups, Roosevelt mixed denunciations of the Republican tariff with calls for greater economic nationalism; condemnation of the Hooverites for centering "control of everything in Washington" with talk of a new industrial and agricultural planning; and biting criticism of Hooverian extravagances and deficits with proposals for greater relief and works expenditures.

Long before election day it was clear that Roosevelt would win. On occasion, notably in Des Moines and at Madison Square Garden, Hoover spoke with force and feeling and was well received. But often the crowds were cold or hostile. And when the votes were counted, the man who had once promised a New Day for the American people was turned out even more decisively than he had beaten Smith in 1928. In the popular column Roosevelt received 27,821,857 votes to 15,761,841 for Hoover and 884,781 for Norman Thomas, the Socialist candidate. In the electoral college Hoover carried only four of the New England states plus Pennsylvania and Delaware, for a total of 59 electoral votes to Roosevelt's 472. Nor did Republican congressional candidates fare much better. In the Senate the Republican contingent was reduced to 36 and in the House of Representatives to only 117. Seen in perspective, the election was another major milestone in the reduction of the Republican party to minority status and the emergence of the Democrats as the nation's normal majority party. The potential for the Roosevelt coalition had now appeared.

In his message to the lame-duck Congress in December 1932, the defeated President outlined another legislative program that would allegedly assist in getting recovery started again. He urged, in particular, new economy and budget balancing measures, a new commission to renegotiate the inter-Allied war debts, a liberalization of the branch banking and bankruptcy laws, and speedy ratification of a Canadian-American treaty calling for joint development of a St. Lawrence Seaway. Subsequently the administration also gave serious consideration to a land-withdrawal program for agriculture and to concerted reemployment plans underwritten by federal credit. But in Congress attention was focused on the President-elect and his plans for action. Of the administration measures, only the bankruptcy reform bill was enacted into law. And of the measures that emerged from congressional initiatives, the only one to get past a presidential veto was a Philippine Independence Act with features so harsh that the Filipinos themselves subsequently rejected the offer. In addition, this last session of the Seventy-second Congress completed action on a proposal to repeal the Prohibition Amendment. Submitted to the states on February 20, 1933, it would be quickly ratified and would take effect before the year ended.

The legislative stalemate at the time was accompanied by a stalemate in international negotiations. There the President's hopes were now tied to the projected world economic conference and to his plans for negotiating new debt settlements in accordance with the "capacity to pay" principle. But efforts to secure Roosevelt's cooperation in implementing this approach were to no avail. Planning for the world conference remained in abeyance. Legislation for a debt commission remained bogged down in Congress. And by March of 1933, two developments abroad had virtually insured that neither the world economic conference nor the reconvened world disarmament conference would find ways to reestablish the kind of liberal international order that Hoover envisioned. One was the decision of the French and other nations following the French lead to default on their war debts and run the risk of whatever retaliatory action the United States might take. The other was the emergence of Adolf Hitler, head of the National Socialist or Nazi party, as Germany's national leader. On January 30 he had assumed the chancellorship, and by late March the Nazi dictatorship was firmly established.

As the international situation deteriorated, the new wave of economic contraction was now bringing down those portions of the banking system that the Reconstruction Finance Corporation had saved in late 1931 and early 1932. A foretaste of what was in store had come during the week before the election, when the governor of Nevada declared a banking holiday to avert the failure of an important chain of banks in his state. But the acute phase of the crisis began in mid-February of 1933, when presidential and RFC efforts to arrange new loans for a banking group in Detroit ended in failure. On February 14 the governor of Michigan declared a banking holiday; and the next two weeks brought a spreading panic, manifested in extensive bank runs, the withdrawal and hoarding of gold, and new measures either declaring holidays or limiting withdrawals. Also contributing to a further loss of confidence in the system were the revelations made at hearings conducted by the Senate Banking and Currency Committee. There some of the most notable banking figures of the 1920s were now confessing to malpractices that, in the lame-duck President's words to his Attorney General, had been far more injurious to the American system than "all the followers of Karl Marx" and "all the incidental operations of Al Capone." By the end of February popular confidence was on the verge of complete collapse, and during the first two days of March so many states joined the bank holiday parade that a general closing seemed all but inevitable.

For Hoover the principal factor behind the deepening crisis was fear of the unsound monetary policies that the new Democratic administration might adopt. This was more important, he seemed to think, than the growing public distrust of bankers and their institutions. Aside from efforts to restore secrecy for RFC loans, his principal attempt to curb the panic took the form of a plea to the President-elect urging that he commit himself to balancing the budget and maintaining the gold standard. Roosevelt, however, was in no mood to cooperate, particularly when the plea came in the form of a thinly veiled accusation that his election was responsible for the crisis. After a perplexing delay, attributed in the response to a "secretary's oversight," he replied that no mere statement could counteract the real trouble. There would be no joint action, and without this Hoover felt that it would be "futile to present anything else."

As the date for Roosevelt's inaugural neared, the deepening crisis seemed destined to leave the country without a functioning monetary system. Under consideration now, both at the White House and by Federal Reserve authorities, were plans for limited deposit guarantees, embargoes on gold withdrawals, issuance of a special scrip, and national closing actions. But disagreements over what should be done, doubts about the power to act, and the President's refusal to act without Roosevelt's formal endorsement prevented any of the plans from being implemented. On Hoover's last night in office the governors of New York and Illinois declared banking holidays. Their actions meant that banks now were either closed or doing business under severe restrictions in nearly every state of the union. And it was against this somber backdrop of impending crisis and economic paralysis that the transfer of power took place. Had the New Dealers planned it that way (and Hoover suspected that they had), they could hardly have arranged a more damning exit for those they had defeated at the polls four months earlier.

AMERICAN SOCIETY IN THE THIRD DEPRESSION WINTER

As the banking system collapsed, the accompanying contraction in economic output and markets also subjected other kinds of institutions to increasingly severe strains. By February of 1933 the ranks of the unemployed had swelled to nearly thirteen million. Savings and credit for those without work or on short hours had been virtually exhausted. And while the new federal relief loans were at last beginning to produce new state relief organizations, their impact was insufficient to compensate for the accelerating collapse of corporate welfare programs, municipal relief systems, and private charity organizations. Social workers in this third winter of extensive unemployment reported increasing misery, malnutrition, and demoralization. Journalists did stories on the new migrants and vagabonds and on the spreading shantytowns that the American public had labeled "Hoovervilles"; while social statistics and surveys told stories of decreasing family formation and new strains in family relations, drastic declines in educational enrollments and expenditures, and increasingly straitened circumstances for churches, health delivery systems, and cultural programs.

There were also expressions of fear that revolution or anarchy might be in the making. These were particularly common in pleas for federal aid or proposals for new welfare services. Yet when pressed on the matter, most of those expressing such fears would concede that the potential anarchists and revolutionaries were still remarkably loyal and docile. More often than not, it seemed, unemployment led to feelings of apathy or personal inadequacy rather than to anger and alienation. At work, too, was a kind of siege mentality that helped to maintain loyalty to established institutions and to make privations more endurable. And reducing disorder and the potential for radicalization still further was what proved to be an amazing capacity of the American social order to cope with the situation by reverting to more primitive forms of economic and social organization.

This reversion, by the third winter of the depression, was apparent in a variety of phenomena. Women and young people were moving back to the home and back to various kinds of household production. Recent migrants to the cities were moving back to the land and the villages. Agriculture seemed to be reverting from highly specialized commerical production back toward its subsistence phase. And unable to find slots in the modern organizational economy, men and women were entering entrepreneurship at the lowest and least rewarding levels. Especially noticeable was the proliferation of hole-in-the-wall shops, street peddlers, and what sophisticated observers called "Mama, Papa, and Rosie" stores. All of this, moreover, was eased by a resurgence of antimodernism that regarded such developments as making for a healthier and more desirable society rather than as indications of social regression or decay. Building on the antimodernism that had persisted during the 1920s, a new set of moral philosophers were telling Americans that the anwer to their present difficulties lay in casting out the false gods of the New Era and returning to simpler and more wholesome forms of social organization.

Even under the conditions of early 1933, then, American society remained remarkably resistant to radicalization. There were, to be sure, outbreaks of violence, the most celebrated incidents being near-lynchings of foreclosing judges and mob seizures of public buildings and food stores. There was also some growth of militant organizations, of such groups, for example, as the Khaki Shirts, the Farm Holiday Association, and Communist-influenced labor unions. But violence and militance were remarkably limited and tended, for the most part, to resemble frontier or community vigilanteism rather than revolutionary action. And what reporters and analysts were calling a "new radicalism" tended to be much more of an intellectual rather than a mass phenomenon. Its principal manifestations were not in mass-based political movements or a mass-supported set of alternative social institutions but rather in new works by Marxist, syndicalist, and fascist theoreticians, in the beginnings of a proletarian literature allegedly arising out of social realities, and in a brief reflowering of the technocratic designs that had first blossomed in the immediate postwar period. The latter were now emanating from a group called Technocracy, under the direction of Howard Scott, the eccentric engineer who had helped to form the Technical Alliance back in 1920. And for a few months, in late 1932 and early 1933, the nation's newspapers carried lengthy discussions of the group's energy surveys, its plans for a new money based on units of energy, and its visions of an economic utopia run by technicians and engineers.

Popular literature and drama, moreover, had remained largely divorced from such radicalization as had occurred in intellectual circles. Curiously, the proletarian works that were supposed to mobilize the masses for action against their enemies seemed to have little mass appeal, and their relative failure left the field to works that tended to enhance rather than reduce the resistance to radicalization. Escape valves for mass anxieties and frustrations remained open, particularly in a plethora of romances, comedies, melodramas, and tales of the bizarre. Consolation remained available in the form of packaged dreams and fantasies or surrogate heroes and lovers. And with the gangster and horror films that dominated popular cinema at the time came both a set of safety valves for antisocial impulses and a set of moral warnings against tampering with established traditions and institutions.

A society resistant to radicalization, however, did not mean a society totally immobilized by safety valves, antimodernist moral philosophies, fatalistic apathy, or the willingness to do penance for its sins. If there was little support for revolutionary action and little response to radical social vision, there was much disillusionment with Hooverian prescriptions and congressional stalemates and hence a disposition to support those segments of the economic and political establishment that proposed to try something different and to expedite this with emergency executive powers. Limited change, in other words, could proceed along the paths outlined by the heirs of McNary-Haugenism, the movement for antitrust revision and business planning, the agitation for compensatory spending and federal welfare supplements, and the spokesmen for utilities, tariff, and monetary reform. In each case energy was mobilized and ready to exploit the collapse of Hooverian barriers and use public and private power in ways previously proscribed. This was energy that the President-elect was preparing to release. And many Americans were disposed to applaud this release and to believe that the man they had elected to the presidency would somehow prove capable of coordinating the conflicting streams of energy, harnessing them to the attainment of national purposes, and correcting any abuses of power that might develop.

What was true of the masses was also true of many of the nation's intellectuals. Convinced now that the depression had opened the way to cultural transformation, they were looking for transforming tools, instruments through which they could supply the new values and insights around which American life could be reintegrated and given meaning and purpose. Potentially, they believed, disillusionment with the New Era could become the basis for a society in which fragmentation would be a passing condition and intellectuals would reassume their rightful place as the creators and defenders of integrating values. And although a considerable number embraced radical political movements as the tools through which these ends were to be achieved, a much larger group looked to the elevation of a powerful national leader who would help to restore intellectuals to their rightful place and would so channel economic and political forces as to further the process of cultural transformation. For some the hopes once invested in Theodore Roosevelt and Woodrow Wilson were now being attached to the incoming President and his much publicized Brains Trust of intellectual advisers and academic experts. For a smaller group he was becoming the embodiment of a new politics capable of achieving ends that were once unrealizable through political tools. And for a few he had become the instrument that Hoover should have been had not the latter been incapacitated by ideological blinders.

THE WATERSHED OF 1933

Meanwhile, as much of the nation invested its hopes in the coming transfer of presidential power, Roosevelt was putting together a cabinet and choosing other advisers and administrators. The first appointments announced were Senator Thomas J. Walsh of Montana for Attorney General and Cordell Hull for Secretary of State. The next was William Woodin, a Republican manufacturer who had contributed generously to Roosevelt's campaign fund, for Secretary of the Treasury; this came after Senator Carter Glass had turned down the post. And following this was the choice of two Republican progressives, Henry A. Wallace for Agriculture and Harold L. Ickes for Interior; the selection of an old Wilson-McAdoo man, Dan Roper, for Secretary of Commerce; and an appointment symbolizing commitment to social welfare and the advancing position of women, that of Frances Perkins for Secretary of Labor. Also decided by March 4 were the positions in which key members of the campaign Brains Trust were to stay on and help to launch the New Deal. Raymond Moley was to be Assistant Secretary of State and Rexford G. Tugwell to serve as Assistant Secretary of Agriculture.

While these appointments were being made, the Roosevelt people were also conferring with and making commitments to the segments of the economic and political establishment that had been pushing for new uses of public and private power. At a series of conferences with representatives of organized agriculture it had become clear that federal agencies were likely to be given large grants of power that could be used either to engage in direct price and production control or to reinforce private activities of this sort. At other conferences there was receptivity to the ideas of federal relief grants, compensatory public works spending, monetary reflation, and some form of wage-and-hour control. At still others it became clear that campaign pledges in regard to new conservation programs, securities regulation, and public development of hydroelectric power were likely to be fulfilled. And forging ties with the incoming Roosevelt Administration were the business officials and former war administrators who wanted to suspend the antitrust laws, transform business associations into government-backed cartels, and use the latter as instruments of economic recovery. In late 1932 and early 1933 this movement had achieved greater unity, and it was now putting forth arguments as to why its envisioned cartels were the instruments that should be used to bring about reemployment and restore mass purchasing power.

During the immediate preinaugural period, however, it was the banking situation that received the most attention. And on this the key development was neither linkages to demands for change in the banking community nor ties to the bank reform initiatives in Congress. It was rather a working association between Roosevelt's appointees and such outgoing Treasury officials as Ogden Mills, Arthur Ballantine, and F. Gloyd Awalt. This was an association that bridged the two administrations; and it was the Hoover men who supplied most of the recommendations that were incorporated in Roosevelt's plan of action and in the Emergency Banking Act that passed Congress on March 9. Hoover was basically incapable of dramatizing the situation and restoring public confidence in the way that Roosevelt would do. But the New Deal's first major piece of banking legislation, especially the scheme under which sound banks would be reopened, was shaped by the same general perspective that had produced the financial legislation of 1932.

There were also other strands of continuity. The distribution of relief and credit, for example, remained mostly in the hands of the same local agencies that had formed the base of the Hooverian administrative network. The new schemes for agricultural and industrial controls, as embodied in the Agricultural Adjustment and National Industrial Recovery acts, were to work through the same private or quasi-private bureaucracies that had been entrusted with implementing Hoover's farm and industrial programs. The purposes of the Economy Act of March 20, 1933, were difficult to distinguish from those of the Economy Act of June 1932. And beyond these individual strands of continuity, there was a broad identity of view as to ultimate goals, technological imperatives, and the institutional gaps or vacuums that were in need of filling. There were some in the new administration who saw its programs as the route to a new kind of collectivist democracy or to the realization of a socialist or syndicalist commonwealth. But they were far outweighed by those who saw them as the route to realizing the kind of America that Hoover had visualized in his New Day speeches of 1928.

The basic difference between the Hooverian system and that emerging from the New Deal measures of 1933 lay in the latter's acceptance of a larger public sector and of a public obligation to enforce privately developed regulations found to be in the public interest. Involved were forms of public enterprise, federal welfare activities, and delegations of federal power that Hoover had continued to regard as incompatible with the maintenance of a liberal order. And involved as well was a rejection of the view that America could find ways of meeting modern needs without developing a welfare and regulatory state. Yet these innovations, too, important as they were, could easily be magnified beyond their real dimensions. Much of the New Deal state was initially conceived of as an emergency government, resembling the emergency structures with which the Hooverites were willing to fight wars, cope with natural disasters, and ward off blows from abroad. And much that was not regarded as temporary was conceived of as being supplementary to private and local programs. To a considerable degree the differences lay in divergent definitions of what constituted an emergency or a necessary supplement rather than in divergent theories of what constituted a liberal polity.

Still, the opening of 1933 was significant for the subsequent development of a federal welfare bureaucracy, a new structure of mass-production unions, a farm program applying cartel principles, and a budgetary policy geared to macroeconomic stabilization. Through it would eventually come the New Deal measures of 1935 to 1938, which did constitute a greater departure from the Hooverian conceptions of a liberal polity. And in the public consciousness it would remain one of the great departures of twentieth-century American history. There the lines of continuity were largely obscured by the contrasting personalities and public images of the two Presidents, by the contrast between the frenetic activism of Roosevelt's Hundred Days and the stalemates of early 1933, and by political oratory that stressed Hoover's "do-nothingism" and Roosevelt's "radicalism."

Thoroughly imbedded in the public consciousness, too, were the images of an inaugural ceremony that seemed to symbolize the passing of an old order and the dawning of a new. As countless journalists and historians would write, March 4, 1933, was a drear and gloomy day, suited, it seemed, to a nation whose financial and economic machinery had come to a virtual standstill and whose outgoing President sat cheerless and immobile like the doomed figure in a Greek tragedy. Then the overcast seemed to break. A new national figure, standing in heavy braces yet exuding energy, confidence, and hope, was ready to turn crisis into challenge. He would banish paralyzing fear, restore the temple of civilization to "social values more noble than mere monetary profit," and seek "broad executive power to wage a war against the emergency." Nor was he ready to accept the constitutional arguments that some opponents of expanded government were now falling back on. "Our Constitution is so simple and practical," he declared, "that it is possible always to meet extraordinary needs by changes in emphasis and arrangement without loss of essential form." In reality the nation had a new crisis manager rather than a leader committed to building a new order; and essentially the crisis was not one of classical capitalism but of the new economic system spawned by the organizational revolution and the institution building of the 1920s. But public psychology was inclined to make the watershed far more pronounced than these realities warranted.

THE HERITAGE OF A SEARCH THAT FAILED

In many respects the central story of the American experience from 1917 to 1933 is the story of a search that failed. It is a story of men deeply influenced by the organizational experience of a democracy at war and seeking, against various obstacles, to draw from that experience a set of liberal ordering mechanisms capable of coordinating an expanding organizational economy and fostering peaceful progress in the social and international spheres. It was a search first manifested in the designs of Wilson and his reconstruction managers in the years from 1918 to 1920. But it did not end when the Wilsonians were ousted from power, not to appear again until the 1930s. A modified form of the search quickly reappeared during the years 1921 and 1922, a form now that held forth the vision of an associational order capable of meeting the needs for coordination and control without creating a welfare, regulatory, or military state. Its tools were to be associational, corporate, foundation, and private planning and welfare bureaucracies assisted by governmental adjuncts working to promote their proper development. And for a time the economic successes of the New Era, coupled with the relative lack of social and international disorder, made it appear that the goals of this vision were being realized. This was appearance, however, not reality. The new order, in so far as it did come into existence, was unable to keep the economy in balance or to overcome the forces that produced the "great contraction" of 1929 to 1933. Failure in the economic sphere subjected its international and social solutions to pressures they could not sustain. Finally, in 1933 the men who still held to this associational vision were removed from power and their places taken by men less resistant to statist coordination and support.

In one sense this search that failed ended up in a blind alley. Or perhaps, as the Hooverites might have put it, it was on a road beset with perils, from which those unwilling to endure temporary privations for the sake of future benefits impatiently turned aside. In any event, the kind of ordering mechanisms it was able to establish proved incapable of doing what had been promised in the time that the American people were willing to allow. Yet in another sense the building and testing of these mechanisms was an important link in the chain of events leading to the New Deal programs and the mechanisms they brought into being. It reflected and reinforced a growing abandonment of classical economic ideas and a growing belief that certain kinds of bureaucracies were necessary to make a modern economy function effectively. It provided a framework in which the ideology of scientific management moved out from the work place to embrace whole industries, whole systems of social activity, and national economic life as a whole. And although the failures of 1931 and 1932 did produce a considerable revival of classical laissez-faire fundamentalism, they also led to the view that other kinds of bureaucracies with different outlooks and more power could be successful. This view was substantially reinforced by the struggle of the failing mechanisms to survive and find new sources of power with which to accomplish the ends they were committed to. Under the pressure of economic contraction the bureaucracies that were to serve as the managerial tools of an associational order turned increasingly to the solution of statist supports, statist protection, or outright movement into the public sector, and thus tended to evolve into instruments for battering down the Hooverian barriers instead of supporting them.

The search that failed, then, had much to do with the creation of an intellectual and political setting in which the New Deal state could become the American response to economic adversity and idled resources. And beyond this it stimulated or allowed organizational developments that were important in determining the eventual form that the New Deal took. If the New Era failed to find the managerial tools and economic coordinators that could bring perpetual growth and prosperity, it was nevertheless a period of extensive organizational and bureaucratic development. The great corporations, the growing network of trade and occupational associations, the foundations and their programs, and the delivery systems for social services all developed a structure of private bureaucracies engaged in planning and rationalizing activities. This was an organizational growth that the New Dealers inherited. And while it provided them with ready-made units of administration, much as it had the Hooverites, it also acted as a barrier against those New Dealers who would build a statist planning apparatus or a statist structure for restoring and maintaining atomistic competition. Significantly, the great organizational changes of the New Deal years were not in these areas but in filling certain organizational vacuums, particularly among mass-production workers and urban ethnics and in the social welfare system.

Finally, it should also be noted that if the Hooverian designs for a "new liberalism" proved defective and politically unsustainable, the same was also true of substantial portions of the New Deal designs. Only a few portions of Roosevelt's National Recovery Administration experiment in government-backed cartelization were able to survive its failure to bring recovery and its generation of a backlash in favor of market restoration. Only isolated portions of the efforts to reunite high culture and national life survived into the 1940s. And as of 1939 the efforts to restore economic balance through attacks on business power, social security measures, and limited bursts of stimulative spending had not brought an economy capable of putting its idle resources to work and rewarding those who participated in it with rising material or social benefits. Full employment and new economic growth would come only with the installation of another war system resembling that installed during the Great War of 1917 and 1918. And the economic miracles of the period from 1945 to 1965 would come less from the heritage of the New Deal programs and initiatives than from new and more successful efforts to adapt the elements of this war system to peacetime needs. If the would-be builders of an associational order in the 1920s opened the way to the political and statist measures of the 1930s, they also created institutions that shaped and limited the results of such measures and became the basis for the new organizational developments of the 1940s. And in many respects, their efforts and designs foreshadowed the institutional arrangements that would be hailed as the true basis of a "new liberalism" in the post–World War II years. Without their handiwork, the America that took shape on the other side of the watershed of 1933 might have developed along quite different lines.

Bibliography

Traditionally, study of America in the 1920s has begun with Frederick Lewis Allen's *Only Yesterday* (New York: Harper, 1931), a work that not only shaped popular stereotypes of the period but also reinforced the tendency of scholars to regard it as a frothy and frivolous interlude between Wilson's New Freedom and Roosevelt's New Deal. Writing on the decade long followed the Allen tradition, resulting in such works as Laurence Greene's *The Era of Wonderful Nonsense* (Indianapolis: Bobbs-Merrill, 1939), Henry M. Robinson's *Fantastic Interim* (New York: Harcourt, Brace, 1943), and Lloyd Morris's *Postcript to Yesterday* (New York: Random House, 1947). Not until the 1950s did historians begin to take a new look, focusing less now on the period's bohemians, bootleggers, and Babbitts and more on its reformist aspects, its technical and organizational innovations, its cultural fragmentation and creativity, and its impulses toward and battles over social modernization. The beginnings of such research were reflected in William E. Leuchtenburg, *The Perils of Prosperity, 1914-1932* (Chicago: University of Chicago Press, 1958). But they had minimal impact on such surveys as Harold U. Faulkner, *From Versailles to the New Deal* (New Haven, Conn.: Yale University Press, 1955), Arthur M. Schlesinger, Jr., *The Crisis of the Old Order, 1919-1933* (Boston: Houghton Mifflin, 1957), and John D. Hicks, *Republican Ascendancy, 1921-1933* (New York: Harper and Row,

1960). And only recently has the new scholarship led to reinterpretations stressing the significance of the period in its own right and not merely for the light it can shed on the fate of progressivism or the origins of the New Deal. For perceptive discussions of this recent scholarship, see Burl Noggle, "The Twenties: A New Historiographical Frontier," *Journal of American History*, LIII (September 1966), 299–314; Joan Hoff Wilson, *The Twenties: The Critical Issues* (Boston: Little, Brown, 1972); and Burl Noggle, "Configurations of the Twenties," in William H. Cartwright and Richard L. Watson, Jr., eds., *The Reinterpretation of American History and Culture* (Washington: National Council for the Social Studies, 1973).

Historical reinterpretation of the 1920s has also been accompanied by changing perceptions of the periods immediately preceding and following the decade. The years 1917–1919 have become significant not only for their impact on liberal reformism and their responses to developments abroad but also for their institutional innovations and especially for their contributions to New Era designs for economic, social, and international order. For a review of recent work on the period, see the bibliographical essay in Burl Noggle's *Into the Twenties* (Urbana: University of Illinois Press, 1974). And at the other end, historians have been restudying the years 1930–1933, seeing them more as a crisis period for the new managerial capitalism and associative designs of the 1920s rather than as a time of retribution for returns to "normalcy" and laissez faire. For a discussion of this work, see especially Robert H. Zieger, "Herbert Hoover: A Reinterpretation," *American Historical Review*, LXXXI (October 1976), 800–810, and the bibliographical essay in Joan Hoff Wilson, *Herbert Hoover: Forgotten Progressive* (Boston: Little, Brown, 1975). For discussions of the new interpretive frameworks that have helped to change perceptions of the New Era and the years preceding and following it, see Louis Galambos, "The Emerging Organizational Synthesis in Modern American History," *Business History Review*, XLIV (Autumn 1970), 279–290; Robert D. Cuff, "American Historians and the 'Organizational Factor,'" *Canadian Review of American Studies*, IV (Spring 1973), 19–31; Irwin Unger, "The 'New Left' and American History—Some Recent Trends in United

States Historiography," *American Historical Review,* LXXII (July 1967), 1237–1263; and John M. Carroll, "Reassessing America's Past," in Charles Bussey, John M. Carroll, William MacDonald, and John W. Storey, eds., *America's Heritage in the Twentieth Century* (St. Louis, Mo.: Forum Press, 1978).

Despite recent trends, the coming of war and the diplomacy of war and peace making still stand as the most intensively researched aspects of the 1917–1933 period. On each there are mountains of literature. Of the older works the most significant are Charles Seymour, *American Diplomacy During the World War* (Baltimore, Md.: Johns Hopkins Press, 1934), Alice M. Morrissey, *The American Defense of Neutral Rights, 1914–1917* (Cambridge, Mass.: Harvard University Press, 1939), Charles C. Tansill, *America Goes to War* (Boston: Little, Brown, 1938), Ray Stannard Baker, *Woodrow Wilson and World Settlement,* 3 vols. (Garden City, N.Y.: Doubleday, Page, 1923), and Thomas A. Bailey, *Woodrow Wilson and the Lost Peace* (New York: Macmillan, 1944). The best of the more recent studies are Ernest R. May, *The World War and American Isolation, 1914–1917* (Cambridge, Mass.: Harvard University Press, 1959), Edward H. Buehrig, *Woodrow Wilson and the Balance of Power* (Bloomington: Indiana University Press, 1955), Arthur S. Link, *Wilson the Diplomatist* (Baltimore, Md.: Johns Hopkins Press, 1957), and Daniel M. Smith, *The Great Departure: The United States and World War I, 1914–1920* (New York: John Wiley, 1965). Also perceptive, especially in illuminating the Wilsonian vision of stability through liberalization, are Arno J. Mayer, *Politics and Diplomacy of Peace-Making* (New York: Knopf, 1968), N. Gordon Levin, Jr., *Woodrow Wilson and World Politics* (New York: Oxford University Press, 1968), and Carl P. Parrini, *Heir to Empire: United States Economic Diplomacy, 1916–1923* (Pittsburgh, Pa.: University of Pittsburgh Press, 1969). In addition, the subjects have been illuminated by a number of outstanding monographs, among which are Lawrence E. Gelfand, *The Inquiry: American Preparations for Peace, 1917–1919* (New Haven, Conn.: Yale University Press, 1963), Karl E. Birnbaum, *Peace Moves and U-Boat Warfare* (Stockholm, Sweden: Almquist and Wiksell, 1958), Ralph Stone, *The Irreconcilables* (Lexington: University Press of Kentucky, 1970), and Daniel M. Smith, *Robert Lansing and*

American Neutrality, 1914-1917 (Berkeley: University of California Press, 1958).

The most detailed account of American military operations during World War I is U.S. Department of the Army, *United States Army in the World War, 1917-1919*, 17 vols. (Washington: Government Printing Office, 1948). Two more recent military histories, both substantial and scholarly, are Edward M. Coffman, *The War to End All Wars: The American Military Experience in World War I* (New York: Oxford University Press, 1968), and Harvey A. DeWeerd, *President Wilson Fights His War* (New York: Macmillan, 1968). Other studies that help clarify the operations of the military agencies, both at home and abroad, are Daniel R. Beaver, *Newton D. Baker and the American War Effort, 1917-1919* (Lincoln: University of Nebraska Press, 1966), Elting E. Morison, *Admiral Sims and the Modern American Navy* (Boston: Houghton Mifflin, 1942), Louis Guichard, *The Naval Blockade, 1914-1918* (New York: Appleton, 1930), and David F. Trask, *The United States in the Supreme War Council* (Middletown, Conn.: Wesleyan University Press, 1961).

Historical study of the wartime mobilization and control agencies has come in three waves. The first produced such immediate postwar publications as Benedict Crowell and Robert F. Wilson, *How America Went to War*, 6 vols. (New Haven, Conn.: Yale University Press, 1921), Grosvenor B. Clarkson, *Industrial America in the World War* (Boston: Houghton Mifflin, 1923), Alexander M. Bing, *Wartime Strikes and Their Adjustment* (New York: Dutton, 1921), and Walker D. Hines, *War History of the American Railroads* (New Haven, Conn.: Yale University Press, 1928). The second, developing in conjunction with concerns about a new mobilization, led to such publications as William C. Mullendore, *History of the United States Food Administration, 1917-1919* (Stanford, Calif.: Stanford University Press, 1941), James R. Mock and Cedric Larson, *Words That Won the War* (Princeton, N.J.: Princeton University Press, 1939), and Richard H. Hippelheuser, ed., *American Industry in the War* (New York: Prentice-Hall, 1941). And the third, arising as one facet of neoinstitutional or managerial history, has produced such detailed analyses of bureaucratic formation and functioning as Robert D. Cuff, *The War Industries Board: Business-Government Relations*

During World War I (Baltimore, Md.: Johns Hopkins Press, 1973) and Burton I. Kaufman, *Efficiency and Expansion: Foreign Trade Organization in the Wilson Administration, 1913–1921* (Westport, Conn.: Greenwood Press, 1974). Also helpful in putting the wartime organizational experience into perspective and illuminating its impact are Frederick L. Paxson, *American Democracy and the World War*, 3 vols. (Boston: Houghton Mifflin, 1936–1948), Seward W. Livermore, *Politics Is Adjourned: Woodrow Wilson and the War Congress, 1916–1918* (Middletown, Conn.: Wesleyan University Press, 1966), Horace C. Peterson and Gilbert C. Fite, *Opponents of War, 1917–1919* (Madison: University of Wisconsin Press, 1957), K. Austin Kerr, *American Railroad Politics, 1914–1920* (Pittsburgh, Pa.: University of Pittsburgh Press, 1968), Robert H. Wiebe, *The Search for Order, 1877–1920* (New York: Hill and Wang, 1967), James Weinstein, *The Corporate Ideal in the Liberal State* (Boston: Beacon, 1968), David Noble, *America by Design* (New York: Knopf, 1977), and Murray N. Rothbard, "War Collectivism in World War I," in Ronald Radosh and Murray N. Rothbard, eds., *A New History of Leviathan* (New York: Dutton, 1972).

Historical study of America's reconversion and demobilization period has tended to focus on antiradical hysteria, setbacks for organized labor, race riots, and the breakup of the Wilsonian coalition. The best accounts of these matters are in Robert K. Murray, *Red Scare: A Study in National Hysteria, 1919–1920* (Minneapolis: University of Minnesota Press, 1955), Stanley Coben, *A. Mitchell Palmer: Politician* (New York: Columbia University Press, 1963), David Brody, *Labor in Crisis: The Steel Strike of 1919* (Philadelphia: Lippincott, 1965), William M. Tuttle, Jr., *Race Riot: Chicago in the Red Summer of 1919* (New York: Atheneum, 1970), and David Burner, "1919: Prelude to Normalcy," in John Braeman *et al.*, eds., *Change and Continuity in Twentieth-Century America: The 1920's* (Columbus: Ohio State University Press, 1968). The efforts to adapt wartime organization to peacetime needs have been less studied. But see Gary Dean Best, *The Politics of American Individualism: Herbert Hoover in Transition, 1918–1921* (Westport, Conn.: Greenwood Press, 1975), Robert Himmelberg, "Business, Antitrust Policy, and the Industrial Board of the Department of Commerce, 1919," *Busi-*

ness History Review, XLIV (Spring 1968), Melvin I. Urofsky, *Big Steel and the Wilson Administration* (Columbus: Ohio State University Press, 1969), James R. Mock and Evangeline Thurber, *Report on Demobilization* (Norman: University of Oklahoma Press, 1944), Stanley Shapiro, "The Great War and Reform," *Labor History*, VII (Summer 1971), and the initial chapters of Burl Noggle, *Into the Twenties* (Urbana: University of Illinois Press, 1974). Still useful as well are Frederic L. Paxson, *The Great Demobilization and Other Essays* (Madison: University of Wisconsin Press, 1941) and John D. Hicks, *Rehearsal for Disaster: The Boom and Collapse of 1919–1920* (Gainesville: University of Florida Press, 1961).

The most detailed account of the politics and policies of the Harding period is Robert K. Murray's *The Harding Era: Warren G. Harding and His Administration* (Minneapolis: University of Minnesota Press, 1969). Less favorable to Harding are Andrew Sinclair, *The Available Man* (New York: Macmillan, 1965), Francis Russell, *The Shadow of Blooming Grove* (New York: McGraw-Hill, 1968), and Eugene P. Trani and David L. Wilson, *The Presidency of Warren G. Harding* (Lawrence: Regents Press of Kansas, 1977). On the Coolidge presidency William Allen White's *A Puritan in Babylon* (New York: Macmillan, 1938) still has value. But the best book is Donald B. McCoy's revisionist study, *Calvin Coolidge: The Quiet President* (New York: Macmillan, 1967). Other works that have helped to clarify New Era political behavior and dispel a variety of myths about it include Wesley M. Bagby, *The Road to Normalcy* (Baltimore, Md.: Johns Hopkins Press, 1962), Burl Noggle, *Teapot Dome: Oil and Politics in the 1920's* (Baton Rouge: Louisiana State University Press, 1962), J. Joseph Huthmacher, *Massachusetts People and Politics, 1919–1933* (Cambridge, Mass.: Harvard University Press, 1959), David Burner, *The Politics of Provincialism: The Democratic Party in Transition, 1918–1932* (New York: Knopf, 1968), Edmund A. Moore, *A Catholic Runs for President* (Gloucester, Mass.: Peter Smith, 1956), Howard Quint and Robert Ferrell, eds., *The Talkative President* (Amherst: University of Massachusetts Press, 1964), Gilbert Fite, *George N. Peek and the Fight for Farm Parity* (Norman: University of Oklahoma Press, 1954), James H. Shideler, *Farm Crisis, 1919–1923* (Berkeley: University of California Press, 1957),

Preston Hubbard, Jr., *Origins of the T.V.A.* (Nashville, Tenn.: Vanderbilt University Press, 1961), Robert Zieger, *Republicans and Labor, 1919–1929* (Lexington: University Press of Kentucky, 1969), and Frank Freidel, *Franklin D. Roosevelt: The Ordeal* (Boston: Little, Brown, 1954).

The most prominent themes in recent work on New Era political history have been the persistence of progressive political modes, the building of administrative networks and domains, and the political manifestations of rural-urban and ethnocultural conflict. On the first of these themes the leading works include Arthur S. Link, "What Happened to the Progressive Movement in the 1920's?" *American Historical Review,* LXIV (July 1959), Clarke A. Chambers, *Seedtime of Reform: American Social Service and Social Action, 1918–1933* (Minneapolis: University of Minnesota Press, 1963), George B. Tindall, "Business Progressivism: Southern Politics in the Twenties," *South Atlantic Quarterly,* LXII (Winter 1963), Paul Glad, "Progressivism and the Business Culture of the 1920's," *Journal of American History,* LIII (June 1966), and Otis L. Graham, Jr., *The Great Campaigns: Reform and War, 1900–1928* (Englewood Cliffs, N.J.: Prentice-Hall, 1971). On administrative developments the most important works include Donald L. Winters, *Henry Cantwell Wallace as Secretary of Agriculture, 1921–1924* (Urbana: University of Illinois Press, 1970), Donald C. Swain, *Federal Conservation Policy, 1921–1933* (Berkeley: University of California Press, 1963), Craig Lloyd, *Aggressive Introvert: Herbert Hoover and Public Relations Management* (Columbus: Ohio State University Press, 1972), G. Cullom Davis, "The Transformation of the Federal Trade Commission, 1914–1929," *Mississippi Valley Historical Review,* XLIX (December 1962), Evan B. Metcalf, "Secretary Hoover and the Emergence of Macroeconomic Management," *Business History Review,* XLIX (Spring 1975), and Ellis W. Hawley, "Herbert Hoover, the Commerce Secretariat, and the Vision of an Associative State, 1921–1928," *Journal of American History,* LXI (June 1974). On rural-urban conflict the most penetrating analyses are in George Mowry, *The Urban Nation, 1920–1960* (New York: Hill and Wang, 1965) and Don S. Kirschner, *City and Country: Rural Responses to Urbanization in the 1920's* (Westport, Conn.: Greenwood, 1970).

And for the most divisive of the ethnocultural issues, see Andrew Sinclair, *Prohibition: Era of Excess* (Boston: Little, Brown, 1962), Norman H. Clark, *Deliver Us from Evil* (New York: Norton, 1976), John Higham, *Strangers in the Land* (New Brunswick, N.J.: Rutgers University Press, 1955), Norman F. Furniss, *The Fundamentalist Controversy, 1918–1931* (New Haven, Conn.: Yale University Press, 1954), and Ruth C. Silva, *Rum, Religion, and Votes* (University Park: Pennsylvania State University Press, 1962).

The story of the anticapitalist left in the 1920s is well told in Theodore Draper, *The Roots of American Communism* (New York: Viking, 1963), David A. Shannon, *The Socialist Party of America* (New York: Macmillan, 1955), James Weinstein, *The Decline of Socialism in America, 1912–1925* (New York: Monthly Review Press, 1967), Robert L. Morlan, *Political Prairie Fire: The Nonpartisan League, 1915–1922* (Minneapolis: University of Minnesota Press, 1956), Melvyn Dubofsky, *We Shall Be All: A History of the Industrial Workers of the World* (Chicago: Quadrangle, 1969), and William E. Akin, *Technocracy and the American Dream* (Berkeley: University of California Press, 1977). The La Follette movement is carefully traced in Kenneth C. McKay's *The Progressive Movement of 1924* (New York: Columbia University Press, 1947), and the development of black nationalism is discussed in E. David Cronon, *Black Moses: The Story of Marcus Garvey and the Universal Negro Improvement Association* (Madison: University of Wisconsin Press, 1962). For the "radical right" of the period, see David M. Chalmers, *Hooded Americanism* (Garden City, N.Y.: Doubleday, 1965), Charles Alexander, *The Ku Klux Klan in the Southwest* (Lexington: University Press of Kentucky, 1965), and Kenneth T. Jackson, *The Ku Klux Klan in the City, 1915–1930* (New York: Oxford University Press, 1967). For rightist groups other than the Klan, the best account, although still an unpublished one, is in George S. May, "Ultra-Conservative Thought in the United States in the 1920's and 1930's" (Ph.D. Dissertation, University of Michigan, 1954).

On American diplomacy, 1920–1932, there is a voluminous literature, much of it synthesized in such surveys as L. Ethan Ellis, *Republican Foreign Policy, 1921–1933* (New Brunswick, N.J.: Rutgers University Press, 1968) and Selig Adler, *The Uncertain Giant,*

1921-1941 (New York: Macmillan, 1965). Among the most important of the specialized studies are Thomas H. Buckley, *The United States and the Washington Conference, 1921-1922* (Knoxville: University of Tennessee Press, 1970), Herbert Feis, *The Diplomacy of the Dollar: First Era, 1919-1932* (Baltimore, Md.: Johns Hopkins Press, 1950), Robert H. Ferrell, *Peace in Their Time: The Origins of the Kellogg-Briand Pact* (New Haven, Conn.: Yale University Press, 1952), Selig Adler, *The Isolationist Impulse* (New York: Abelard-Schuman, 1957), Akira Iriye, *After Imperialism: The Search for a New Order in the Far East, 1921-1931* (Cambridge, Mass.: Harvard University Press, 1965), Betty Glad, *Charles Evans Hughes and the Illusions of Innocence* (Urbana: University of Illinois Press, 1966), Joseph Tulchin, *The Aftermath of War: World War I and U.S. Policy Toward Latin America* (New York: New York University Press, 1971), Joseph Brandes, *Herbert Hoover and Economic Diplomacy* (Pittsburgh, Pa.: University of Pittsburgh Press, 1962), Robert H. Ferrell, *American Diplomacy in the Great Depression: Hoover-Stimson Foreign Policy, 1929-1933* (New Haven, Conn.: Yale University Press, 1957), Alexander DeConde, *Herbert Hoover's Latin American Policy* (Stanford, Calif.: Stanford University Press, 1951), Edward M. Bennett, *Recognition of Russia* (Waltham, Mass.: Ginn, Blaisdell, 1970), and Armin Rappaport, *Henry L. Stimson and Japan* (Chicago: University of Chicago Press, 1963).

In recent years a number of important works have also illuminated the relationships between the New Era political economy and the diplomacy of the period. Among these are William Appleman Williams, "The Legend of Isolationism in the 1920's," *Science and Society,* XVIII (Winter 1954), Joan Hoff Wilson, *American Business and Foreign Policy, 1920-1933* (Lexington: University Press of Kentucky, 1971), Carl P. Parrini, *Heir to Empire: United States Economic Diplomacy, 1916-1923* (Pittsburgh, Pa.: University of Pittsburgh Press, 1969), Michael J. Hogan, *Informal Entente: The Private Structure of Cooperation in Anglo-American Economic Diplomacy, 1918-1928* (Columbia: University of Missouri Press, 1977), Melvyn P. Leffler, "Political Isolationsim, Economic Expansion, or Diplomatic Realism: American Policy Toward Western Europe, 1921-1933," *Perspectives in American History,* VIII (1974), Robert N.

Seidel, *Progressive Pan Americanism* (Ithaca, N.Y.: Cornell University Latin American Studies Program, 1973), and Robert F. Smith, *The United States and Revolutionary Nationalism in Mexico, 1916–32* (Chicago: University of Chicago Press, 1972).

The standard work on economic developments during the period is George Soule, *Prosperity Decade: From War to Depression, 1917–1929* (New York: Holt, Rinehart, 1947). Also good on particular aspects and sectors of economic behavior are Irving Bernstein, *The Lean Years: A History of the American Worker, 1920–1933* (Boston: Houghton Mifflin, 1960), Elmus R. Wicker, *Federal Reserve Monetary Policy, 1917–1933* (New York: Random House, 1966), Wassily W. Leontief, *The Structure of the American Economy, 1919–1929* (Cambridge, Mass.: Harvard University Press, 1941), Simon Kuznets, *National Income and Its Composition, 1919–1938* (New York: National Bureau of Economic Research, 1941), Harold Barger and Hans H. Landsberg, *American Agriculture, 1899–1939* (New York: National Bureau of Economic Research, 1942), John B. Rae, *The American Automobile* (Chicago: University of Chicago Press, 1965), and Milton J. Nadworny, *Scientific Management and the Unions, 1900–1932* (Cambridge, Mass.: Harvard University Press, 1955). On business organization and practice during the period, see Thomas C. Cochran, *The American Business System: A Historical Perspective, 1900–1955* (Cambridge, Mass.: Harvard University Press, 1957), Louis Galambos, *Competition and Cooperation: The Emergence of a National Trade Association* (Baltimore, Md.: Johns Hopkins Press, 1966), Alfred D. Chandler, *Strategy and Structure: Chapters in the History of the Industrial Enterprise* (Cambrdige, Mass.: M.I.T. Press, 1962), Robert F. Himmelberg, *The Origins of the National Recovery Administration: Business, Government, and the Trade Association Issue, 1921–1933* (New York: Fordham University Press, 1976), Loren Baritz, *The Servants of Power* (Middletown, Conn.: Wesleyan University Press, 1960), Stuart D. Brandes, *American Welfare Capitalism, 1880–1940* (Chicago: University of Chicago Press, 1976), and Morrell Heald, *The Social Responsibilities of Business* (Cleveland, Ohio: Case Western Reserve University Press, 1970). And for differing views on the origins and coming of the depression, see John K. Galbraith, *The Great Crash*

(Boston: Houghton Mifflin, 1955), Milton Friedman and Anna Schwartz, *The Great Contraction, 1929–1933* (Princeton, N.J.,: Princeton University Press, 1965), Peter Temin, *Did Monetary Forces Cause the Great Depression?* (New York: Norton, 1976), Derek Aldcroft, *From Versailles to Wall Street* (Berkeley: University of California Press, 1977), and Charles P. Kindleberger, *The World in Depression, 1929–1939* (Berkeley: University of California Press, 1973). Still useful as well is the President's Conference on Unemployment, *Recent Economic Changes in the United States,* 2 vols. (New York: McGraw-Hill, 1929).

For the social history of the 1920s historians have continued to rely heavily on Robert S. and Helen M. Lynd, *Middletown: A Study in Contemporary American Culture* (New York: Harcourt, Brace, 1929), the President's Research Committee on Social Trends, *Recent Social Trends in the United States,* 2 vols. (New York: McGraw-Hill, 1933), and the relevant volume in the "History of American Life" series, Preston W. Slosson's *The Great Crusade and After, 1914–1928* (New York: Macmillan, 1931). Recent years, however, have witnessed the appearance of a growing number of specialized studies illuminating various aspects of the decade's popular life and arts, its social institutions, its subcultures, and its community and welfare structures. Among these are Paul A. Carter, *The Decline and Revival of the Social Gospel* (Ithaca, N.Y.: Cornell University Press, 1954), Gilbert Osofsky, *Harlem: The Making of a Ghetto* (New York: Harper and Row, 1966), Paula S. Fass, *The Damned and the Beautiful: American Youth in the 1920's* (New York: Oxford University Press, 1971), Paul A. Carter, *Another Part of the Twenties* (New York: Columbia University Press, 1971), Gunther Schuller, *Early Jazz: Its Roots and Musical Development* (New York: Oxford University Press, 1971), J. Stanley Lemons, *The Woman Citizen: Social Feminism in the 1920's* (Urbana: University of Illinois Press, 1973), Erick Barnouw, *A Tower in Babel: A History of Broadcasting in the United States to 1933* (New York: Oxford University Press, 1966), James J. Flink, *The Car Culture* (Cambridge, Mass.: M.I.T. Press, 1975), David Robinson, *Hollywood in the Twenties* (New York: A. S. Barnes, 1968), Raymond Callahan, *Education and the Cult of Efficiency* (Chicago: University of Chicago Press, 1962), Lawrence A. Cremin,

The Transformation of the School (New York: Knopf, 1961), Roy Lubove, *Community Planning in the 1920's* (Pittsburgh, Pa.: University of Pittsburgh Press, 1963), Daniel Nelson, *Unemployment Insurance: The American Experience, 1915–1935* (Madison: University of Wisconsin Press, 1969), and Ernest Sandeen, *The Roots of Fundamentalism* (Chicago: University of Chicago Press, 1970). In addition, see Paul A. Carter, *The Twenties in America* (New York: T. Y. Crowell, 1968), Gilman Ostrander, *American Civilization in the First Machine Age, 1890–1940* (New York: Harper and Row, 1970), Elizabeth Stevenson, *Babbits and Bohemians* (New York: Macmillan, 1967), Mark Sullivan, *Our Times,* Vol. VI (New York: Scribner's, 1946), and Gilbert Seldes, *The Seven Lively Arts* (New York: Sagamore, 1957 ed.).

The best survey of intellectual and artistic developments in the 1920s, and one upon which I have drawn heavily, is Roderick Nash, *The Nervous Generation: American Thought, 1917–1930* (Chicago: Rand McNally, 1970). Other major works illuminating various aspects of these developments are Frederick J. Hoffman, *The Twenties: American Writing in the Postwar Decade* (New York: Viking, 1955), Thomas R. West, *Flesh of Steel* (Nashville, Tenn.: Vanderbilt University Press, 1967), Robert M. Crunden, *From Self to Society, 1919–1941* (Englewood Cliffs, N.J.: Prentice-Hall, 1972), Nathan I. Huggins, *The Harlem Renaissance* (New York: Oxford University Press, 1971), Nathan G. Hale, *Freud and the Americans* (New York: Oxford University Press, 1971), Robert Faris, *Chicago Sociology, 1920–1932* (San Francisco: Chandler, 1967), Edward A. Purcell, Jr., *The Crisis of Democratic Theory: Scientific Naturalism and the Problem of Value* (Lexington: University Press of Kentucky, 1973), Ronald C. Tobey, *The American Ideology of National Science, 1919–1930* (Pittsburgh, Pa.: University of Pittsburgh Press, 1971), G. Louis Joughin and Edmund Morgan, *The Legacy of Sacco and Vanzetti* (New York: Harcourt, Brace, 1948), David Felix, *Protest: Sacco-Vanzetti and the Intellectuals* (Bloomington: Indiana University Press, 1965), and Milton W. Brown, *American Painting from the Armory Show to the Depression* (Princeton, N.J.: Princeton University Press, 1955). See also Caroline F. Ware, *Greenwich Village, 1920–1933* (Boston: Houghton Mifflin, 1935), John Malcolm

Brinnin, *The Third Rose: Gertrude Stein and Her World* (Boston: Little, Brown, 1959), and Robert Crunden, ed., *The Superfluous Men: Conservative Critics of American Culture* (Austin: University of Texas Press, 1977).

The standard surveys of the Hoover programs and policies, 1929–1933, are Albert U. Romasco, *The Poverty of Abundance: Hoover, the Nation, the Depression* (New York; Oxford University Press, 1965) and Harris G. Warren, *Herbert Hoover and the Great Depression* (New York: Oxford University Press, 1959). Also useful within limits are such defenses of Hoover as William Myers and Walter Newton, *The Hoover Administration* (New York: Scribner's, 1936), Ray Lyman Wilbur and Arthur M. Hyde, *The Hoover Policies* (New York: Scribner's, 1937), Edgar Robinson and Vaughn Bornet, *Herbert Hoover: President of the United States* (Stanford, Calif.: Hoover Institution Press, 1975), and Herbert C. Hoover, *The Memoirs of Herbert Hoover: The Great Depression* (New York: Macmillan, 1952). All these surveys, however, either predate or largely ignore the scholarship that has appeared since the opening of the Hoover papers at the Hoover Presidential Library in 1966. Among the most important of these recent works are Joan Hoff Wilson, *Herbert Hoover: Forgotten Progressive* (Boston: Little, Brown, 1975), David Burner, *Herbert Hoover: A Public Life* (New York: Knopf, 1978), Ellis W. Hawley and others, *Herbert Hoover and the Crisis of American Capitalism* (Cambridge, Mass.: Schenkman, 1973), Martin L. Fausold and George T. Mazuzan, eds., *The Hoover Presidency: A Reappraisal* (Albany: State University of New York Press, 1974), Donald J. Lisio, *The President and Protest: Hoover, Conspiracy, and the Bonus Riot* (Columbia: University of Missouri Press, 1974), Roger Daniels, *The Bonus March* (Westport, Conn.: Greenwood, 1971), Jordan A. Schwarz, *Interregnum of Despair: Hoover, Congress, and the Depression* (Urbana: University of Illinois Press, 1970), James S. Olson, *Herbert Hoover and the Reconstruction Finance Corporation, 1931–1933* (Ames: Iowa State University Press, 1977), and Herbert Stein, *The Fiscal Revolution in America* (Chicago: University of Chicago Press, 1969). In addition, there are a number of seminally interpretive works on Hooverian ideology and policy, among them Richard Hofstadter's "Herbert Hoover and the Crisis of American Individualism," in *The American*

Political Tradition and the Men Who Made It (New York: Knopf, 1948), William Appleman Williams's "The Central Role of Herbert Hoover in the Maturation of an Industrial Gentry," in *The Contours of American History* (Cleveland, Ohio: World Publishing Company, 1961), Carl N. Degler's "The Ordeal of Herbert Hoover," *Yale Review*, LII (Summer 1963), Barry D. Karl's "Presidential Planning and Social Science Research: Mr. Hoover's Experts," *Perspectives in American History*, III (1969), Peri Arnold's "Herbert Hoover and the Continuity of American Public Policy," *Public Policy*, XX (Fall 1972), Bruce A. Lohoff's "Herbert Hoover, Spokesman of Humane Efficiency," *American Quarterly*, XXII (Fall 1970), and Grant McConnell's discussion of Hoover in his *Private Power and American Democracy* (New York: Knopf, 1966).

Finally, on the interregum period and the coming of the New Deal, see especially Frank Freidel, *Franklin D. Roosevelt: Launching the New Deal* (Boston: Little, Brown, 1973), Susan Estabrook Kennedy, *The Banking Crisis of 1933* (Lexington: University Press of Kentucky, 1973), Rexford G. Tugwell, *The Brains Trust* (New York: Viking, 1968), Raymond Moley, *The First New Deal* (New York: Harcourt, Brace, 1966), Herbert Feis, *1933: Characters in a Crisis* (Boston: Little, Brown, 1966), and Laurin L. Henry, *Presidential Transitions* (Washington: Brookings Institution, 1960). A dissent, both from the standard scholarship on the period and from the recent revisionism on the Hoover Administration, is Elliot A. Rosen's *Hoover, Roosevelt, and the Brains Trust: From Depression to New Deal* (New York: Columbia University Press, 1977).

Index